AF646728

INTEGRATED RURAL DEVELOPMENT IN ASIA
Learning from Recent Experience

INTEGRATED RURAL DEVELOPMENT IN ASIA

Learning from Recent Experience

Edited by

H. RAMACHANDRAN

J.P. DE CAMPOS GUIMARAES

CONCEPT PUBLISHING COMPANY, NEW DELHI 110059

© Institute for Social and Economic Change

All rights reserved. No part of this work may be reproduced, stored, adapted, or transmitted in any form or by any means, electronic, mechanical, photocopying, micro-filming recording or otherwise, or translated in any language, without the prior written permission of the copyright owner and the publisher. The book is sold subject to the condition that it shall not, by way of trade or otherwise, be lent, resold, hired out, or otherwise circulated without the prior publisher's written consent in any form of binding or cover other than that in which it is published.

The views and opinions expressed in this book are author(s) own and the facts reported by him/her have been verified to the extent possible, and the publishers are not in any way liable for the same.

ISBN-13: 978-81-8069-881-1 (PB)

Reprinted 2018
First Published 1991

Published and Printed by

Concept
Since 1974

Concept Publishing Company Pvt. Ltd.
A/15-16, Commercial Block, Mohan Garden
New Delhi-110059 (India)
T: 25351460, 25351794, *F*: 091-11-25357109
E: publishing@conceptpub.com, W: www.conceptpub.com

Cataloging in Publication Data--Courtesy: D.K. Agencies (P) Ltd. <docinfo@dkagencies.com>

Integrated rural development in Asia : learning from recent experience / edited by H. Ramachandran, J.P. de Campos Guimaraes.
pages cm
"First published 1991"--Title page verso.
Papers presented at an international seminar held at Bangalore on 7-9th July 1988.
Includes bibliographical references and index.
ISBN 9788170223344 (HB)
ISBN 9788180698811 (PB)

1. Rural development projects--Asia--Congresses. I. Ramachandran, H. (Hariharan), 1947- editor. II. Guimaraes, J. P. de Campos, editor.

LCC HN655.2.C6I58 2018 | DDC 307.1412095 23

DEDICATION

The inaugural session of the International Seminar on which this book is based was presided over by Professor V.K.R.V. Rao, the doyen of social sciences in India and a builder of great academic institutions. It was a happy coincidence that the seminar was inaugurated under his chairmanship on his 80th birthday. The editors and the institutions that sponsored the seminar deem it a privilege and an honour to dedicate this volume, as a mark of respect and appreciation, to Prof. V.K.R.V. Rao.

V.K.R.V. RAO : A PROFILE

Prof. V.K.R.V. Rao completed 80 years of his life on 8th July, 1988 much of which was devoted to selfless service to the people of India. He has been active in many fields – as a thinker with vision, a teacher, a researcher, an activist, an institution builder, an administrator and a politician – and continues to be a highly respected and admired public figure as well as an active researcher. He has an enviable record of achievements in every facet of his academic and public life which invokes inspiration and admiration.

The important role that economists in India today play in planning and policy formulation is to a large extent attributed to him, not only because he himself was a prime consultant on major economic policies and a member of various committees constituted by the Government of India during the founding years of Indian Planning, but with his vision and organising capacity he had established such institutions of international repute as the Delhi School of Economics, that provided the base for training young social scientists. Subsequently he founded the Institute of Economic Growth, Agro-economic Research Centres and the Institute for Social and Economic Change. It is in these centres that he encouraged and promoted young social scientists with promise many of whom are occupying important positions in various parts of the world.

Having realised the mutually strengthening role of social sciences in addressing developmental issues of a developing economy, he played a crucial role in establishing the Indian Council for Social Science Research – the institution that promotes and funds research in Social Sciences in India.

Prof. Rao has served the country in various capacities – among others as a Vice-Chancellor of Delhi University, as a member of Planning Commission, as a Union Minister. While these were exacting positions he was far from inactive in his intelectual pursuits of refining research tools, of reflecting on various development issues confronting the society. Starting from his pioneering work *National Income of the*

British India, 1931-32, published five decades ago he has authored about 40 books and monographs, over 150 articles, several committee reports and addresses. The themes include development problems, planning, public finance, education, agriculture, urbanisation, rural development, student unrest, socialism and religion.

In recognition of his contribution to the Nation, he has been honoured with several awards, and awards have been instituted in his name for excellence in social science research. The country honoured him with *Padma Vibhushan* in the seventies. The dedication of this volume to Prof. Rao is but a small token of appreciation and admiration.

PREFACE

Over the past two decades, Asian countries have accumulated considerable experience with Integrated Rural Development (IRD). IRD programmes have been in existence long enough for it to be possible to assess both their achievements and their limitations. As a result, IRD has been subjected to well-known – and often well-founded – criticism concerning the difficulties that have been experienced in changing significantly the situation of the rural poor and in achieving high degrees of effectiveness, replicability and sustainability.

The question at the core of this book is what has been learnt from past experience with – and past criticism of – the IRD approach. The international seminar at its origin was organised with the intention of providing an opportunity for professionals and scholars, working in the field of rural development and particularly of IRD in Asia, to meet and address this question.

The seminar took place in the campus of the Institute for Social and Economic Change (ISEC), on the outskirts of Bangalore, from 7 to 9 July, 1988, and was co-organised by ISEC, by the Institute of Social Studies (ISS) of The Hague, Netherlands, and by the Asian Institute of Technology (AIT) of Bangkok, Thailand, the latter two institutions through the AIT/ISS Project of International Co-operation of the Division of Human Settlements Development of AIT.

All three organising institutions are widely known and acknowledged as centres of excellence in their respective fields. The Institute for Social and Economic Change is an autonomous research institution, essentially supported by the Government of Karnataka and the Union Government of India, which was established in 1973 by Prof. V.K.R.V. Rao. A large part of the Institute's work is in the field of rural economics, agricultural development, development administration, rural sociology and education.

The Asian Institute of Technology is an independent international institute that provides advanced training in engineering, science, human settlements development and related fields to students from all countries of Asia, through a variety of post-graduate diploma and degree courses, as well as short in-service training courses, seminars and international conferences. Created in 1977, the Division of Human Settlements Development (HSD) represents one of the most significant efforts of AIT to diversify its training activities away from infrastructure-oriented engineering, into fields that are directly relevant to national development processes, needs and priorities of Asian countries. HSD has programmes at the Master level in Urban Planning, Housing and Land Development, Rural Development Planning and Rural Regional Development Planning. It also has a Ph.D. programme.

The Institute of Social Studies is one of Europe's oldest and most distinguished centres of higher education and research in development studies. The Institute currently offers a total of 13 teaching programmes, ranging from short-term courses of 6 weeks to 15 months for the M.A. programme and even longer for the M.Phil. and Ph.D. programmes. All the programmes at ISS are oriented towards policy problems, are interdisciplinary in nature and relate to current needs, complementing rather than duplicating education and training available in Third World countries. ISS also has considerable experience in institutional development in the Third World, where it has helped set up a variety of national and international training programmes in development studies at the post-graduate level.

Initiated in 1984 with financial support from the Government of the Netherlands, the AIT/ISS Project of International Education and Research in Rural Regional Development Planning combined the expertise of ISS and of HSD to create and consolidate, at AIT, a programme in rural regional development planning at the Master level. At the same time, and to maximise the potential benefits of the project for the Asian region as a whole, it pursued the parallel objective of stimulating the creation and supporting the development of the Rural Regional Development Network (RRDN), a horizontal network of Asian institutions active in training and research in the fields of rural and regional planning. With a regular Newsletter and the organisation of several international meetings and workshops and other activities of international co-operation to its credit, the RRDN is now a consolidated reality.

This volume includes edited versions of fourteen of the papers presented at the Bangalore seminar and is divided into two main parts. Part I contains papers dealing with various country experiences or reviewing specific IRD projects or programmes; these contributions include papers from Bangladesh, India, Indonesia, Nepal, the Philippines and Sri Lanka, which provide a wealth of material for international comparisons. Part II includes papers dealing with issues more specific to India, reflecting the magnitude and complexity of the problems of rural development in this country and its long experience with IRD programmes.

The book closes with a postscript which contains an attempt by the editors to draw some conclusions from the seminar, in terms of planning and implementation practice, and to identify a number of areas where further research is likely to prove useful.

Most of the papers in this book are written either by professionals directly or indirectly involved in IRD, or by academics with considerable experience of the practical problems of designing and implementing IRD programmes. As a consequence of this, there is a strong emphasis on the concrete practice of IRD and on how it addresses the fundamental questions of rural development. This practical emphasis is one of the main strengths of the book, particularly given the wealth and variety of personal and national experience on which the authors draw.

As organisers of the seminar and editors of this volume, we owe a considerable debt to all the people who contributed to make the former a success and the latter a possibility. We are particularly grateful to Professor M.N. Srinivas, the noted sociologist and chairman, Board of Governors, ISEC, for his inaugural address. We owe our thanks to the authors of the papers the discussants, the rapporteurs and the participants in the seminar; T.R. Satish Chandran the director, Dr. C.S. Nagaraju the Registrar and staff - both academic and administrative - of ISEC, who hosted the seminar and provided local support to its organisation; Dr. H. Demaine and Ms. L. Porteria, of the HSD Division of AIT, who played a central role in the organisation of the international contributions; the administrative staff of HSD; the Project Office and the Typing Service of the ISS; and, last but not least, the Department of International Co-operation of the Government of the Netherlands, whose funding of the AIT/ISS Project and thus, indirectly, of a substantial part of the seminar was a *sine qua non* condition of it taking place at all.

H. RAMACHANDRAN
J.P.DE CAMPOS GUIMARÃES

CONTENTS

PART II
IRD Experiences Indian Specificities

PARTICIPANTS IN THE SEMINAR

Harvey Demaine, Associate Professor, Division of Human Settlements Development, Asian Institute of Technology, G.P.O. Box 2754, Bangkok 10501.

Dwarika Dhungel, Joint Secretary Coordination and Planning Division, Ministry of Panchayat and Local Development, Pulchowk Lalitpur, Kathmandu, Nepal.

David Field, Agrologist, Canadian Executing Agency (Co-water International), K-BIRD Project, Box 1762, Kathmandu, Nepal.

Manuel P. Garcia, Research Management Center, University of the Philippines at Los Banos, College, Laguna, 3720, Philippines.

J.P. de Campos Guimarães, Lecturer in Regional Development Planning, Institute of Social Studies, P.O. Box 90733, 2509LS The Hague, Netherlands.

Manel Jayamanne, Director, Integrated Rural Development Project, Ratnapura, No. 19, Pothgul Vihara Mawatha, Getangama, Ratnapura, Sri Lanka.

Moeljarto Tjokrowinoto, Research Centre of Rural and Regional Development, Gadjah Mada University, Bulak Sumur, G/7, P.O. Box 2 UGM, Indonesia.

Pulcra Nietes, Deputy Executive Director, National Council on Integrated Area Development (NACIAD), FBI Bldg., 60 Timog Avenue, Quezon City, Philippines.

Lilian A. Porteria, Research Associate, Division of Human Settlements Development, Asian Institute of Technology, G.P.O. Box 2754, Bangkok 10501, Thailand.

Zillur Rahman[1], Joint Chief, Rural Institution Division, Planning Commission, Government of Bangladesh, Sher-e-Bangla Nagar, Dhaka, Bangladesh.

---

1. Could not attend the Seminar.

K.B.S. Rasheed, Department of Geography, University of Dhaka, Dhaka 1000, Bangladesh.

E. Desingu Setty, Associate Professor, Division of Human Settlements Development, Asian Institute of Technology, G.P.O. Box 2754, Bangkok 10501, Thailand.

Abdul Aziz, Professor, Institute for Social and Economic Change, Bangalore.

K.S Jagadish, Professor, Indian Institute of Science, Bangalore.

K. Jayalakshmi, Asst. Director, National Institute of Rural Development, Hyderabad.

P.M. Kulkarni, Associate Professor, Institute for Social and Economic Change, Bangalore.

N.J. Kurian, Director, Department of Rural Development, Ministry of Agriculture, New Delhi.

K.N. Ninan, Assistant Professor, Institute for Social and Ecnomic Change, Bangalore.

V.S. Parthasarathy, Assistant Professor, Institute for Social and Economic Change, Bangalore.

H. Ramachandran, Associate Professor, Institute for Social and Economic Change, Bangalore.

V.M. Rao, Professor, Institute for Social and Economic Change, Bangalore.

Amal Ray, Professor, Institute for Social and Economic Change, Bangalore.

S.N. Sangitha, Associate Professor, Institute for Social and Economic Change, Bangalore.

T.R. Satish Chandran, Director, Institute for Social and Economic Change, Bangalore.

A.S. Seetharamu, Professor, Institute for Social and Economic Change, Bangalore.

J. Tharamangalam, Professor, Institute for Social and Economic Change, Bangalore.

V. Vyasulu, Professor, Institute for Social and Economic Change, Bangalore.

PART I

IRD EXPERIENCES FROM SIX ASIAN COUNTRIES

1

INTRODUCTION TO COUNTRY EXPERIENCES

In the past twenty or thirty years, a majority of developing countries in Asia has achieved remarkable success in improving rural infrastructure, modernising agriculture and increasing agricultural production and rural incomes. Such growth has, however, largely by-passed sizeable segments of the rural population, and most of these countries continue to be plagued by serious problems of rural unemployment and widespread rural poverty. Concern with this situation has led to the explicit adoption of rural development as a policy objective and of a variety of programmes aiming at the alleviation of rural poverty, which include, among others, the so-called Integrated Rural Development (IRD) programmes. In this respect international assistance donors, both multilateral and bilateral, played a key role in encouraging the adoption of the IRD approach to rural development and in funding projects formulated according to this new format.

Unlike "rural development", which is — sometimes confusingly — used to denote both processes and certain types of intervention, "integrated rural development" normally denotes exclusively interventions, i.e. projects or programmes, carried out in rural areas by government or, occasionally, by non-governmental organisations. The exact meaning of the expression "integrated rural development" is not easy to establish unambiguously: in fact this expression has been applied to projects which differ substantially from each other, both in concept and in format. There are, however, certain common elements that give most of these projects at least a family resemblance. Without attempting to define IRD, we may characterise most IRD projects as (i) being multi-sectoral, (ii) including an explicit concern with poverty alleviation and (iii) being designed with the explicit aim of achieving a complementarity of interventions likely to potentiate their impact, so that the delivery of the various project components in a co-ordinated way will achieve a greater effect than the sum of the partial effects attributable to each component separately. This orientation is reflected in the use of the word "integrated", much in the same way as the multi-sectoral nature of IRD is associated with the use of "rural" rather than "agricultural": project interventions and development objectives span a wide range of rural activities, including, in addition to agriculture, off-farm production and physical and social infrastructure.

It may be useful to reflect briefly on the *objectives* of IRD projects, and on some of their implications. IRD projects seem to have two main types of explicit objectives, which we could characterise as *economic growth* and *poverty alleviation*. The first type includes objectives such as increased agricultural and off-farm production, increased productivity, higher rural incomes, improved infrastructure and technological modernisation in the countryside. The second involves the transfer of assets to and/or the creation of jobs for the poor, and the satisfaction of their basic minimum needs.

In spite of the fact that they are often found side-by-side in the same projects, these two types of objectives do not always or necessarily have much to do with each other. The consistent failure of the trickle-down mechanisms postulated in the sixties to operate according to expectations means that growth will not necessarily decrease poverty. This is indeed one of the main reasons why it has been found necessary to add poverty alleviation to the list of objectives of rural development. Rural economic growth, in Asia as elsewhere, is not a process where the poor play a particularly important or conspicuous role, if they play one at all; on the contrary, as has been found again and again, it is the relatively well-off peasants, who control enough land to provide a living to their families and a modest surplus for sale in the market, that are normally the principal beneficiaries of successful rural development programmes, at least when these are not simply appropriated by the rural rich. The benefits for the poorest sections of rural society that follow from such programmes tend to be incidental and relatively unimportant, and to take a long time in reaching them.

Conversely, poverty alleviation measures will by definition be directed towards, and primarily benefit, the poor (or at least some of them: the poor do not form a homogeneous group). This means that IRD projects are often addressed at two or even more client or beneficiary groups, very different from each other. This places considerable constraints on the degree of integration which can be achieved in such projects, since for example certain growth-oriented components of an IRD project are likely to concern primarily the moderately well-off, while poverty-oriented components concern mainly the poor, or at least some of them.

As was suggested above, IRD projects differ substantially from each other. The scopes of the programmes, the mechanics of their implementation and the socio-political contexts within which they are formulated and implemented vary considerably across countries and even across different periods in the same country. Such wide variation does not, however, negate the advantages of comparing different national experiences; on the contrary, the richer and more varied the experiences, the greater the potential for learning from their comparison, provided of course that we are still talking about the same type, or similar types, of programme, so that comparison remains legitimate.

The different policy contexts in which they are formulated have important implications for the specific forms given to IRD projects. Each project will tend to address primarily problems and needs which were not solved or satisfactorily dealt with by pre-existing policies and programmes and to leave aside those that were. Furthermore, no matter how well designed and implemented, projects are often limited in their ability to generate economic growth and to reduce rural poverty and income disparities by the nature of macro-economic policies and national development strategies. This implies that the policy contexts in which different projects or programmes are formulated need to be taken into account when evaluating and when attempting to compare them, without which both evaluation and comparison may turn out to be almost totally meaningless.

The dependence of the effectiveness of IRD projects on the national policy context within which they are implemented has another important implication. In addition to explicit objectives of the kind mentioned above, it is imperative to keep in mind the possibility that certain IRD projects may be designed to serve certain other objectives, for example of a political nature, which may not be explicitly formulated or even officially acknowledged by the authorities, but are nevertheless assigned great importance by them. This is the case, for example, of the use of IRD as an instrument of counter-insurgency, or of public relations (as when it is used in areas of low priority to give the local population the impression — or the illusion — that the government is actively looking after their development needs). Dunham (1983) analyses the use of rural development as "(in addition to its economic logic) a means of countering the potential threat of rural unrest or of insurrection generated by existing agrarian structures, by severe and very conspicuous inequalities, mounting landlessness and chronic poverty", and "the significance and role of middle and richer peasants . . . in containing class conflicts and generating support and political control for dominant groups at national and international level". The existence of such 'hidden agendas' — and of corresponding unstated evaluation criteria — may help to explain the remarkable persistence of IRD and similar programmes of rural development, in spite of considerable and justified criticism of their ability to reach their explicit objectives.

To provide additional focus — and thus make sure that they *were* writing about more or less the same thing — the contributors to this volume were asked not only to provide critical reviews of their countries' recent experience with IRD, but also to centre their contributions around three main topics, which correspond to important facets of IRD strategy. These topics are:

(i) The strategy of spatial integration and of expansion of the rural economy through the establishment of linkages with, and integration into, wider economic spaces, with greater diversity of activities, resources and linkages, so as to enhance its capacity for sustained development.

(ii) The strategy of de-linking the poor from the prevailing patterns of asset-ownership, i.e. of trying to bring about their autonomous development by severing the links of dependence that tie them to the rural rich. Of particular interest in this regard are the inter-related questions of what will replace those dependence relations and of the conditions under which such a strategy can be sustained over a long enough period to bring about genuine and significant social and economic change.

(iii) The decentralisation of organisational structures and the use of decentralised organisations in trying to change the structure of local power in rural areas, so as to improve the social and economic opportunities of the poor and their access to productive resources.

Together, these three topics clearly cover a wide area of past criticism of IRD projects and programmes. As will be seen below, the contributions vary in the degree to which they actually address these topics and in the way of approaching them.

Designed to extend and develop the note of invitation to the seminar and aimed at providing a focus and a framework for the discussions, the paper by Guimaraes differs from the others in this part in that it deals with a number of general questions rather than with specific country experiences. After a discussion of the IRD approach, its achievements and some of its implicit assumptions, the paper takes up and discusses the three strategies mentioned above, tries to assess how likely they are to lead to better results than earlier approaches and draws some of their implications for the design and implementation of IRD projects.

The remaining papers in Part I deal with various aspects of the IRD experiences of six Asian developing countries — Bangladesh, India, Nepal, Sri Lanka, Indonesia and the Philippines. Table 1.1 below gives some background information on these countries, in the form of a number of indicators for each of the six plus three other countries which are added in order to strengthen the comparative character of the table, namely Pakistan, Thailand and China.

Table 1.1: Development Indicators for Selected Asian Countries

Country	GNP Per Capita		Share of Agriculture in GDP (%)		Daily Calorie Supply (Per Capita)	
	Dollars	Av. Annual Growth Rate (per cent)				
	1986	1965-86	1965	1986	1965	1985
Bangladesh	160	0.4	53	47	1,964	1,804
India	290	1.8	47	32	2,100	2,126
Nepal	150	1.9	65	..	1,931	1,997
Pakistan	350	2.4	40	24	1,747	2,180
Sri Lanka	400	2.9	28	26	2,155	2,485
Thailand	810	4.0	35	17	2,200	2,399
Indonesia	490	4.6	56	26	1,792	2,476
Philippines	560	1.9	26	26	1,936	2,260
China	300	5.1	39	31	2,034	2,620

Source: World Bank, *World Development Report, 1988.*

In Bangladesh, the implementation of rural development programmes does not seem to have been able to stop the growth of rural poverty and landlessness. This can probably be partly explained by the stagnation of the economy (see Table 1.1), and partly by the fact that the main beneficiaries of the measures aimed at stimulating rural development were relatively large land owners, many of whom evicted tenants or/and bought additional land from poor neighbours, thus increasing the incidence of landlessness and rural poverty (de Vylder and Asplund, 1979).

In his paper, Z. Rahman traces the origins of IRD in Bangladesh and describes the latest approach adopted following the failure of earlier efforts to address the problem of rural poverty in an effective way. This new approach has been adopted comparatively recently and there is as yet no indication of whether it is more successful than earlier ones. The paper closes with an outline of the approach and measures that, in his view, should be implemented in Bangladesh for the alleviation of rural poverty. The author advocates a shift from the community to the household as the basic unit of planned intervention, particularly in target group-oriented programmes, so as to avoid by-passing the poor because of the rural power structure. He also stresses the crucial importance of land reform as a precondition for other poverty alleviation measures, and the need to set up systems capable of monitoring impacts on an ongoing basis, both at the sectoral and at the project levels.

Although it contains inevitable areas of overlap with that of Z. Rahman, the paper by K.S. Rasheed also provides some complementary information. After a brief review of the history of IRD in Bangladesh, the author describes the recent administrative reorganisation in the course of which the old *thanas* or police station areas (the administrative unit below the level of the district) were upgraded and renamed *upazilas*, and given increased functional responsibilities, including a greatly enhanced role in decentralised planning and implementation. He then advocates a major re-organisation of *upazila* boundaries, so as to achieve approximately equal number of people in each *upazila*; at a much more pragmatic level, he also puts forth the idea that afforestation and social forestry schemes be brought under the IRDP jurisdiction in Bangladesh.

The Integrated Rural Development Programme in India must be seen as only one of a cluster of programmes that includes a national rural employment programme, a rural landless employment guarantee programme and a variety of agricultural schemes, the overall purpose of which is to alleviate poverty through infrastructure development and the promotion of viable economic activities. IRDP, which is the most important anti-poverty programme, is strongly target group-oriented, in the sense that it consists primarily of assisting poor families to cross the poverty line by providing them with income-generating assets.

After reviewing the criticisms to which IRDP has been subjected in India, N.J. Kurian's paper presents a number of findings based on the data generated by the Concurrent Evaluation Survey of IRDP carried out by several research institutions on behalf of the Department of Rural Development during 1985-86. His conclusions are critical but cautiously positive in relation to the way in which the IRDP is run and to its ability to target the poor and to help increase their income. Although many IRDP beneficiaries — especially the poorest among them — fail to cross the poverty line as a result of the programme, most of them experience significant increases in income, which means that the programme is as relevant for them as for those who do cross the poverty line. Among the weaknesses and areas where IRDP could be improved, Kurian includes greater participation in the planning and implementation of the programme and improvement in the planning and implementation capacity of bureaucratic structures at district and block levels.

The paper by D.N. Dhungel and D.I. Field is the first in this collection to deal with the experience of a particular project, in this case the Karnali-Bheri IRDP (K-BIRD), covering three districts in Nepal. Two major characteristics of the policy context are important for a proper understanding of the way in which this project functions: first, the shift of emphasis in development policy that began with the Fifth Plan in 1975, away from the development of physical infrastructure and towards the growth of agricultural production and, somewhat later, the satisfaction of basic needs; second, the 1982 Decentralisation Act and its by-laws, according to which all local level and district level projects are required to be formally approved by the concerned district panchayats. According to the Act, all district level offices — including those of the line ministries — are under the district panchayat secretariat. Its head, the Local Development Officer (LDO), who is both a member and the secretary of the district panchayat, plays a key role in co-ordinating all the district level offices and helping the district panchayat in its functions of planning, implementation and evaluation. The line agency offices in a district thus have a double set of responsibilities: towards their own ministries, who provide them with resources and policy guidance, and towards the LDO as the executive officer of the district panchayat secretariat, who co-ordinates the programmes of all the district level offices (Amatya, 1987: 98-100).

K-BIRD, like the other Integrated Rural Development Projects in the country, is a foreign assisted project which finds itself in a situation where there are already the usual problems of conflict between functional-based and territorial-based co-ordinating structures. Apart from certain functions like training and the hiring of consultants which it implements directly, K-BIRD does not implement any separate programmes itself, but provides funds to implementing agencies instead. From the administrative point of view such a position is understandably rather awkward, and the paper is particularly interesting for its perspective on the difficulties faced by the project, the ways in which it dealt with them and its record of achievement.

As in Nepal, all the IRD projects in Sri Lanka are foreign-funded, through bilateral or multi-lateral agencies. In terms of national priorities, IRD in Sri Lanka has not been at the top, a position reserved for large scale capital-intensive programmes like the Mahaweli Programme of river basin development, the Million Houses Programme and the development of the Free Trade Zone. All the IRD projects are carried out in areas which do not derive significant benefits from either of the three major programmes mentioned, which may indicate that politically they play a role of "consolation prizes" for the areas which were not favoured by the major programmes.

In her paper, M. Jayamane deals with a specific project in Sri Lanka — IRDP-Ratnapura. The author gives special emphasis to questions of planning and implementation methodology, and particularly to what she calls the key-area approach, whereby planners facilitate integration and participation and, at the same time, minimise the difficulties of problem identification, planning and implementation, by initially reducing the area of intervention to relatively small "key areas", selected on the basis of geographical homogeneity, administrative unity and degree of under-development. She also makes the useful point that the impact of the IRD project varies greatly among key areas, and identifies as the main reason for that fact the differences in development potential of the areas.

The distinction made in the paper between the two main types of approach adopted by foreign donors towards IRD projects, namely the blue-print approach adopted by the World Bank and the annual planning approach adopted by a number of bilateral agencies, like the Scandinavian and the Dutch international co-operation agencies, deserves some additional comment. In the first case, funding is allocated for a period of five years, by sectors, and the implementation is consequently rather rigid. The second approach, by contrast, is characterised by year-to-year allocations, allowing people to introduce changes and to reformulate at least some components of the projects, and thus the incorporation of what is learnt about the area and the project. Considering the importance of learning processes of various kinds in IRD projects — where both individuals and organisations must learn a great deal about both the areas and the groups they work with, and where implementing agencies used to vertical lines of authority, responsibility and co-ordination must learn the art of co-ordinating interventions with those of other agencies in the interests of a common purpose — the advantage of the second, more flexible approach is considerable.

A comparison between two approaches to IRD is also one of the main themes of the paper by Moeljarto on IRD in Indonesia. Following the adoption of a clearly growth-oriented economic strategy in the mid-sixties, Indonesia implemented a series of sectoral programmes in order to increase agricultural production, covering the whole country and dealing with food production, smallholder plantations, small-scale livestock and fishery development and other productive activities. Thanks to these policies the country made great progress and achieved self-sufficiency in rice. From 1978 onwards, this orientation was supplemented with a set of equity-oriented programmes among the objectives of which rural development and poverty eradication figured prominently. Among these programmes are the two described and compared by Moeljarto, namely (i) the UKPD accentuating the objective of transition from traditional to modern villages and adopting a blue-print approach based on the manipulation of a number of facets of the socio-economic life of the village; and (ii) the PDP laying greater emphasis to on the alleviation of rural poverty through institutional development and social experimentation. The author's conclusion clearly favours the second, more flexible and open-ended approach over the first, the main result of which he describes as "the ritualisation of organisational behaviour imposed from above".

The last two papers in this part both refer to the Integrated Area Development approach, which is the version of IRD adopted and implemented in the Philippines since the early 1970s. This approach aims at achieving integration and breaking sectoral approaches by directing sectoral interventions, in a co-ordinated fashion, at specific areas, an approach that may at least in part be explained by the importance given in the Philippines to regional development. In her paper, P.

Nietes gives an authoritative description of the evolution of perspectives on and approaches to IAD in the Philippines, from the earlier generation of projects, through a second to the current third generation. This evolution was characterised by a decreasing emphasis on infrastructure and a correspondingly greater stress being placed on productive activities, human resource development and institutional development, in order to achieve greater sustainability. The paper ends with a brief description of one of the second generation IAD projects, the Palawan IAD, which both incorporates some of the lessons of the first generation and constitutes a clear indication of the direction in which IAD is evolving.

In spite of efforts by the editors to minimise duplication, the paper by M. Garcia inevitably overlaps with that of P. Nietes. At the same time, the differences in perspective between the two papers — one written from very close to the organisational core where the IAD strategy was developed and revised, the other written from outside with a deliberately critical perspective — makes them well worth reading side by side. Garcia's stress on certain aspects of organisation and management of IAD usefully complements the description and analysis in Nietes's paper. Garcia explicitly assesses the IAD experience and track record in relation to each of the three strategies mentioned at the beginning of this introduction: spatial integration and expansion of the rural economy, development of the poor and structural decentralisation. His main conclusions are the that the shift in strategy from infrastructure to livelihood support should continue, as should the efforts to develop grassroots organisations and to stimulate institutional development so as to enhance the sustainability of projects. A very useful reminder that rural development cannot and should not be reduced to IRD comes at the end of the paper in the recommendation that IAD areas should be made into priority areas for the implementation of the agrarian reform envisaged by the current administration of the Philippines.

REFERENCES

Amatya, S.L. (1987) "Decentralisation in Nepal: an Overview", in H. Demaine and R.E. Malong (ed.), *Decentralization: Area Development in Practice in Asia*, Rural-Regional Development Network, AIT, Bangkok.

Dunham, D. (1983) "Rural Development as Counter-Insurgency: Notes on the Political Dimensions of 'Small-Farmer' Policies", Inst. of Social Studies, the Hague (Mimeo).

de Vylder, S. and Asplund, D. (1979) "Contradictions and Distortions in a Rural Economy: The Case of Bangladesh", Stockholm: Swedish International Development Authority.

2

INTEGRATED RURAL DEVELOPMENT: What Have We Learnt?

J. P. de Campos Guimaraes

1. Introduction

Integrated Rural Development (IRD) has been in existence for a significant period of time, and much has been written about it. It has been evaluated, criticised and discussed in a variety of national and organisational contexts (Ruttan, 1975 and 1984; Cohen, 1980; Birgegaard, 1987).

The main thesis of this paper is that, in the design and evaluation of IRD projects and programmes, too much attention has been paid to the organisational and administrative problems of implementation, at the expense of better understanding of the nature, problems and dynamics of the rural societies for which the projects and programmes are designed. More emphasis needs to be laid on the substantive problems of rural development projects and programmes, which are too often overshadowed or even completely hidden by an excessive concern with the administrative problems of implementation.

Section 2 contains a brief discussion of the nature and main characteristics of IRD, in the sense in which the term is used in this paper. Reference is also made to the antecedents and origins of the approach. Section 3 then presents a number of comments on the achievements of IRD, particularly from the point of view of effectiveness, sustainability and replicability. Not surprisingly, the approach does not seem to have fared particularly well according to these criteria. This leads to the question of whether IRD *could* have fared much better, given the nature of the approach and what we know about the structure and dynamics of rural societies. In connection with this question, section 4 contains a brief discussion of two main underlying assumptions of the

IRD approach and of how well they fit in with what we know about rural development processes. The argument continues in section 5, where three strategies which have some novel characteristics, namely (i) de-linking the poor, (ii) spatial integration and (iii) decentralisation, are discussed in order to see whether they are likely to lead to better results than the earlier ones. Finally, section 6 analyses some implications of the argument for the way in which IRD projects are designed and implemented.

2. The Nature of Integrated Rural Development

Partly no doubt as a result of its widespread use, the expression 'Integrated Rural Development' has become rather ambiguous, requiring clarification as to the precise set of objectives and approaches it denotes in each case (Cohen, 1980). Perhaps the best way of achieving clarity in this respect is to recall briefly the main influences that led to the development of IRD as a recognisably new approach to rural development.

First, a reference must be made to the Community Development (CD) approach that prevailed in the 1950s, first in India and later in many other developing countries. IRD shares several of the characteristics of CD, particularly the importance attributed to poverty and the stress laid on multi-sectoral activities, on bottom-up planning and on local participation and mobilisation.

Following the decline of the Community Development approach, consequent on its limited impact, the 1960s were characterised by growth-oriented development strategies, emphasising interventions aiming at technological and infrastructural development and at the increase of production. Unfortunately, the trickle-down mechanisms which provided an important rationalisation for the new strategy did not work as effectively as expected, if they worked at all. One key consequence of this fact was that, in spite of reasonable rates of economic growth in many developing countries, poverty continued to increase, to the point of becoming a major political problem and of occupying a predominant position in the development debate. Equally significant was the fact that poverty remained, to a large extent, *rural* poverty. This was a major influence in the development of the IRD approach.

Another important factor in that development was the growing awareness, among planners and administrators, of what may be described as the multi-dimensional nature of rural problems. Partly as a result of project failures, these people came to realise that the majority of, say, economic problems in rural areas cannot be solved by economic means alone, because they are embedded in very complex situations, with cultural, political, social, technical and other dimensions. The word 'integrated' in the expression 'integrated rural development' is, in its most common usage, related more or less directly with this question, in that it denotes the attempt to tackle rural development problems on several fronts at the same time. As Ruttan (1984: 394) puts it, 'recognition that rural development involves the interaction of a large number of interrelated activities was interpreted to imply that integrated programme implementation could contribute to the achievement of rapid and measurable gains in agricultural production and rural welfare'.

The concept of IRD was also significantly influenced by the basic needs strategy of development, introduced in the early 1970s and adopted by the ILO. This strategy displaced growth as the principal objective and yardstick of development; instead of growth, meeting the basic minimum needs of the poor became the central concern of development planning and policy. Under the influence of this approach, combating poverty and meeting the basic needs of the poorest people in the rural areas became central objectives for rural development programmes and projects in the 1970s.

As a result of all these influences, IRD projects evolved a typical format. It is important to stress here that IRD is indeed basically that: a project format. The lack of a solid theoretical basis for IRD has been reiterated so often as to have become almost trivial. IRD has developed not as a result of a particular theoretical or analytical insight but as a consequence of a change in perspective concerning the ends and means of rural development programmes. Although the typical IRD project has a number of points in common with Community Development projects, it differs from them by a greater awareness of the stratified nature of rural communities and of the importance of conflict in those communities, and by the emphasis on basic needs and income generation. Birgegaard (1984: 2) identifies the main characteristics of this format as:

(a) Multi-sectoral nature of the projects, which are usually implemented by several agencies;
(b) Limitation of the area of intervention (area planning, district planning, etc.);

(c) Emphasis on local participation and mobilisation; and
(d) Explicit reference to poverty alleviation and to the basic minimum needs of the poor.

It must be stressed that even these characteristics define no more than a rather broad range of different approaches. Participation, for instance, is perhaps the most ambiguous of all the words used in the context of rural development projects. In practice it has been given meanings that range from exercises in public relations designed to increase a project's capacity to manipulate the local population, to varying degrees of genuine involvement of that population in the assessment of local needs, the design of projects and/or their implementation (Cohen and Uphoff, 1980). In a similar way, the poverty orientation of IRD projects has also received different interpretations, reflecting different degrees of commitment to the objective of fighting poverty. However, most IRD projects share one important negative characteristic, common also to the community development projects of the 1950s, namely that they do not address the structural questions that are so frequently at the root of poverty. As a consequence, the poverty-related elements of these projects are often limited to the provision of delivery systems addressed at the poor, at best accompanied by organisational efforts designed to maximise the benefits that the poor derive from them. This point is dealt with at greater length below.

3. The Performance of IRD

Several publications in the recent literature detail the achievements and failures of IRD and provide explanations for one or the other type of result (e.g. Crener *et al*, 1983; Lele, 1975; Ruttan, 1975). At the risk of being somewhat unfair to certain individual projects, we could summarise the track record of IRD in the following propositions:

I. From the point of view of *effectiveness*, programmes and projects based on the IRD approach have generally failed to achieve substantial and reliable increases in food production and to make a significant dent in the problem of rural poverty. A large part of the projects that may be described as successful consists of pilot projects, where it has been possible to achieve an intensive use of human and material resources.

II. Even when effective, many pilot projects turn out not to be *replicable*, because the high intensity of resource inputs cannot be sustained when attempts are made to extend the pilot projects to national or regional rural development programmes.

III. As for *sustainability*, projects which are implemented with special administrative arrangements and with comparatively abundant resources (often associated with the existence of a foreign assistance component) frequently experience difficulties once the pilot stage is over and they find themselves integrated into an existing bureaucratic structure and forced to compete with other projects or activities for the resources they need to continue functioning.

Furthermore, as Ruttan (1984: 398) puts it,

> . . . access to the higher decision-making levels of government and the administrative freedom to tailor programmes precisely to local natural and human resource endowments and capacities and to priority development problems that is often available to directors of pilot projects is frequently sacrificed to administrative convenience when the projects are generalised in the form of provincial or national programmes. Highly centralised administration of national programmes makes it difficult to carry out the experiments with programme content and delivery methods that are essential if rural development programmes are to meet the diverse needs of rural areas.

In the light of this assessment, it is reasonable to ask what causes have been identified for the rather poor performance of IRD projects. This question is addressed in a recent paper, based on an extensive literature review and some field studies (Birgegaard, 1987). In this paper, the author provides a tentative summary of arguments concerning the reasons for the poor performance of IRD. Slightly edited, the summary is as follows (Birgegaard, 1987: 11):

(1) Implementation of multi-sectoral IRD projects has met with serious organisational and managerial problems limiting the scope for replicability and for a wide coverage of the rural population.

(2) Co-ordination is the single most important management

problem reported from implementation of IRD projects.

(3) The difficulties in finding effective organisational designs explain many of what are generally identified as managerial problems.

(4) By-pass [defined not only as the establishment of autonomous project organisations which do not depend on the existing bureaucratic structures but also as deviation from the bureaucracy's prevailing rules in planning, implementation and financial management of projects] is hard to avoid in IRD projects, raising serious questions concerning project sustainability.

(5) Integration [defined as the selection and design of activities which together contribute to solve a particular problem] seems hard to achieve. A multi-sectoral project format has to be justified primarily on other grounds.

(6) A multi-sectoral project design is more relevant than a mono-sectoral design when attempts are made to promote people's participation through e.g. local government.

It is interesting and revealing that, although there are references in the paper to substantive difficulties found in the course of implementation, *all six* paragraphs in the summary concern characteristics of what we might call the planning and management system of the IRD projects, and their impact upon project performance. A first implication of this is that in IRD projects the planning and management system itself must be dealt with explicitly as part of the problem to be solved, rather than merely as part of the solution.

Perhaps even more interesting, however, is the fact that, in spite of being fully aware of the theoretical weakness of the IRD approach, Birgegaard makes no reference to the possibility that such weakness might affect performance, and limits his summary to organisational and administrative aspects. This reflects a common attitude among professionals involved in IRD projects, for whom the only serious problems are those related to organisation, co-ordination and the efficiency with which project activities are carried out. Although it is easy to sympathise with this attitude, there is in it the hidden – and dangerous – assumption that the project design itself is unquestionable, and that if only the implementation problems are solved the project is bound to reach its objectives. In other words, there is the risk that implementation problems may overshadow other, perhaps critical, problems of a substantive nature. This danger is greater because of the lack of a solid theoretical foundation for IRD.

It is imperative that rural development professionals become conscious of at least the possibility that organisational and administrative difficulties may conceal the irrelevance of a particular project. Projects may fail to work simply because their design is flawed and misses crucial points in the situation or problem they are designed to deal with. This is even more important because the IRD approach is beset by obvious theoretical weaknesses. One way of bringing these to light is to analyse some of the main underlying assumptions of IRD.

4. Some Assumptions of IRD

In a World Bank publication, Uma Lele (1975: 20) defines rural development as 'improving living standards of the mass of the low-income population residing in rural areas and making the process of their development self-sustaining'. As for the reduction of poverty, the following quotation clearly indicates the way in which rural development projects are expected to help:

> Since rural development is intended to reduce poverty, it must be clearly designed to increase production and raise productivity. Rural development recognises that improved food supplies and nutrition, together with basic services, such as health and education, not only directly improve the physical well-being and quality of life of the rural poor, but can also indirectly enhance their productivity and their ability to contribute to the national economy (IBRD, 1975: 3).

In practice, IRD projects employ a number of instruments, which normally include (i) some form of local participation in the identification of needs and even in the planning of interventions; (ii) a multi-sectoral delivery system, covering as a rule agricultural infrastructure and inputs, credit and social services like health and education; (iii) an organisational mechanism of co-ordination of the delivery of various inputs and resources to the community. The question is then whether these instruments are likely to have the expected impact, particularly on poverty.

In order to address this question we must first discuss, even if briefly, how people and organisations conceptualise 'poverty' and its causes. If poverty is simply equated with lack of resources, if it is considered as a state in which people or groups may find themselves, then the delivery of resources by an IRD project may, if carried out properly, be expected to have a significant impact on poverty. 'Properly' here means that the delivery should be made to the right people, in a co-ordinated (or integrated) manner and in sufficient amounts and for a sufficiently long period to make a difference.

When, however, we consider that poverty is to a very large extent the result of ongoing social *processes* and social *relations* that bring about a redistribution of resources away from the poor and in favour of some of the higher income groups, then clearly the delivery of resources to the poor, no matter how well co-ordinated and implemented, is not enough. Only if a way is found to stop that redistribution from taking place, either by neutralising the effects of the social processes at work or by actually attempting to change both processes and relations, is IRD likely to have an impact.

A very simple and clear case may help illustrate this statement. In south-west Bangladesh, where sharecropping is widespread, a practice exists that is clearly connected with the relative scarcity of land. This practice, named '*salami*', consists of the payment by sharecroppers of a certain quantity of money to their landlords, for the use of the land (van Roosmalen and Guimaraes, 1981: 57). This payment is repeated every season and is made *in addition* to the payment of a share (which is normally 50 per cent of the crop, with all costs borne by the sharecropper). Under the prevailing conditions of land scarcity, the landlords can easily appropriate any increase in the productivity of the land simply by raising the *salami*, since they are always able to find sharecroppers willing to pay the increased *salami*. In this situation, even an efficient system for the delivery of resources to the poor – who, as is easy to understand given the conditions described, include many sharecroppers - will not be able to avoid the appropriation of a significant part of those resources by the landowners. For such a system to function effectively it would be necessary first to find a way of preventing the transfer of resources associated with the *salami* – and with other mechanisms of the same type, including sharecropping itself – on a reliable and sustainable basis.

The case just described is clearly not an isolated one, and represents only one aspect of the complex social relations between rich and poor in a particular society. In one form or another, however, similar mechanisms are at work in the majority of rural societies. This means that the question of the dependence relations that exist between rich and poor in rural areas, and of the way in which they will influence the impact of IRD projects, has general relevance for IRD.

It must be stressed that there *are* situations where it may be legitimate to ascribe poverty to lack of resources or a low carrying capacity of the environment, not necessarily because there are no mechanisms of exploitation at work in the rural community, but because the general lack of resources affects the whole community to such a degree that it overshadows wealth differentials within the community. In such cases, the setting up of delivery systems following the IRD model may indeed have an important impact on the welfare of the rural community, including the poor. But these cases are arguably in a minority when compared to situations where social relations and social processes are at the root of rural poverty.

The identification of rural poverty with lack of resources is a basic assumption, as well as a basic source of weakness, of most IRD projects. Such projects reflect awareness of the existence of poverty as well as the desire to do something about it, but poverty itself is conceived in a static way, and the question of what mechanisms and relations beget it is hardly ever allowed to influence project design. In these circumstances, improvements in co-ordination or participation do not offer a solution to the problem, since its existence does not follow from poor co-ordination or from a lack of participation, but from a mismatch between the models underlying project design and the way in which the community actually functions. Participation, especially in the way in which it is normally practised, is also very vulnerable to appropriation by the rich and powerful in the rural areas (who are in general better educated and more articulate than the poor), in much the same way as happens with resources.

A second weakness of the IRD approach stems from its almost exclusively rural focus, which affects not only objectives but also problem identification, analysis and intervention. The implicit assumption behind this rural focus is that rural areas are closed systems, or at least may be treated as such from the point of view of rural development. This is tantamount to disregarding the role and importance of urban systems for the development of rural areas. Project designs predicated on this type of assumption are inevitably less effective than they could be, since they disregard the influence, and fail to benefit from the use, of a set of variables that significantly influence rural development.

In most cases, the key to the development of rural areas does not lie entirely within those areas but also – and sometimes principally – in their relations with the outside world, normally mediated by the urban system. A solid understanding of the various ways in which rural and urban areas interact, and of how these interactions influence rural development, is essential for planners who have to deal with the problems of rural development. It must be stressed that this does not represent an attempt to re-colonise rural development by bringing back an urban-based perspective, as was done in the 1960s with growth pole strategies which relied on trickle-down to bring about rural development. On the contrary, it is because we take the objective of rural development seriously that rural-urban relations must be explicitly included in the analysis and realistically planned for. In this way, analytical and policy issues, e.g. the marketing of agricultural products, rural-urban migration and the structure of central place systems can be given the importance they deserve, in the design and implementation of rural development projects.

At the same time, however, the tendency for reification that follows from an increased emphasis on rural-urban relations must be avoided. The interactions between rural and urban areas are primarily interactions between individuals, organisations, groups or classes, *not* between 'areas' endowed with fictitious personality and/or unity of purpose. For this reason, it is important to adopt a political economy approach to the study of those interactions, interpreting rural-urban relations, in a second stage of the analysis, as a spatial expression of socio-economic and political processes that cannot and should not be reduced to their spatial dimensions alone. Of course, the spatial dimension is in turn irreducible to others, in that the distribution of natural resources and, to a certain extent, also population, is area-specific and may in general be treated as given. This makes it imperative for rural planners to complement other approaches with a careful analysis, at the local level, of the relations between population and natural resources.

To sum up, what is proposed above is the replacement of the rather simplistic model of society that underlies much of IRD practice with a more accurate and realistic one, where (i) the implementing capacity of the existing administrative system is considered as part of the problem to be solved, and taken into account in the design and planning of implementation; (ii) the simple identification of poverty with lack of resources is replaced by a deliberate attempt to understand and influence the socio-economic processes that are so often at its root and

(iii) the openness of the rural systems and the importance for rural development of their links to urban and other rural systems is recognised. This model shift has important practical implications, as will be made clear in section 5, where three approaches to rural development which hold out the promise of overcoming some of the difficulties of previous approaches is discussed. The three approaches in question have some novel aspects and are representative of recent attempts to explore new and innovative paths to rural development.

5. Some New Approaches to Rural Development

In this section we shall discuss three very different, and to some extent complementary, approaches to rural development, namely (i) de-linking the poor, (ii) decentralisation and (iii) spatial integration.

The rationale for the strategy often described as 'de-linking the poor' is well known: given the dependence relations that tie the rural poor to the rich, and their role in the perpetuation of rural poverty, one of the ways of fighting poverty consists of breaking those relationships. This, it is expected, will allow the poor to develop independently from the rich and give them a better chance of escaping from poverty, or at least improving their own lot significantly. Two important questions arise immediately in connection with this strategy: *first*, by what can these relations of dependence be replaced; *second*, how sustainable is a strategy of this type. However exploitative, the relations between rich and poor in rural areas have functional aspects that result in benefits for the poor, even if only occasional or short-term. Patronage gives protection to the poor in a variety of situations where their welfare or even their survival may be threatened. It also plays a particularly important role in societies riven by factionalism and ethnic and religious divides. This means that it is important to be clearly aware, in each concrete historical situation, of the nature, strength and role of the relations that link rich and poor, and of the benefits that the poor derive from them, before discussing the question of replacing them. But replaced they must be, since it will be necessary to fill in some way the vacuum caused by their disappearance. The transition from dependence to self-sufficiency is not easy, and needs support along the way. The concrete forms of this support and the costs associated with it in turn largely determine the answer to the question of sustainability.

Two main types of answer have in practice been given to the first of the two questions above. In its most extreme form, the first of these consists of replacing dependence on the rich with dependence on a particular project or organisation which, rather than exploit the poor, supports them and provides them with access to economic resources. This is an approach typical of relief projects and of certain non-governmental organisations (NGOs) which provide resources (e.g. credit, tools, technology, designs, etc.) to the rural poor and then buy and market the production themselves. It has the advantage of producing an immediate impact, which is why it is adopted in short-term relief projects where immediate efficacy is essential. If, however, no serious attempt is made to eliminate dependence and bring about some kind of self-reliance, the improvement in the situation of the poor will remain dependent on the continuing presence of the project or organisation, and if this presence is terminated the most likely outcome will be a return to the original situation, or to one not very different from it. In other words, the sustainability of this type of project is generally not very high.

Again in an extreme form, the second type of answer given to the question of what will replace dependence consists of providing no resources to the poor and focusing all efforts on their socio-political organisation and conscientisation on the basis of common interests and class solidarity. For obvious reasons, this type of approach is more common among NGOs than among government organisations. These NGOs see their primary task as one of helping the poor to organise themselves, and consider that the improvement of access to resources and the consequent amelioration of their socio-economic situation can only occur in the long run. They will however have a greater likelihood of being sustained, as a result of the increase in the capacity of the poor to make demands of the system (and particularly of the government), itself a consequence of their organisation and greater level of political consciousness.

In practice, neither extreme position is often found in a pure form. Organisations and projects which lay emphasis on the provision of resources to the poor also, in general, attempt to raise their consciousness and to stimulate their organisation, and even radical advocates of the second type of approach use at least the expectation of economic benefits to motivate the members of the organisations they set up. Also, interventions of the second type frequently require a measure of support and protection, easier to obtain if their projects contain at least some recognisable elements of resource provision.

These are, however, two basically different approaches to the same problem, and most attempts at putting into practice the strategy of delinking the poor may be classified according to which of the two receives most emphasis.

There seems to exist a trade-off, in these two types of approach, between effectiveness – especially immediate effectiveness – on the one hand, and replicability and sustainability, on the other. As mentioned above, the first type of approach is much more effective in the short-term but requires the ongoing presence of the project or organisation if the benefits are to be sustained. The second type of approach is normally much slower in generating palpable improvements – if indeed it can be said to generate them at all, at least directly. On the other hand, it holds the promise of greater sustainability, once the level of social and political awareness of the poor and the size of their organisations have crossed certain thresholds. The same may be said for replicability, since at least the organisational process, once successfully initiated, will tend to spread almost by itself.

An important unanswered question in this respect concerns the possibility and the consequences of moving from one type of approach to the other, as time passes and situations change: could it be possible, for instance, for a project to evolve from an emphasis on relief and income generation to an emphasis on political organisation and self-reliance? Or for a project focused on organisation to arrive at a stage where the provision of resources to the poor will no longer risk compromising their socio-political organisation, their autonomy and solidarity? Based on my own experience, I would expect the second situation to occur more easily than the first. This is an important field of research, with direct policy relevance. More generally, there is much in the experience of both NGOs and of government projects with these approaches that is directly relevant for the design and planning of IRD projects. To mention only an example, a solid organisation may be the only possibility that the poor have of playing an active role in the participation exercises associated with IRD projects.

Another important approach to rural development that is closely connected with the question of participation is organisational decentralisation. By increasing decision-making capacity at the local level, decentralisation creates conditions where, at least in principle, decisions can be made by people who are closer to the problems, and presumably understand them better, than decision-makers at the national or even regional levels.

Because of the closeness of the decision-makers to the population, decentralisation also has the potential to achieve greater and more genuine participation. However, two 'caveats' seem essential: first, decentralisation may, if unsupported by clear norms from the centre and by an effective monitoring system, easily give rise to arbitrariness and corruption. Secondly, there is a significant possibility that an effective process of decentralisation may, if it is not carefully prepared and monitored, result merely in the reinforcement of the position of the local elites and in the virtual appropriation by them of the decentralised decision-making capacity, with dire consequences for the welfare of the rural poor. Instead of changing the rural power structure, decentralisation under these conditions reinforces it and makes the poor more, not less, dependent on the rich.

The implications of what has just been said are clear: decentralisation should come at the end of a long process of preparation designed to ensure that it fulfils its promise. This process will minimally involve the drawing up of a monitoring and control system based on a carefully designed set of norms and criteria of evaluation and the investment of time and effort in the socio-political organisation of the rural poor on the basis of solidarity and common interests. Under these conditions decentralisation may indeed bring about, or at least greatly facilitate, rural social change, and contribute to redress the imbalance between rich and poor in the countryside.

Finally, a reference must be made to what was described above as the strategy of spatial integration. This consists of adding to the spatial integration that is normally achieved at the local level (by devising programmes or projects that reinforce each other's effects) an integration between actions and projects at the higher spatial level of the micro-region, including the cities that it may contain. This means that variables like employment creation in urban areas may be included in the analysis and plan, and that rural development projects are devised and planned in the context, not purely of the rural areas where they are going to be implemented, but of the whole rural region which contains these areas. It also means that it becomes possible to plan and implement region-wide programmes and to achieve a better compatibility between interventions aimed at urban and at rural areas. In other words, this strategy consists of introducing a regional dimension in rural development planning and implementation. In the past few years, the rural region has progressively come to be seen as a more appropriate level for analysis and intervention aimed at rural development than the village or even the group of villages. The main reason for this departure from earlier thinking is the growing awareness of the strong influence of the urban and industrial system, and particularly the nearby urban centres, on the development of rural areas. The adoption of a regional framework for a rural development planning permits the explicit inclusion of rural-urban relations in the planning of rural development.

Rural regional development planning, with its explicit consideration of the structure and role of marketing systems for agricultural produce, agricultural inputs and consumer goods, of flows of people, commodities and finance through the settlement hierarchy, has the potential of allowing rural development planners to design and implement programmes and projects integrated into economic spaces with greater diversity of resources, activities and linkages. In this way, rural development projects become *integrated* in a new sense which creates special opportunities as well as special constraints for rural development. Of course, it would be wrong to forget the very real dangers of what Pearse (1971) calls "the persistent process of penetration and incorporation of rural areas in the system of market relations", particularly the creation of economic and social dependence on the urban sector, the destruction of traditional solidarity, the subordination of traditional production to the modern sector of the economy and the polarisation that is usually associated with it, all of which are often accompanied by a deterioration in the wealth and welfare of the majority of the rural population. It can, however, also be argued that such processes of penetration and incorporation are taking place all the time, and that the adoption of a deliberate, planning approach to them at least offers the hope of minimising their negative aspects while taking advantage of the advantages and opportunities that are also associated with them.

The development of rural areas usually entails a mixture of diversification and specialisation. The potential for the success of either of these two types of change and the limitations of such change are largely determined not at the local but at the regional or even higher levels. Thus, the regional level may well be the lowest spatial level at which it makes sense to plan for rural development.

Having said all this, however, it must also be admitted that strategies for rural development which could appropriately be classified as rural regional, like agropolitan planning as first proposed by J. Friedmann and M. Douglass, or the Urban Functions in Rural Development approach normally associated with the name of D. Rondinelli, often lack a solid basis of factual knowledge, which they replace by a mixture of guesswork and wishful thinking that is frequently proven wrong by experience. A great deal of research is necessary on the conditions under which each of these approaches to the development of rural areas is likely to succeed, and thus also on when they should be adopted.

Before concluding, it should be stressed that the three approaches discussed in this section are very different in nature, and at the same time are perfectly compatible with each other, if not actually complementary. They all reflect an improved model of rural development and rural planning, and for that reason are more likely to achieve at least a measure of success than was the case with earlier approaches.

6. Some Implications

Given the purpose of this paper, of stimulating discussion, it would be inappropriate to try to draw a large number of conclusions from what has been said above. There are, however, some implications that deserve to be spelled out, because of their considerable practical importance.

If we take seriously the objective of fighting poverty, then it seems clear that something more than the traditional IRD approaches will be necessary for our interventions to have a significant impact. The strategy which was designated above by 'de-linking the poor' has the advantage of taking into account the processes and relationships that play a role in the creation and maintenance of poverty. In connection with this strategy, the need to organise the poor on the basis of common interests and class or group solidarity follows more or less directly from the requirements of sustainability and replicability, as well as from the objectives of self-reliance and unbiased participation. This organisation will almost inevitably have an important political dimension and this, in turn, may imply that under certain political conditions government organisations or projects are not the ideal vehicle for it. NGOs, often less committed to the existing political system, may be more effective organisers. One possible combination that has given promising results is for a project which has among its objectives the delivery of resources to bring in an NGO, whose function it will be to organise the poor. For such an arrangement to work, the responsibilities of the two organisations should be well divided and clearly established, and they should work as independently from each other as possible, except from the point of view of co-ordination of activities. This may also have the advantage of avoiding an identification between the NGO and the project, which could seriously compromise the effectiveness of the work of organisation.

An important implication of such a combination of activities aiming at organising the poor with others aiming at the provision of economic resources concerns the *timing* of the two types of activity. The time scale of organisation is much longer than that of other activities, such as the provision of infrastructure, of inputs, credit, or other services. This implies that, in order to avoid situations where one type of activity hinders the other, the work of organising the poor should start long in advance of the other types of project activities. This is not always easy to achieve, and conflicts may ensue within projects because of the different time scales of different activities. The interesting aspect here is that these conflicts often result, not from lack of co-operation (say, between engineers and socio-economists), but from the differences in the logic of each of the activities. They can, therefore, only be resolved through a process of project planning that takes such differences into account.

A second observation concerns the implications of adopting an approach characterised by decentralised planning and by the use of a rural regional planning framework. The requirements of decentralisation and participation, on the one hand, and those that follow from the need to achieve a spatial integration of projects, in the sense in which the term was used above, on the other, place considerable strain upon the planning system, which will have to achieve compatibility between top-down and bottom-up planning. This is the price that must be paid for the greater effectiveness that is expected to follow from the adoption of a planning framework that permits the integration of rural development and the urban-industrial sectors into a unified system of intervention.

REFERENCES

Biregard, L. (1987) 'A Review of Experiences with Integrated Rural Development', *Issue Paper No. 3*, International Rural Development Centre, Swedish University of Agricultural Sciences, Uppsala.

Cohen, J.M. (1980) 'Integrated Rural Development: Clearing Out the Underbrush', *Sociologia Ruralis*, Vol. 20, No. 3.

Cohen, J.M. and N.T. Uphoff (1980) 'Participation's Place in Rural Development: Seeking Clarity Through Specificity', *World Development*, vol. 8, pp. 213 - 235.

Crener, M.A. *et al.*, (1983) 'Integrated Rural Development, State of the Art Review 1982/83', *CIDA*, Quebec.

I.B.R.D. (1975) 'Rural Development', in *The Assault on World Poverty,* Baltimore and London.

Lele, U. (1975) *The Design of Rural Development: Lessons from Africa*, Johns Hopkins, Baltimore and London.

Pearse, A. (1971) 'Metropolis and Peasant: The Expansion of the Urban- Industrial Complex and the Changing Rural Structure", in T. Shanin (ed.), *Peasants and Peasant Societies*, Penguin, Harmondsworth, 1971.

Roosmalen, H. van and J. Guimaraes (1981) 'Preliminary Notes on the Socio-Economic Situation in Polder 22', *Delta Development Project*, Dhaka.

Ruttan, V.W. (1975) 'Integrated Rural Development Programs: A Sceptical Perspective', *International Development Review*, Vol. 17, No. 4.

Ruttan, V.W. (1984) 'Integrated Rural Development Programs: A Historical Perspective', *World Development*, Vol. 12, No. 4.

Waterstone, A. (1975) 'A Viable Model for Rural Development', *Integrated Rural Development*, Vol. 1, No. 1.

Weitz, R. (1979) *Integrated Rural Development: The Rehovot Approach*, Settlement Study Centre, Rehovot.

3

INTEGRATED RURAL DEVELOPMENT AND POVERTY ALLEVIATION : The Bangladesh Experience

M. Zillur Rahman

1.0 Introduction

Development economists and historians may find it difficult to locate the origin of Integrated Rural Development (IRD) as an approach to rural development. IRD is definitely not a product or a by-product of an identifiable body of development theories, but rather the outcome of assessments of performance of development efforts in the past, contributions particularly from social science research, political considerations in the face of increasing polarisation in the rural areas and the omnipresent need in the donor community for new and hopefully more promising avenues than those followed in the past. Some of the influences which resulted in IRD are as follows:

- Relative and absolute poverty grew in rural areas in most developing countries, despite declared intentions of Governments and reasonable overall performance of economic development.
- Infrastructural investment turned out to be largely irrelevant to the rural poor, while asset owners benefited substantially, at no cost to them.
- The trickle-down hypothesis turned out to be irrelevant for poverty alleviation.
- Social science researchers developed the concept of multi-dimensional rural problems, which in turn necessitated the adoption of broader development approaches.
- The ILO-triggered basic minimum needs strategy substantially

helped formulate the broader approach.

- Involvement of the beneficiaries in the planning and implementation of projects led to emphasis being laid on a broader approach and on participation.
- The containment of social and political tensions in the rural areas may also have contributed to the IRD concept. Implicitly, the intention may have been to blunt the sharpness of the class struggle.

Mention may be made in this respect of the Comilla model which was a forerunner of a number of similar programmes, like Cadu, Puebla, Ujamaa, etc., to mention only a few, popularly known as IRD projects.

It was the donor community, rather than the development planners and the governments of the developing countries, who played the dominant role in promoting IRD as an approach to rural development. The rapid expansion of the numbers of IRD projects in the seventies was initiated by donor agencies like USAID, ODA, GTZ, the World Bank and ADB. Soon other countries, especially the Nordic countries, adopted the IRD strategy. IRD became a centre-piece in the debate on rural development. Like its forerunner Community Development, IRD turned almost into a movement with its own promoters, vested interests and a kind of euphoria which contributed to its expansion. Workshops, symposia, seminars, etc. multiplied. At one time there was competition among the donors, both multilateral and bilateral, to get IRD projects introduced in specific areas. In Bangladesh the donors followed what could be described as the policy of "Rent a Thana", as a consequence of which a large number of area development projects started functioning with considerable vigour and energy but little pragmatism and knowledge, ultimately resulting largely in failures.

The IRD approach has been tried in different ways, with both successes and failures, in a number of developing countries. The approach may have an attractive and appealing flavour, but its complexity, excessive number of components, complex management and coordination problems compromise its viability. In particular, this model has failed to alleviate poverty, rather it accentuated it. In this paper, an attempt is made to describe and examine the experience of Bangladesh in the field of integrated rural development, especially from the perspective of poverty alleviation.

2.0 IRD in Bangladesh

Bangladesh is overwhelmingly rural, its economy is predominantly agrarian, and about 87 per cent of its population lives in rural areas. The rural sector is the most important in the economy in terms of both Gross Domestic Product (GDP) and the labour force. Poverty, which is widespread, is basically a rural phenomenon. The size and importance of the rural sector and the existence of massive rural poverty have necessitated a special focus on rural development. Over the years, different concepts and approaches have been tried and changes have been made in the context of changing demands and experience gained from past efforts.

A rudimentary notion of integrated rural development can be traced to the community development activities organised in the pre-partition days in British India by zealous social workers, civil servants and eminent personalities. They attempted to improve the socio-economic and cultural conditions of communities in selected areas through the involvement of people and the initiation of activities in the fields of agriculture, health, education, sanitation, etc. But these efforts were sporadic and did not crystallise into a systematic programme for extensive implementation. During the fifties, community development projects, under the designation of Village Agricultural and Industrial Development (VAID), started and, after a few years of fanfare, collapsed in 1960/61.

2.1 *The Comilla Model*

A beginning in systematic conceptualisation and programme development in the field of integrated rural development was made in the sixties with the development of the Comilla Model, which evolved out of experimentation made by the Comilla-based erstwhile Pakistan Academy for Rural Development (now Bangladesh Academy for Rural Development). The model envisaged construction of physical infrastructure, development of irrigation facilities and organisation of groups to make optimum use of such facilities, development of rural institutions for mobilisation of savings and delivery of agricultural inputs, provision of training on improved agricultural practices and a system for its dissemination. It had the following four components:

1. *The KSS-TCCA Co-operative System*: This is a two-tier system

to organise village-based peasant co-operatives called 'KSS' (Krishak Samabay Samity, or peasants' co-operative association), and to federate them into the Thana Central Co-operative Association (TCCA) at the *thana* (now, *Upazila*) level. The functions of the co-operatives were to raise savings deposits at weekly meetings of members, to ensure the management of irrigation equipment on a group basis, and to supply institutional credit and other supplementary inputs to overcome the limitations associated with small fragmented holdings, the use of bigger inputs by smaller farmers, and the problem of agricultural credit. The TCCA was designed as the support and servicing apex organisation to provide credit and other inputs and to provide overall co-ordination, supervision, training and support services to the KSSs.

2. *The Thana Training and Development Centre (TTDC)*: The idea of the centre was to co-ordinate all the specialist government departments concerned with rural administration at the thana level, and to make these services available to village people. It was intended to be a transmission centre for the diffusion of agricultural technology and modern agricultural practices by training chairmen, managers and model farmers for the KSSs at the centre.
3. *Thana Irrigation Plan (TIP)*: The plan was designed to organise peasants into groups to control irrigation equipment like low-lift pumps, Deep Tubewells (DTW) and Shallow Tubewells (STW), to provide maintenance services from *thana* workshops, to train equipment operators and managers of irrigation groups, and to construct field and distribution channels. The groups were eventually to be transformed into co-operatives and federated with TCCA.
4. *Rural Works Programme (RWP)*: This was designed to construct rural physical infrastructure, like roads, flood protection embankments, irrigation and drainage canals, etc., and to provide employment opportunities to the rural poor during slack seasons. The initial emphasis was on infrastructures that would directly promote agricultural growth.

2.2 *Area Development Programme*

In the mid-1970s, the 'area development' programme was initiated, on an experimental basis, to develop a project model for rural development. The first constituent project (Rural Development I) was undertaken in 1976 in seven *thanas* located in two districts. The major components of the project were to develop irrigation and physical infrastructure and to strengthen the TCCA/KSS system in the project areas. The second project, which was known as the Serajgonj Integrated Rural Development Project (SIRDP), was launched in July 1977 in four thanas. The project focused on irrigation and infrastructure development, flood control, and the development of social service facilities, such as health, family planning and community education. A third project, the Noakhali Integrated Rural Development Project (NIRDP), was implemented in July 1978 in three *thanas*. In addition to the major components of the other two projects, this project emphasised social service components, such as health and education. The fourth project, South-West Rural Development Project (SWRDP), covered 44 *Upazilas* in two districts with activities relating to infrastructure development, irrigated agriculture, fisheries development, co-operatives and employment programmes for the poor. Of the above four area development projects, the first three were completed after some time over-run. These three completed projects had a total cost of Tk 101.4 million. The fourth project has been completed in June 1988.

' Under each of these area development projects, multi-sectoral development activities were initiated in selected areas. With successive projects, the scope of the programmes gradually expanded to include social services. The specific form of the projects, especially SIRDP and NIRDP, was analogous to the concept of integrated rural development designed for specific project locations.

The area development projects designed for integrated development of selected rural areas emphasised agricultural development and included provisions for the development of physical infrastructure, but in practice very little for the rural poor. The programmes experienced time over-runs mainly because of difficulties in co-ordination among various implementing agencies at the field level. The inadequacy of the programmes for the rural poor and the emphasis laid on agriculture within the present structure of ownership of land have not led to improvements in the lot of the rural poor. The excessive numbers of components of the projects created problems of co-ordination and management and made benefits intractable. So far, only one area development project, namely RD-I, has been evaluated by the Bangladesh Institute of Development Studies, which detected no discernible impact on agriculture as distinct from areas outside the project, while management of project co-operatives was found to be dominated by relatively well-off households. It is felt that the programme failed to make any noticeable impact on alleviation of poverty; one important reason for this was the absence of specific activities for the rural poor.

2.3 *New Strategy for Rural Development Projects*

In view of the inadequacy of past efforts to address the problem of rural poverty in an effective manner and of the emergent need to alleviate poverty over a wide area, the need for a new strategy for rural development projects was felt. Accordingly, a new strategy was formulated in the Third Five Year Plan (TFYP) (1985-86 to 1989-90). The new strategy envisages that in an agrarian economy like Bangladesh agricultural development must remain a top priority and infrastructure, like roads and markets, is needed for agricultural development but, along with the development of these sectors, production and employment programmes in both farm and non-farm sectors for the rural poor must form an integral part of rural development programmes. According to this strategy, Rural Development (RD) projects will have one or a combination of the following three major components:

a. Development of physical infrastructure, including roads.
b. Irrigated agriculture, minor drainage and flood control works.
c. Production and Employment Programme (PEP) for the rural poor (landless and those having up to 0.5 acre of land).

While all the three components are important, special emphasis has been laid on the Production and Employment Programme for the rural poor. Each individual RD project may take the components separately or in combination but must cover a minimum of one full district. The strategy has been built on the principles of having a small number of important components but with wider area coverage, and of having specific programmes for the rural poor.

The new RD projects initiated during the period of the TFYP are being modelled on the new strategy with one or more of the three components mentioned above. A brief description of the components, together with the coverage envisaged for these components during the TFYP, is presented below:

(a) *Development of Physical Infrastructure*: This component envisages construction or improvement of feeder roads connecting growth centres with *Upazila* Headquarters or the arterial road system (B-type feeder roads) and development of growth centres. A number of new projects has been identified in these areas in the TFYP. It is envisaged that fourteen old districts will be covered by these new projects. They are expected to generate employment opportunities for the rural poor during the construction or improvement phase of the works.

(b) *Irrigated Agriculture, Minor Drainage and Flood Control*: It envisages extension of minor irrigation and flood control facilities, provision of production inputs like fertiliser and seeds and provision of adequate credit to the farmers. No specific new project under the programme in the rural development and institutions sector could yet be taken up. However, some new projects dealing with the development of physical infrastructure include construction/development of small flood control structures (embankments, sluice gates, etc.) and drainage channels. Efforts for the extension of irrigation facilities continued under some ongoing projects carried over from the Second Five Year Plan.

(c) *Production and Employment Programme for the Rural Poor*: The programme envisages the creation of employment opportunities and increased incomes for the rural poor for alleviation of poverty in a gradual manner. The programme has been conceived as an integrated package of five components, viz. (i) institution-building, (ii) training, (iii) credit, (iv) supply of other inputs, and (v) marketing. The TFYP identified a number of projects for the poor covering 17 old districts.

Some RD projects are made up of one component, some of two components and some others comprise all three components. In those RD projects which consist of more than one component, an integrated approach among the components has been aimed at.

One of the important elements of PEP is institution-building, which entails the formation of BSS (co-operatives for assetless men) and MSS (co-operative for assetless women). Separate institutions for the rural poor are considered essential in view of the fact that the KSS/UCCA system developed in the sixties could not provide any appreciable relief to the landless rural poor. At present, BSSs and MSSs are federated into the Upazila Central Co-operative Association (UCCA), which is also the federation of the KSSs.

It is envisaged that there should be at least three representatives from BSS and MSS, including one woman, in each UCCA. It can be argued that the participation of these three members in the UCCA (where large farmers usually dominate) can be nominal rather than real. These institutions are, however, a recent phenomenon, and their coverage is still very limited. It is too early to draw conclusions on the performance of these institutions. However, indications are positive and suggest that these organisations can eventually take off if provided with the necessary support and impetus and some innovations in programmes. It is also envisaged that when such institutions grow to substantial numbers they shall have the option to break away from the UCCA and form their own federation. In fact, in six old districts a separate UCCA of the assetless co-operatives will start functioning from July 1988.

3.0 **Alleviation of Rural Poverty: Approach and Imperatives**

For the alleviation of rural poverty, clear policies with strategies favouring the rural poor, with provision of access to resources and benefits for the poor, need to be developed and pursued. In this respect it is relevant to mention that alleviation of poverty should not be considered in isolation but within the framework of a macro-development process. To achieve this, the following approaches could be adopted:

(i) A thrust on macro development with sufficiently high GDP growth rate and equity to satisfy the basic needs of the poor. The GDP growth rate must be significantly higher than that of population if more goods and services are to become available.

(ii) Secondly, emphasis on the sectoral priorities through which the questions of increased employment, income and consumption will be addressed. Sectors like Agriculture, Rural Development, Rural Industries, Rural Energy, Health, Education and Rural Infrastructure are critically important.

(iii) Thirdly, rural poverty-specific target group-oriented programme interventions based on the idea of direct efforts to reach the poor.

The implementation of these approaches would help realise the goal of alleviating poverty. In the second and third approaches, the basic way to reach the poor is to shift from the community to the household as the basic unit of planned intervention. The principle here is "not lose to sight of the trees because of the wood". In the macro-delivery system, the poor are often by-passed because of the power structure. The household approach would help minimise this deprivation.

In view of the existing production relations, overriding power structure and steady erosion of the asset base of the poor, institutional reforms and policy changes in favour of the rural poor are necessary. It is generally stressed that any meaningful programme for alleviation of rural poverty will call for redistribution of assets like land, to be closely followed by expansion of employment both in agriculture and in non-agricultural sectors. Land reform is considered as an important precondition to proceed with other poverty alleviation programmes. This will bring about the key institutional change that will make the difference.

The ultimate merits of poverty alleviation efforts should not be judged simply by assessing the achievement of physical or financial targets but by ascertaining the effect of such efforts on the target group, i.e. the rural poor. The present system, whereby every five years we evaluate and give an account of bad performance of development efforts in terms of their contribution to alleviation of rural poverty, does little to help in detecting and correcting mistakes or inappropriate interventions. It is, therefore, essential that a continuous impact monitoring system be set up, both sectorally and programme or project-wise. It may be developed in each sector of the Planning Commission to assess the flow of benefits or income among different groups. This will help redirect the allocation of resources and redesign plans if necessary. At the project level, the establishment of an impact monitoring unit will help management in ascertaining whether the project is on course in delivering the desired benefits to the target groups and if not, what could be the possible reasons and what corrective measures could be taken. Monitoring of impact is, therefore, a critical element in any poverty alleviation programme which has been seriously lacking in IRD projects.

4

CHANGING PERSPECTIVES OF IRD PROGRAMMES IN BANGLADESH

K.B. Sajjadur Rasheed

Introduction

The betterment of the socio-economic life of the rural poor is the long-run goal of any rural development scheme. And in Bangladesh, where over 48 per cent of the rural households are functionally landless (BBS 1986a), it is doubtlessly a programme of the greatest significance . Rural development in Bangladesh cannot be merely centred on raising agricultural productivity, but must concern itself with the development of a strategy which can halt or slow down the pace of progressive pauperisation of the rural population.

The history of rural development in Bangladesh covers a short period of only three decades, yet it is a story of inspiring leadership, challenging concepts and changing perspectives to meet dynamic needs. This paper seeks to evaluate the experiences from Bangladesh's rural development efforts and to suggest some modifications with a view to achieving better spatial linkages and increased diversification. The achievements and constraints of rural development programmes in Bangladesh have to be perceived in the context of a dyadic tradition of an individualistic and autonomous social structure and a simultaneous capability of the peasantry to organise and respond to efforts for agricultural progress (Bertocci, 1976).

Pre-Independence Strategy in IRD

In the decade following World War II, developing countries showed a tendency to assign a residual role to agriculture in their national growth plans. Bangladesh had its first experience with agricultural development in 1953 when the V-AID (Village Agricultural and Industrial Development) programme was started with the central theme of extension work. Soon, the flaws of unplanned training of multi-purpose village workers were recognised and the V-AID Academy was instituted to train workers and administrators and to undertake research. The realisation of the importance of the rural population in the country's economy was still in its nascent phase.

True comprehensive rural development in Bangladesh owes its origin to Dr. Akhtar Hameed Khan, a man of extraordinary vision whose dedication and altruism enabled his Comilla Model to become a textbook example of co-operation among the peasantry (Raper, 1970). Khan headed the academy at Comilla – which is now known as Bangladesh Academy for Rural Development (BARD) – from its foundation in 1959. He was convinced that mere agricultural development was not bringing a better quality of life to the rural mass and at the Academy he moulded an innovative strategy of rural institutional development.

The Comilla experiment reasoned that all developmental tasks in the village must involve the villagers and could not be imposed upon them from the top. Hence, the locus of interaction with the rural population was brought to the thana (now upazila) level from the district level; the remoteness of the district bureaucracy had been one basic weakness in the former V-AID programme. The basic approach in the Comilla Model was to organise a two-tier co-operative structure for a total development process in the villages. The bottom tier of the co-operative was formed by the village-based *Krishi Samabay Samiti* (KSS) or farmers' co-operative societies; the KSSs were federated at the *thana* (*upazila*) level in a Thana Central Co-operative Association (TCCA, now UCCA). Each KSS consisted of about 50 farmers who would promote new technology, receive inputs and credit, and plan a cropping strategy through co-operative schemes. Comilla *thana* served as the laboratory for this experiment with the objective of spatially expanding the co-operatives throughout the country. As a more effective approach to rural development, including training programmes, the Thana Training and Development Centres (TTDC) were organised, whose soundness was proved by subsequent financial support by the World Bank (Thomas, 1971a). Two other innovative institutional contributions of the Comilla Model were the Thana Irrigation Programme (TIP) and the Rural Works Programme (RWP). The TIP was aimed at organising farmers into co-operatives to receive credit and help for indivisible irrigation equipment like low-lift pumps and tubewells, while the RWP was concerned with building much needed infrastructural facilities like roads, drainage canals, embankments, etc. while at the same time creating job opportunities for the rural poor – a task in which the programme was found to be admirably successful (Thomas, 1971b).

In the ten-year period following the launching of the Comilla experiment, the scheme was transformed into an Integrated Rural Development Programme (IRDP). The administration was buoyed by the Comilla Model's functional stability and promise. It was hoped that within the next decade the IRDP would cover all the rural thanas of the country. However, the Comilla Model was not without shortcomings. It was not always possible to prevent the control of cooperatives falling into the hands of richer landed elites (Khan, 1971). Besides, landlessness was much larger in reality than envisioned and the co-operative efforts often failed to create employment for the rural poor. Yet, the fundamental precept that village development can be truly attained only through a bottom-up approach remains valid in Bangladesh, and most of the rural institutional developments in Bangladesh since independence in 1971 basically draw inspiration from the Comilla experience.

Post-Independence Dynamics

The events of 1971 leading to the emergence of Bangladesh as a sovereign country offered an opportunity to the administration to redesign the dimensions of rural institutional development. The Comilla Model was to be followed and replicated, but enthusiasm was somewhat muted (Alamgir, 1980), presumably because most of the national programmes were laced with ideological phrases where pragmatism had little place. Nevertheless, the First Five Year Plan (1973-78) did give rural development a place of priority in the total development of the nation. The co-operative framework of IRDP was continued while a new dimension was added to it by initiating an area development approach (TFYP, 1985). These area development projects had their basis on co-operative spirit and credit facilities, and also included several socio-economic aspects of rural life (including health) within the planning process. But the project implementation performance was less than satisfactory, mainly due to inadequacies in management. Besides, centralised agencies like the Bangladesh Water

Development Board and the Bangladesh Agricultural Development Corporation (BADC) assumed greater control, leading to an erosion of participatory development at the bottom level (Stepanek, 1979). Consequently, rural development programmes in independent Bangladesh experienced misleading signals from the outset.

The scene was further complicated with newer experimentation in the mid-1970s. A very different rural development approach from the IRDP was initiated in 1975 under the name of *Shwanirbhar* movement (Johnson, 1982). Shwanirbhar means self-reliance and the fundamental goal of this approach was to eliminate dependency and promote the use of unutilised and underutilised local resources through collective efforts. It also envisaged mass mobilisation of voluntary labour and creation of self-governing institutions at the village level – 'Gram Sharkar'. A widely publicised example of the Shwanirbhar approach was the Ulashi canal-digging programme (at Sarsha upazila of Jessore district), aimed at draining a swampy tract by cutting a 5 km canal with the use of voluntary labour. Subsequently, a self-reliant area development plan was also launched at Ulashi and the principles of the Shwanirbhar model were to be extended to other parts of the country. The basic philosophy of the Shwanirbhar approach was somewhat similar to that of the V-AID programme of the 1950s. True, it was an example of bottom-up planning where local participation was expected. As a result, local development initiatives did have a chance to secure bureaucratic response. On the other hand, however, it remained basically a production-oriented approach which failed to address or mitigate the problems of landlessness, skewed class structure and progressive pauperisation of the rural poor (Jahangir, 1981). The majority of the benefits derived from the Shwanirbhar movement were enjoyed by the large landowners (de Vylder and Asplund, 1979).

The Second Five Year Plan (SFYP) of 1980-85 aimed at strengthening the IRDP and organised the Bangladesh Rural Development Board (BRDB) to oversee and manage area development projects. Comprehensive planning for the rural population was stressed, encompassing – besides agriculture – irrigation, flood control, fisheries, health, education, etc. During the mid-1980s, a new strategy was developed for rural development projects. This comprised three components: (a) development of physical infrastructure; (b) irrigated agriculture, drainage and flood control and (c) employment programme for the rural poor (TFYP, 1985). The Rural Works Programme was accelerated through a decentralised participatory planning and execution process, while the two-tier co-operative scheme (KSS and UCCA, formerly TCCA) was boosted to attain maximum spatial coverage. By the end of the Second Five Year Plan period, the KSS programme was operating throughout the whole country in over 63,000 villages (BBS, 1986b).

Integrated rural development in Bangladesh experienced yet another new dimension in 1982 when 460 of the 495 *thanas* of the country were upgraded and labelled as *upazilas*. The rationale behind this reorganisation of administrative units was to prevent the by-passing of the local rural communities in the national planning process. The *upazilas*, having representative local governments, were entrusted with additional functional responsibilities including the planning and implementation of the Rural Works Programme. It is further envisioned in the Third Five Year Plan (1985-90) that the Upazila headquarters will be promoted to the status of growth centres and that jobs will be created in them to absorb the rural landless population. Indeed, the *upazila* scheme, if efficiently managed, should provide a wider economic base to the rural economy and help to maximise horizontal as well as vertical linkages of rural development activities. The Third Five Year Plan (1985-90) reiterates the three components of the national rural development strategy. Special stress is given in the Plan to the alleviation of rural poverty through planning for employment facilities, especially in the non-farm sector. The expansion of employment both in agriculture and in non-farm occupations to cater for the increase of entrants to the rural labour force and the currently unemployed is one of the primary objectives of rural development (Kamiya, 1980). Besides, the *upazilas* and the unions under them are also expected to draw up their respective development plans and this would ensure a greater realisation of a bottom-up approach and enhance participatory development in the rural areas.

Spatial Reorganisation and IRD Strategy

In view of the pre-eminent role of *upazilas* in rural development in Bangladesh, it is pertinent to examine the spatial efficiency of these administrative units. Optimal spatial efficiency can in principle be attained through the maximisation of contact between the administrative agencies and the population in each *upazila*. In a theoretically ideal world, the *upazila* headquarters should be located at the geometric centre of the upazila, which should be circular in shape. Since none of these conditions can be expected or achieved in reality, it is argued here that a reorganisation of *upazila* perimeters should be carried out in order to obtain optimal spatial efficiency. The concept underlying this exercise is that all administrative units (*upazilas*) should be so constructed as to have approximately equal numbers of population (Rasheed, 1986). As the administrative agencies seated at the *upazila* headquarters serve the entire population of the *upazila,* it is logical to propose that each *upazila* administration be loaded with the responsibilities of rural development for an equal number of customers.

The distribution of the rural population in Bangladesh is far from uniform and consequently, the populations of different *upazilas* vary between 80,000 and over 400,000 (excluding the three hilly districts in the south-east where the density is lower) (BBS, 1986a). Certain *upazilas* thus have much larger rural populations than others. On the basis of the 1985 estimates of the rural population of Bangladesh, each rural *upazila* should ideally have a population of around 190,000. But the reality is different. Hence, it is suggested that an attempt be made to redefine *upazila* boundaries in such a manner as to include an approximately equal rural population (i.e., 190,000 persons) in each. This would ensure that no *upazila* would be entrusted with rural development responsibilities out of proportion with the national norm. These redefined *upazilas* are called here Equal-Population Optimal Upazilas. The areas of such *upazilas* would surely vary, but the size of the target population would be more or less uniform. It should, however, be parenthetically added that such an exercise of relocating *upazila* boundaries would necessarily involve cognizance of certain pragmatic circumstances like transport routes, alignment of rivers and streams, locational orientation of *upazila* headquarters, etc. But the results to be achieved from this exercise are worth the effort.

Expansion of IRD Services

The nature of the rural economy in Bangladesh dictates that the the scope of IRDP activities should be broadened to include afforestation schemes. Like many other developing countries, Bangladesh has witnessed an ever increasing process of deforestation in the past 25 years to meet woodfuel needs of the growing population. Bangladesh's forest wealth is dismally poor. State forest lands, controlled by the Forest Department, account for a mere 9.6 per cent of the total land area. In addition, there are about 3,000 sq. km of homestead forest groves (of tree and/or bamboo) on private lands (Magno, 1986). Although this privately-owned forest wealth constitutes only 12 per cent of the total forest land, it meets nearly 80 per cent of the national fuelwood requirements (Alim and Choudhury, n.d.). Among the conventional biomass fuels, fuelwood is one of the dominant sources of energy in both urban and rural sectors of Bangladesh. But the present per capita consumption of wood (0.099 cubic metres) is among the lowest in the world (Magno, 1986), mainly due to the paucity of forest wealth. Per capita consumption will tend to decrease further as population increases, unless wood production is augmented. An afforestation programme is within the purview of the Forest Department. While the Forest Department should be involved in the reafforestation of the state forest lands, afforestation in the rural landscape should become a part of the IRD programme. Since the significance of woodfuel for the rural population is vital, IRD services have to be expanded to incorporate social or community forestry schemes. Social forestry in Bangladesh had its origin in 1982 when the programme was launched to cover the seven north-western districts of Dinajpur, Rangpur, Bogra, Pabna, Rajshahi, Kushtia and Jessore. The six-year project is funded by the Asian Development Bank and executed by the Forest Department. Besides augmenting supplies of fuelwood and timber, the project also aims at playing a catalytic role in creating community awareness in the rural population through participatory involvement. More precisely, the social forestry project in north-western Bangladesh plans to (a) replenish homestead wood-lots with the villagers' participation; (b) establish strip plantations along roads, railway lines and canal embankments; and (c) start pilot agro-forestry model units. In each of the schemes, the co-operation and participation of the rural population are sought and utilised. This is especially true for strip plantations on public lands where the rural poor and the landless can get an opportunity to earn through a benefit-sharing enterprise. Moreover, it would be advisable to plant fast-growing trees around homesteads which make the yield of wood possible in a shorter period than the traditional tree varieties (Nannen-Gethmann, 1983) and thus, help to meet the demand for fuelwood. Hence, it is advocated here that the social forestry scheme should be brought under the jurisdiction of the IRDP although the Forest Department might serve in an advisory role. The idea of expanding IRD services to include social forestry is certain to arouse bureaucratic passions, yet such a measure would bring long-run benefits to the target population of the IRDP, i.e., the rural poor.

REFERENCES

Alamgir, M.K. 1980 *Development Strategy for Bangladesh.* Dhaka: Centre for Social Studies, University of Dhaka.

Alim, A. and Choudhury, A.H. n.d. *Community Forestry in Bangladesh: An Analytical Review.* Dhaka: Forest Department, Government of Bangladesh.

BBS (Banglades Bureau of Statistics) 1986a *Statistical Pocket Book of Bangladesh 1986.* Dhaka: Ministry of Planning, Statistics Division.

BBS (Banglades Bureau of Statistics) 1986b *Statistical Yearbook of Bangladesh.* Dhaka: Ministry of Planning, Statistics Division.

Bertocci, P.J. 1976 "Rural Development in Bangladesh: An Introduction" in *Rural Development in Bangladesh and Pakistan*, (eds) R.D. Stevens, H. Alavi and P.J. Bertocci. Honolulu: The University Press of Hawaii, pp. 3-8.

Jahangir, B.K. 1981 "Local Action for Self-reliant Development in Bangladesh" in *Rural Development in Bangladesh: Trends and Issues*, (eds) M.M. Khan and H. M. Zafarullah. Dhaka: Centre for Administrative Studies, University of Dhaka, pp. 123-146.

Johnson, B.L.C. 1982 *Bangladesh.* London: Heinemann Educational Books. 2nd edition.

Kamiya, M. 1980 "Grow More Food and Rural Development Programmes" in New *Directions of Asia's Development Strategies*, (ed.) Economic Growth Department, I.D.E. Tokyo: Institute of Development Economics, pp. 237- 245.

Khan, A.H. 1971 Tour of 20 *Thanas.* Comilla: Pakistan Academy for Rural Development.

Magno, V.C. 1986 *Bangladesh: Community Forestry Handbook.* Dhaka: Forestry Department and F.A.O. Asian Development Bank Community Forestry Project, Field Document No. 1.

Nannen-Gethmann, Folence 1983 *Energy in the Rural Economy: A Case Study of the Philippines and Bangladesh.* Saarbrucken: W.G. Verlag breitenbach Publishers.

Raper, A.E. 1970 *Rural Development in Action - The Comprehensive Experiment at Comilla.* Ithaca, N.Y.: Cornell University Press.

Rasheed, K.B.S. 1986 "The Spatial Efficiency of Administrative Units in Bangladesh", *Geografiska Annaler*, 68B: 21-28.

Stepanek, J.F. 1979 *Bangladesh - Equitable Growth.* New York: Pergamon Press Inc.

TFYP (Third Five Year Plan) 1985 The *Third five Year Plan 1985-90.* Dhaka: Ministry of Planning, Planning Commission.

Thomas, J.W. 1971a "Agricultural Production, Equity and Rural Organization in East Pakistan". Preliminary draft presented to Research Workshop on Rural Development in Pakistan, Asian Studies Centre, Michigan State University.

Thomas, J.W. 1971b "The Rural Public Works Programme in East Pakistan" in *Developing Policy II: The Pakistan Experience*, (eds) W.P. Falcon and G.F. Papenek. Cambridge, Mass: Harvard University Press, pp. 186-236.

de Vylder, S. and Asplund, D. 1979 *Contradictions and Distortions in a Rural Economy: The Case of Bangladesh.* Stockholm: Swedish International Development Authority.

5

INTEGRATED RURAL DEVELOPMENT PROGRAMME IN INDIA: A Review of Performance*

N.J. Kurian

1. Introduction

The Integrated Rural Development Programme (IRDP), which was introduced on a modest scale during the Fifth Five Year Plan period was extended to cover the entire rural areas of India during the Sixth Plan. The IRDP continues to be the centre-piece of anti-poverty programmes in the Seventh Plan. The cover, the IRDP is to provide poor families with income generating assets to enable them to generate the requisite incremental incomes to cross the poverty line.[1] The objective of the Sixth Plan was to assist 15 million rural families for which a total allocation of Rs. 4,50 million including bank credit was made. The number of beneficiaries to be assisted and the amount allocated are even higher in the Seventh Plan.[2] More than 16.5 million families were assisted during the Sixth Plan. Thus, on the face of it, the achievement exceeded the target.

IRDP is, perhaps, the one programme which has attracted the maximum public attention among all the development/redistributive programmes introduced in this country over the years. A large volume of literature on this programme has been generated. The vast majority of this literature has been rather critical of the programme. While much

* (The views expressed in this paper are strictly the personal views of the author. I am grateful to D Bandyopadhyay, Ake Blomqvist, Yogesh Chandra, Mathew Kurien, D.S. Tyagi and S.D. Tendulkar for helpful comments on an earlier draft of this paper. None of them, however, shares, esponsibility for the errors that remain).

of the newspapers write-up and popular literature about the programme deals with vivid descriptions of corruption, malpractices and inefficiencies involved in the implementation of the programme, the more serious criticisms relate to the basic philosophy of the programme, its economic rationality and its viability. It is argued that even if the programme is implemented as planned, without any malpractices or leakages, the benefits to the poor may not be significant or sustainable. A good part of what is given to the poor through IRDP will be taken away, through the social process and market operations dominated by the rich and powerful. This line of thinking is very succinctly presented by Dantwala[3] when he writes: "Equity-oriented policies and programmes pursued within the cast iron inequitous economic structure – of ownership of assets – will not only be self-defeating, but may prove counter-productive through a 'trickle up'. More simply, a direct attack on poverty without an equally direct attack on the structure, which has bred poverty and continues to do so, is an illusion at best, fraud at worst". Though Dantwala himself does not agree with this 'structuralist' view he recommends it for a serious debate.

A second set of major critiques arises not so much out of structural issues but because of a well articulated preference for wage employment over asset distribution as more beneficial to the poor. Any one who is wanting employment at a basic subsistence wage rate should be provided with the opportunity to earn an income. In this, there is no demand on his entrepreneurial skills, no worry about input and output linkages, no demoralising pursuit of an overstretched bureaucracy and no worry about repayment of loan. In the relatively backward regions where lack of basic social and economic infrastructures such as roads, water supply, schools, health centres, housing, etc., stand in the way of development, employment programmes could be directed at creating such facilities. Wage employment generation could also be used for development of irrigation systems, soil conservation, etc., which will significantly improve agricultural productivity and incomes. And that is the stage at which IRDP type of programmes can be effectively implemented. This line of thinking is put forward by Rath,[4] Dandekar,[5] and others.

A third set of critiques is based on the argument that the low-end poverty in its worst forms cannot be ameliorated by providing them with opportunities for self-employment or wage employment. The worst-placed among the poor are those who are not able to participate in economic activity on account of old age, physical and mental handicaps, various disabilities due to morbidity, etc. These contingencies need to be relieved by measures that are specifically directed towards the target groups. In the absence or inadequacy of such measures, the burden has to be borne, if at all, by the families, relatives and local communities of those affected. Informal social security of this kind shifts the hardship to those who are themselves most often under the poverty line and ill-placed to support dependents. Increasingly, community and familial support cultures and systems are also weakening. A publicly funded and manageable – admininstratively viable and financially feasible – social security system must be an essential component of an anti-poverty package to take care of the poorest. A forceful and persuasive argument for this is put forward by Guhan.[6]

The main objective of this paper is not to join issues with these major critiques of the programme. Our purpose is rather modest: To have an objective and dispassionate look at the IRDP as it is articulated and implemented today, to seek answers to a few specific questions which are often raised but remain mostly unanswered. What proportion of the assistance goes to the deserving poor? What are the kinds of asset they are provided with? How much over-valuation of assistance due to market factors, leakages and other inefficiencies takes place? What are the problems associated with bank financing of IRDP? Are there sufficient backward and forward linkages established for the successful operation of the schemes? Do the assets remain with the beneficiaries? Do they generate sufficient incomes to enable the assisted families to cross the poverty line? Even if they are not crossing the poverty line are they significantly better off after the IRDP assistance? In other words, we examine the programme to see whether the resources spent on IRDP can be justified on the grounds of equity and social justice as well as economic efficiency. Or in other words we try to assess whether IRDP is a worthwhile endeavour on balance. Also an attempt is made to place the programme in correct perspective *vis-a-vis* the skepticism of the academics and intellectuals and the excessive optimism of bureaucracy and politicians. An issue of deeper significance is whether IRDP is just another bureaucratic construct devoid of any conceptual framework? And finally a few concluding comments are drawn in the light of the major critiques referred to earlier.

Our analyses and discussions of the various issues involved are based on the massive primary data/information generated by the Concurrent Evaluation Survey of IRDP carried out by reputed research institutions in the country on behalf of the Department of Rural Development of the Government of India during 1985-86. This novel scheme of data collection by non-government agencies for monitoring the implementation of the programme and evaluating its impact on the beneficiaries was the result of wide criticism of the implementation of the programme during the Sixth Plan. Though most of the shortcomings of the implementation of IRDP were known to the concerned implementing agencies and the public at large as a result of experience and on the basis of various localised and micro-level evaluation studies, a national level debate of a serious nature[7] took place only after the publication of a few evaluation studies of all India coverage.[8]

As a result of the serious criticisms of the programme, a number of improvements have been incorporated in the IRDP during the Seventh Plan. In this context, it was felt that the official monitoring of the programme based on periodic progress reports furnished by the field level functionaries and implementing agencies are not effective. Further, such official reports invariably projected the weaknesses of the programme. It was also felt that involvement of reputed and independent research institutions in monitoring the programme will have salutary effects on the programme in more ways than one. Also they will use the detailed data/information for their own research and analysis which can be quite valuable for regional and local level policy planning and programme implementation. The survey was carried out during the period October 1985 to September 1986. All the districts in the country were covered on a rotation basis. In each district a sample of 40 IRDP beneficiaries were studied in detail. The method of sampling followed was a stratified four-stage random scheme.

A combination of interview, observations and verification of records was used for fulfilling up the pre-coded and structured household schedule specifically prepared for this purpose by an expert group. The schedule was divided into 11 blocks to collect data on identification details of the beneficiaries, selection procedure for assistance, provision of assets, details for the benefits, details of the loan, maintenance of assets, insurance of assets, training, linkages and after care, income from assets and other details. Apart from collecting objective data, an attempt was made to look at the programme from the point of view of the beneficiaries. Hence, a few pointed questions were included in the schedule to ascertain the perception of the beneficiaries about some of the critical points. Though the. survey covered both current and old beneficiaries who were assisted two years before the survey. The total sample size of such beneficiaries was 8,640. However, due to various reasons only 8,024 schedules were available for processing. The present analysis is based on this sample of 8,024 beneficiaries.

The plan of the rest of the paper is as follows: In Sections 2 to the main findings based on the survey are presented. The topics covered are : who received the IRDP assistance?; sectoral distribution of the schemes, over-valuation of assets; status of the assets after two years; bank financing of IRDP; increase in incomes of IRDP beneficiaries and crossing the poverty line. Section 9 is devoted to a discussion of issues involved and a few concluding comments are offered.

2. Who Received IRDP Assistance?

The poverty line of Rs. 3,500 per annum for an average family of size five, arrived at on the basis of 32nd round of NSS (1977-78), continued to be the official cut-off level for IRDP assistance throughout the Sixth Plan period even though the purchasing power of rupee was significantly eroded by inflation since 1977-78. As a consequence, even when non-poor were assisted under the programme, their annual family incomes were invariably entered in the official records as below Rs. 3,500. The true pre-assistance incomes of the sample beneficiaries[9] as assessed from the survey data reveal that at the national level only 80 per cent of the sample beneficiaries had pre-assistance income below Rs. 3,500. That is, 20 per cent of the beneficiaries had incomes more than Rs. 3,500. The under reporting of family income might have been deliberately done by the beneficiary with or without the knowledge of the government functionaries involved in the assessment of the income. Out of the 80 per cent beneficiaries who satisfied the eligibility criterion according to official guidelines, 38 per cent belonged to the income group Rs. 0-2,265 who are categorised as 'destitutes' and the remaining 42 per cent belonged to the income group Rs. 2,266-3,500 who are categorised as 'very very poor'. Of the 20 per cent non-eligible beneficiaries, 12 per cent belonged to the income group Rs. 3,501-4,800 who are categorised as 'very poor' and are treated as eligible for assistance during the Seventh Plan. Out of the remaining 8 per cent non-eligible beneficiaries, 4 per cent belonged to the income group Rs. 4,801-6,400 and the balance 4 per cent had pre-assistance income more than even Rs. 6,400 which is the revised poverty line for the Seventh Plan. It may be observed in this connection that the four national level evaluation studies of IRDP conducted earlier[10] had reported assistance of non-eligible beneficiaries ranging from 15 to 26 percent as against 20 per cent in the pre sent case.

As per official guidelines, the list of identified potential beneficiaries prepared by the officials has to be presented in the gram sabha meeting and got ratified by it before they are actually assisted.[11] This is to ensure that the most deserving poor get priority over others and that no non-poor or non-eligible families get IRDP assistance through suppression of incomes or through collusion with government functionaries. However, in actual practice, this procedure of public participation and open selection did not take place everywhere. At the national level, 55 per cent of the beneficiaries were selected in the *gram sabha* meetings, 40 per cent by officials and the remaining 5 per cent by others including members of Parliament and of Legislative Assemblies.

Wherever *gram sabhas* made the final selection in 80 per cent or more cases, have selected more than 90 per cent of the beneficiaries from among 'destitutes' and 'very very poor'. The *gram sabha* selection and the proportion of deserving beneficiaries under-scores the need for more public participation in the selection for IRDP assistance.[12]

3. Sectoral Distribution

One of the repeated criticisms of IRDP is that it is nothing but a 'milch animal' and 'sewing machine' programme. Though detailed guidelines have been issued by the Central Government regarding conduct of resource surveys and resource analysis for assessing the viability of various schemes before the preparation of family plans, cluster plans and block plans, in actual practice, a rather weak block machinery[13] could not do anything more than meeting the 'target' by providing assets to 600 families in a year. In chasing this target, quite often, the government functionaries preferred to provide 'easily manageable' assets to the beneficiaries irrespective of their income generating potential and in some cases even against the preference of the beneficiaries. Thus, in the extreme, absurd cases were reported where hundreds of milch animals were distributed in drought affected areas and dozens of sewing machines were supplied to different women beneficiaries in a single village.

About 55 per cent of the beneficiaries had assets in the primary sector and 35 per cent in the tertiary sector. In fact, this is much more even, as compared to the highly skewed distribution in favour of the primary sector in the early years of the Sixth Plan.[14]

4. **Over-valuation of Assets**

Much of the public criticism of IRDP is concerned about corruption, malpractices, bribery and other leakages at the stage of implementation of the programme. Extreme forms of corruption and malpractices are the cases where the government functionaries and bankers involved in the implementation of the programme along with the beneficiary (usually an intelligible one) take or dispose of the asset immediately after the purchase and share the subsidy component of the assistance. A lesser, but more common, type of corruption is the payment of bribes by the beneficiary from his own resources to the individual functionaries of the government or bank who are involved in processing the application and acquiring the asset. The former type of corruption is rather rare, especially in well-administered states[15] The latter is quite common in number of States but the information is extremely difficult to elicit and the amounts involved are difficult to quantify.[16]

According to the guidelines, the asset has to be purchased by a committee consisting of the representatives of the block, bank and the beneficiary. And, the survey has revealed that in vast majority of the cases, indeed, the purchase was done by the committee.[17] But, in actual practice, in many instances, the involvement of the beneficiary in the purchase decision, especially about the price, is rather minimal. Quite often there may be a mark-up in the price or for the standard price the beneficiary may be getting an inferior quality asset. And the difference will be shared by the various parties involved on the basis of a 'pre-determined' formula.[18] Another reason for higher prices for IRDP assets is the market process itself. To illustrate, take the case of milch animals. During the Sixth Plan period, this programme alone created demand for roughly 4 to 5 million milch animals at the All India level. But, there was hardly any scheme for augmentation of supply of milch animals to meet this unprecedented demand either at the macro-level or at the regional and sub-regional levels. In fact, the demand for cows, especially that of better breed, under the programme in some regions shot up fast to make 'IRDP cow' a premium product.[19] Obviously, the market absorbed the excess demand via adjustments in prices. The net result was that the IRDP beneficiary ended up paying a significantly higher price for his 'cow' than under normal conditions. Though the case of milch animals is an extreme one, similar excess demands of a lesser order were created for a number of assets due to the operation of IRDP programme.[20]

To capture the extent of excess cost the beneficiary incurred due to the two factors noted in the preceding paragraph the beneficiary was asked to give his estimate of the 'value of asset' when it was acquired. At the national level, as much as 68 per cent of the sample beneficiaries thought that the asset they got was worth the cost. Of course, the value of asset as judged by the beneficiary may have an unknown measure of 'bias' due to the subjectivity of his perception.[21]

Out of the remaining 32 per cent sample beneficiaries who thought that the cost of the asset was more than its values, 11 per cent reported that the excess cost was not more than Rs. 250, 9 per cent reported that it was between Rs. 250 and Rs. 500, 5 per cent reported that it was between Rs. 500 and Rs. 1,000 and the remaining 7 per cent thought that it was even more than Rs. 1,000.

The really alarming cases are the ones where differences are more than Rs. 1,000 which work out to more than one-third of the average cost of the asset. Indeed, these are likely to be the cases where the various functionaries involved in the implementation of IRDP alongwith the middlemen had taken the poor beneficiaries for a ride. The national average of such cases from the sample being 7 per cent, one can tentatively suggest that more than one million out of the sixteen million and odd beneficiaries assisted during the Sixth Plan had to pay Rs. 1,000 or more as extra cost, in other words than one million beneficiaries ended up paying an average amount of Rs. 3,000 for an asset which was worth less than Rs. 2,000.

5. Status of the Asset After Two Years

An aspect of the programme which has come up for considerable public discussion and criticism is the durability of the IRDP asset in the custody of the beneficiary. To start with, whether the beneficiary actually takes physical possession of the asset? Or is it only in the records of the concerned offices? Or is it only a transitory change of hand for the purpose of meeting the guidelines in letter though not in spirit at least for a short while? It is in this context that 'IRDP cow' is known as 'circulating capital'. Then there are cases about giving defective assets which may not generate much of an income and hence cannot last any way. Another argument is that in any case the beneficiary normally being very poor, has a high propensity to sell the asset away to meet his immediate pressing needs and hence is unlikely to maintain the asset in an intact form for a long time.[22] In fact, quite a number of instances have been reported by IRDP valuation studies, individual researchers and other observers, which fall into one or the other of the above categories. And also there are other reasons for the beneficiary not to possess the asset for long.[23]

With the above observations as background, the finding of the IRDP Concurrent Evaluation Survey that 71 per cent of the beneficiaries at the national level have the asset intact with them two years after the assistance is quite encouraging. Indeed, this finding is quite consistent with the estimates generated by the earlier national level studies.[24] The remaining 29 per cent 'cases of asset not intact' comprise of cases where the assets were 'sold', 'fully perished', 'partly perished/defective' and 'others' which include the cases where the assets were not even purchased. It may be noted that situations where a part of the asset has perished, has become defective or has been sold out are also included in 'not intact' cases.[25]

The broad distribution of the reasons for the asset not intact on the basis of the sample is, unexpected event – 22 per cent, not enough income generated – 19 per cent, defective asset - 16 per cent and maintenance of the asset costly – 8 per cent and other reasons – 35 per cent.

Contingencies include disposal of asset to meet unexpected family crisis like illness or death of family members or unexpected loss of the asset due to accident, theft or disease/death in the case of animals.[26] Inadequate income generation and high cost of maintenance are related in as much as both relate to income from the asset, one in relation to the fixed capital cost of the asset and the other in relation to the working capital requirements. An asset may be defective because it was so at the time of its acquisition[27] or it might have become defective subsequently. 'Other reasons' could be a variety of miscellaneous reasons which may vary from family to family, but they also include cases where the assets were not even given to the beneficiary or the asset was given but the purpose was not so much to keep the asset for generating income. Rather it was only intended to be disposed of to get the cash benefit of subsidy.

6. Bank Financing of IRDP

The IRDP programme is financed partly by government grants and partly by bank credit. The Sixth Plan outlay for IRDP of Rs. 45,000 million consisted of Rs. 15,000 million of budgetary grants and Rs. 30,000 million of bank credit. Thus, the government share and bank share in IRDP financing were in the ratio of 1:2 during the Sixth Plan. And roughly the same ratio between government financing and bank financing is being maintained in the Seventh Plan. As the major financier of the programme, the banks are thus expected to play a very important role in the implementation of IRDP. However, there is general criticism that banks are rather unwilling partners in the joint programme. Unlike in the case of District Rural Development Agencies (DRDAs) and block offices, banks are not allotted specific financial and physical targets to be achieved under IRDP. True, IRDP is one of the programmes in the priority sector for which the banks have to fulfil a 40 per cent lending target. But, normally banks prefer to achieve this target by lending to 'more credit worthy' customers whose projects are financially more 'viable'.

On the other hand, the number of lending cases the banks have to handle on the IRDP front is very large as compared to other borrowers and as such the workload increases considerably since the staff strength is normally determined on the basis of the volume of transactions, the rural branches are usually understaffed. According to the IRDP guidelines, banks should not ask for or get any surety for a loan up to Rs. 5,000 except for the asset procured under the programme which will be hypothecated to the bank.[28] Also the block machinery which is highly enthusiastic about securing bank loans for providing assistance to IRDP beneficiaries, is usually not of much help in ensuring repayment of the loan. These factors together provide a kind of rationale and justification on the part of bankers to keep their involvement in IRDP to the minimum.

One of the important concerns of the critics of IRDP and also of the public at large is relating to the repayment of loans by the beneficiaries. This is, indeed, a very valid concern as the experiences of the banking sector in the past other priority lending areas have been rather depressing.[29] One of the cardinal principles of banking, and for that matter financial intermediation in general, is the uninterrupted flow of finances from the bank to the creditors and back. This is essential for recycling of the loans. The banking industry may come to a grinding halt if substantial portions of the bank finances are tied up with the borrowers as overdues. IRDP beneficiaries being not credit-worthy in the conventional sense, bankers often invoke the issue of overdues, even from better endowed borrowers, to express their concerns. This makes an objective review of the overdues position of IRDP loans all the more important.

The overdues of sample beneficiaries according to the quantum of overdues[30] indicates that 45 per cent of the sample beneficiaries had no overdues at the national level. Another 8 per cent of the beneficiaries had an amount of overdue of up to Rs. 250 only. For all practical purposes this category also can be treated as non-defaulters. Thus, more than half of the IRDP beneficiaries were prompt in repaying their dues to the banks which, indeed, is a very positive finding and compares favourably with the situation in the case of other borrowers.[31] This was also the finding from the earlier studies.

Out of the remaining 47 per cent of cases, 25 per cent had overdues between Rs. 251 and Rs. 1,000, 16 per cent had overdues between Rs. 1,001 and Rs. 2,000 and the balance 6 per cent had overdues beyond Rs. 2,000. The range of Rs. 251 to Rs. 1,000 is indeed a very broad one and an overdue closer to Rs. 251 may very well mean a very different thing as compared to an overdue of Rs. 1,000.[32]

It may be of great policy relevance for the banks to conduct an indepth analysis of the causes of 'bad debts' in the case of IRDP beneficiaries. It is quite likely that some of these high overdues are the results of unrealistic repayment schedules. Others may be due to non-viability of the scheme which could have been avoided by proper project appraisal or the scheme could have been made viable by proper resource planning or by providing needed linkages. There may be other cases where the asset provided was not insured and subsequently perished due to accident or death. There may be still other cases of 'bad debts' where the beneficiaries get the assistance/asset without any intention to repay the loans.[33] Identifying these and other possible factors for large overdues is an important prerequisite for improving the profile of the IRDP programme as well as the liquidity of the banking industry in the country.

A limited amount of information relating to the reasons for

overdues was collected in the concurrent evaluation survey. Those sample beneficiaries who reported overdues were asked to state the main reason and second reasons, if any, from the given category of reasons viz., inadequate income, unforeseen calamity, tight repayment schedule and 'other reasons'. From the distribution of the sample beneficiaries on the basis of the reported first reasons for overdues we find that 59 per cent reported inadequate income generation from the given asset as the main reason for overdues. Tight repayment schedule was the reason next in importance which accounted for 30 per cent of the cases of overdues. In fact, both these reasons are quite related. In a way, a repayment schedule which does not realistically relate to the income generation schedule is bound to cause overdues. The beneficiary may have all the good intentions to repay the loan. But the income generated may not be adequate to meet the tight and hence unrealistic repayment schedule. Unforeseen calamities account for 8 per cent of the overdues cases and 'other reasons' account for the remaining 3 per cent of such cases.

7. Increases in Income of IRDP Beneficiaries

Exceptions apart, most of the evaluation studies and almost all the general critiques of IRDP, concentrate on the single criterion of 'crossing the poverty line' to judge the impact of the programme. This excessive pre-occupation with poverty line and using it as the sole criterion to judge the performance of the programme has led some critics to reach dramatic conclusions about the wastages involved in the programme.[34] An asset might prove to be highly productive and generate an income beyond expectations. In the present scheme of things, it is possible that still the beneficiary may not cross the poverty line. This happens in situations where the beneficiary's pre-assistance income was substantially lower than the poverty line and the value of asset was very small compared to the requirements. Such cases are quite common. This is because the investment opportunities for the 'destitutes' and 'very very poor' are normally not those involving lumpy assets unlike in the case of say, small farmers who prefer pumpsets/tube-wells, etc., which involve large outlays. Also preparation of viable schemes or packages of such schemes for individual members of those families is a time consuming process and the programme implementors just do not have the time, patience or motivation to do such exercises. Further, the very poor do not have the clout to demand and get adequate assistance to cross the poverty line. One the other hand an asset may prove to be highly unproductive but still the beneficiary may cross the poverty line. Such is the case when the pre-assistance income of the beneficiary is very close to the poverty line and he is given a large quantum of assistance. Thus in judging the effectiveness of IRDP assistance, in addition to the criterion of 'crossing the poverty line' one has to take into account the pre-assistance or the value of the asset provided.

The issue of 'what should constitute a poverty line' is not a settled one.[35] Even if it is conceded that the poverty line concept used at present is irrevocable from the policy planners' point of view, the poor, who are the victims of poverty and the beneficiaries of the IRDP assistance may have entirely different perception about their condition and they may judge the effectiveness of the programme quite differently. To illustrate, a destitute family with meagre and irregular pre-assistance income may find a small steady income from an IRDP asset extremely valuable even if it does not take the family above the poverty line. What matters to it is the absolute quantum of incremental income and its relative importance with reference to the pre-assistance level of income? It is so because even a small quantum increase in disposable income, especially if it is of a steady nature based on an owned asset, can make a substantial difference in the well-being of the family.[36] In other words, each poor family may have its own perception of poverty line threshold pending upon the intensity of its own destitution. And this may have very little to do with an official poverty line, however, sophisticated its instruments are and however important it may be for the policy-makers and programme planners. In view of this reasoning, before we examine the effects of IRDP on our sample beneficiaries in terms of crossing the poverty line, we shall have look at the income generation effects of the programme in an absolute and relative sense. The per centage share of sample beneficiaries in whose case the asset did not generate any income at all was 24 per cent at the national level. The finding that almost one-fourth of the IRDP assets have not generated any income at all is, indeed, a damning commentary on the implementation of the programme.

The distribution of the 76 per cent of sample beneficiaries at the national level for whom the assets generated non-zero income is 11 per cent cases with income upto Rs. 500, 15 per cent cases with income between Rs. 501 and Rs. 1,000, 24 per cent cases with income between Rs. 1,001 and Rs. 2,000. In this context it may be recalled that the

Sixth Plan total outlay of Rs. 45,000 million to assist 15 million beneficiaries (i.e. at the average rate of Rs. 3,000 per beneficiary) on the assumption of an incremental capital output ratio (ICOR) of 1.5 implied that on the average the income increment per family will be Rs. 2,000. The evaluation studies conducted during the Sixth Plan had revealed that an ICOR of 1.5 is too optimistic even for IRDP programmes[37] and that in reality it was closer to three. As a consequence, the ICOR assumed for the Seventh Plan is 2.7. In the light of these facts the finding that half the sample beneficiaries had more than Rs. 1,000 income from assets (for 24 per cent between Rs. 1,001 and Rs. 2,000 and for 26 per cent more than Rs. 2,000) is indeed commendable. And that too, after reckoning the fact that in 29 per cent cases the assets were not intact. It is likely that there may be other important variables like the input and output linkages, after care support, etc., which we have not included in the present analysis. Further probing and analysis of the underlying factors, especially in respect of extreme cases will be a rewarding exercise in terms of practical policy planning and programme implementation.

So far our concern was mainly with respect to the success or failure of IRDP assistance in terms of the absolute incremental income from the asset. But what is more important and what ultimately determines the welfare of the family is the change in the total family income and more so in a relative sense. An IRDP asset might have changed the status of a beneficiary from a wage earner to a self-employed without substantially changing the family income. It may be a highly successful case of IRDP assistance in terms of the absolute income generated by the asset, but may not necessarily improve the net disposable income of the family. Similarly an absolute income of say Rs. 1,000 from an asset may have very different welfare implications for a 'destitute' family and a 'poor' family. A more sensitive measure of improvement in the levels of living may be the per centage increase in the family income preferably after correcting for price changes. Besides IRDP assistance, there could be other factors also which might have affected the incomes of the families. In fact, for a more scientific analysis, one should have observed the differences in incomes during the same period of a 'control group' of families which were identical to the assisted sample beneficiaries, except for the IRDP assistance. However, the changes in incomes of the assisted families, by the large, can be attributed to IRDP assistance[38].

From the analysis of our survey data we find that 16 per cent of the sample beneficiaries at the national level experienced a decline or no increase in family income after the IRDP assistance. Such a sad situation might have arisen due to a number of factors. If the beneficiary did not get the asset or if the asset was totally defective or if it got destroyed, 'no income' would be generated. The process of acquiring the IRDP asset might have led to other costs, monetary or others. Or the opportunity cost of IRDP might be reduced income from other sources, say wage labour. As a result, if the asset does not generate any net income the family income might, in fact, decline.

Out of the remaining 84 per cent sample beneficiaries who experienced increase in family income during the post-assistance period, 24 per cent had an increase of up to 25 per cent of the pre-assistance income, 22 per cent had an increase between 26 and 50 per cent, 28 per cent had an increase between 51 and 100 per cent. The remaining 15 per cent sample beneficiaries experienced more than 100 per cent increase in the family income from IRDP assistance. Irrespective of the pre-assistance income level, doubling of the family income as a result of IRDP assistance might have had a profound impact on the overall well-being of the family. Even an increase of more than 50 per cent in the family income over a short period can be deemed to be of significant welfare implications for the family. Thus, a total of 38 per cent of the sample beneficiaries who have experienced more than 50 per cent increase in the family income, irrespective of the value of assets given to them or the absolute increase in their income can be considered to have gained significantly in terms of family welfare.

8. Crossing the Poverty Line

In the previous section our concern was with the incremental incomes accruing to the IRDP beneficiaries from the assets given to them under the programme as well as with the increment in the family income from all sources (from the given asset as well as from other sources) as a proportion of the pre-assistance income. The former measures the direct income generation impact of the asset on the beneficiary and is more relevant in working out the productivity of the asset and estimating the incremental capital output ratios (ICORs). The latter is more meaningful for measuring the total welfare effect of the programme on the beneficiary family. It is the net increment in family income in relation to the pre-assistance level of income which is the relevant measure.[39]

In the present section we shall evaluate the effect and impact of IRDP on the beneficiaries in terms of the more commonly used criterion of 'crossing the poverty line'. Before we examine the results, let us clarify a few conceptual and measurement issues. First of all, as we have discussed elsewhere, the definition of poverty line and its measurements are unsettled issues. More importantly, since the poverty line is measured in monetary terms, the inflation factor or price changes have to be incorporated into the poverty line. However, as we have noted earlier, this dynamic aspect of poverty line was ignored throughout the Sixth Plan in the identification of beneficiaries as well as in determining the quantum of assistance. As a result, even in 1984-85, the poverty line remained at Rs. 3,500 for the purpose of IRDP assistance, when the actual poverty line had become Rs. 6,400. According to the guidelines, only those whose incomes were below Rs. 3,500 were eligible for assistance. About 41 per cent of the eligible beneficiaries crossed the poverty line of Rs. 3,500 at the national level.

Basically the factors that determine the proportion of beneficiaries who cross the poverty line are: (i) the pre-assistance level of income; (ii) the level of assistance; and (iii) the actual ICORs of the projects.

9. Summary and Concluding Remarks

To sum up, we have found: that in vast majority of cases, the assistance has gone to the deserving poor; that the village assemblies were fully involved in the final selection of the beneficiaries; that the sectoral distribution of assets under the programme which was quite skewed in favour of the primary sector and in particular milch animals initially has become gradually more evenly distributed among various sectors; that even in the face of sudden spurt in demand due to IRDP, majority of the beneficiaries got assets which justify their costs; that in more than seventy per cent of the cases, the assets are with the beneficiaries in an intact condition even after two years; that commercial banks have involved themselves in a very big way in IRDP financing; that the record of repayment of loans by IRDP beneficiaries is no worse than that of other debtors who generally are better off economically; that in vast majority of cases the assets generated net incremental income; and that most of the beneficiaries were relatively better off after the assistance as compared to the pre-assistance days in the sense that there was a significant per centage increase in the family income in the latter period. Thus, the findings generally vindicate the stand taken by the protagonists of IRDP.

We have also found: that in about one-fifth of the entire sample beneficiaries at the time of selection had income more than the cut-off point for selection; quite often the sectoral distribution of the schemes/assets was influenced by simple expedients like easy accessibility, personal biases[40] of the government functionaries, etc., rather than suitability to local conditions and income generating ability; that a significant share of assets in at least a few States was highly overpriced, which in no way can be justified; that banks were reluctant partners in the programme in many cases, the schemes were not properly appraised and the repayment schedules were too short and unrealistic in many cases; that in a considerable proportion of cases the programme has not improved the lot of the poor families at all; that only a very small per centage of the assisted poor could actually cross the poverty line; and that in a majority of cases the assistance was too inadequate to expect them to cross the poverty line. And these findings certainly vindicate some of the criticisms of the antagonists of IRDP.

Obviously, IRDP has many strong points and many weaknesses, as it often happens with most of the development programmes whether they are growth-oriented or equity-oriented. There is nothing singularly bad about IRDP. Also it is not a panacea for all our ills. The truth is in between the extremes. The substantive issue is whether IRDP is a worthwhile endeavour on balance. But this can be answered only in relation to two basic issues. First, what is the objective of the programme? Second, what are the alternatives to achieve the same objective? We shall briefly take up these issues one by one.

The objective of anti-poverty programmes, of which IRDP is the centre-piece, is removal of rural poverty in the country. One of the criticisms of rural development programmes in the country, from the days of community development (CD) programmes onwards including the green revolution technology is that in most cases, the better off sections of the rural society were benefited to the exclusion of the very poor. In fact, this apprehension was there at the very genesis of anti-poverty programmes.[41] Our findings clearly show that, as far as IRDP is concerned, the results are a mixed bag.

As we have noted in the introductory section, some of the critiques of IRDP are concerned about the alternatives to achieve the same objective. The structuralist stance is that a direct attack on poverty without an equally direct attack on the inequitous ownership of assets will not yield results. The experience of the past four decades in regard to land redistribution,[42] the socio-political realities of our highly complex society and the emerging political power equations clearly indicate that any romantic ideas about significant redistribution of existing assets have to be ruled out as a viable propositions. Another alternative is provision of wage employment to the poor. Though wage employment has a number of merits over IRDP in specific contexts as noted in the introductory section, it cannot be thought of as a permanent cure to poverty in the country. To ensure a minimum subsistence income to all the rural poor, the employment requirements will have to be several times that provided by the existing employment schemes. The benefits of community asset creation and augmentation of value to private assets via employment generation will provide disproportionate advantages to the better off sections of the rural society. The hypothesis that these in turn will generate sufficient private employment via multiplier effects needs to be empirically tested. Of course, the very poor and old who suffer extreme forms of physical and mental disabilities have to be taken care of by publicly funded and well-administered social security schemes. But this alternative can possibly take care of only those at the low-end of the poverty spectrum. Thus, one cannot escape the conclusion that the IRDP approach is quite relevant in the present Indian context. The substantive issue is how to make it more effective than what it has been evidenced by the findings presented in the previous sections.

Even the staunchest critics agree[43] that IRDP as a concept has great merit. First, major development programme which directly addresses itself specifically to the poor families and offers direct assistance in the form of income earning assets. Since the scope for redistribution of the existing main rural asset, viz., farm land is rather limited, the idea of provision of newly created assets to the poor is a welcome one. The visibility and the direct approach involved in IRDP have both strengths and weaknesses. The substantive issue is whether the strategy can be used as an instrument to transform the political process and to initiate changes in the structural characteristics of the economy. The IRDP strategy has the latent potential to change the structural characteristics.[44] It is based on the principle that even the poorest in the society have rights. It introduced an element of accountability in the administrative system. It opens up the possibility of participation in the development process. If these latent potentials can be energised, they can be used to mount pressure from below to loosen some of the rigidities of the system and to ensure that growth becomes socially more responsive and equitable. The task, however, is not an easy one.

Though originally IRDP was introduced as a truly integrated rural development programme, the rather hurried expansion of the programme to cover the entire rural areas at the beginning of the Sixth Plan has resulted in the dilution of this integration, at least in practice, if not in concept. This has been a major reason for much of the undesirable results we have noted earlier and a lot of criticism. At the same time the commitment on the part of the government to expand the outreach of the programme had its own positive effect. Once an undertaking is given, there is hardly any going back on this responsibility. Now it is mainly a matter of improving the quality and efficiency of the programme. This however, requires significant strengthening of the planning, implementing and monitoring machinery at the district level and below. On the planning side, too much is expected from the very nominal personnel and expertise available at the district and block levels.[45] Considering the mammoth dimensions of IRDP in terms of the number of beneficiaries covered and the various stages of planning and implementation according to the guidelines, no doubt, the bureaucratic limits have been reached during the Sixth Plan in a literal sense and perhaps more so in a logical sense. This may be an important reason for the emphasis in the Seventh Plan on people's involvement in the planning, implementation and monitoring of IRDP and other anti-poverty programmes by involving elected bodies and people's representatives, voluntary agencies (NGOs) and promoting organisations of the rural poor.

Another aspect of the bureaucratic involvement, in programmes of this type which needs a lot of motivation and involvement on the part of the implementors, is precisely the lack of the same positive factors. For, the bureaucracy has its own system of postings and transfers, career prospects and reward structures and incentives and disincentives which have very little to do with the efficient and successful implementation of the programmes and their effects and impacts on the affected individuals and society at large. Also the management information system developed for the purpose of monitoring of these programmes is, by and large, weighted in favour of assessing the results in terms of expenditure incurred (higher the better) and physical achievements in terms of numbers, irrespective of the physical quality of the achievements. A number of these issues were, indeed, deliberated upon in very great detail by the high level committee on administrative arrangements for rural development and poverty alleviation programmes[46] and a number of significant recommendations in the directions indicated above have been made by the Committee. The report is under the active consideration of the Government of India and the State governments. It all depends on whether the major recommendations will be accepted for implementation and if so how soon they are going to be implemented.

We have to place this programme in its correct perspective. It is only one of a packages of anti-poverty and minimum needs programmes. As we have seen earlier, there is much to be desired in the planning and execution of IRDP. Its success critically depends on how well integrated it is with the various other programmes. Integration or co-ordination is an aspect which is extremely important at all stages but is sadly missing at all stages including policy planning at the central level to implementation at the grass-roots level.

Proper integration of all anti-poverty programmes, other target group-oriented programmes and major minimum needs programmes like primary education, primary health, nutrition, rural drinking water supply, sanitation and rural roads at the stages of planning and implementation including pooling together of resources, both physical and human, can lead to results far beyond the sum total of what we achieve today. The present IRDP need be considered only the entry point to a vast area of activity. The IRDP cannot only provide assets to the poor families but also can create awareness among the poor about the possibility of a better life and their right to achieve it and the means of achieving it. They will be enabled to appreciate the importance of our cherished national objectives like universal literacy and small family norm and may like to adopt them on their own. Removal of poverty involves issues far beyond providing income for enough calorie or food or even private consumer items. In fact, it implies providing a dignified existence.

The concurrent evaluation of IRDP has clearly brought out the fact that the programme has great potential, though it suffers from a number of limitations at present. Most of the serious critics of the prog ramme also have recognised this fact. Another important aspect which was brought out by the survey is the fact that the programme is too important to be left entirely in the hands of bureaucracy, professional politicians and the middlemen. It requires much more intellectual inputs and clarity of thought for conceptualisation and planning at all levels than what is provided at present. The implementation and monitoring have to be necessarily a much more involved and co-operative effort between the implementors and beneficiaries actual as well as potential.

NOTES

1. The poor are identified in India on the basis of a very modestly defined poverty line to ensure a consumption basket which includes the minimum calorie requirements. The poverty line is usually measured as the mid-point of the frequency class interval of National Sample Survey (NSS) consumer expenditure estimates, which contains the minimum calorie requirements.
2. The target for the Seventh Plan is fixed at 20 million beneficiaries. The total amount allocated including bank credit is about Rs. 70,000 million.
3. See Dantwala (1986). For a more detailed discussion of this theme, see Dantwala et al. (1986). Especially the articles by C.T. Kurian on "Reconcilling Growth and Social justice: Strategies versus Structure?" and M.L. Dantwala on "Reconciling Growth and Social Justice: Agrarian Structure and Poverty" raise a number of important issues in this connection.
4. Rath (1985).
5. Dandekar (1986).
6. Guhan (1986).
7. Besides the references given in notes 3 to 6 above, also see Bagchee (1987), Dantwala (1985), Hirway (1985), Jodha (1986), (though this article is not a direct critiques of IRDP or anti-poverty programme as such, it is quite relevant in our context); Mukund Kanakalata (1986), Parthasarathy (1985), Rao (1987), Subbarao (1985), Sandaram and Tendulkar (1983) and Tendulkar (1983). (Again, though the last two articles preceded in National Level Evaluation Studies, they are quite relevant for our purpose).
8. The more important evaluation studies are the ones by (1) Programme Evaluation Organisation (PEO) of the Planning Commission, which covered 16 States, 33 districts, 66 blocks and 1,179 households and was released in May 1985, (2) Reserve Bank of India which covered 16 districts in 16 States (3) NABARD which covered 30 districts and 60 blocks in 16 States and (4) Institute for Financial Management and Research, which covered 17 blocks and 5 districts in 3 States. The IFMR sample size in terms of beneficiary families was 1857 besides a control group of 1007 non-beneficiary families.
9. The investigator assessed the annual family income by asking probing questions regarding (a) various sources of incomes and (b) earning of different members of the family. Item (goods and services) which were not traded or which were barted were imputed appropriate values based on ongoing market prices. Net farm income, if any, was assessed after accounting for paid out costs.
10. Same as the four listed in note 8 *ante.*
11. *Gram sabha* is the traditional village assembly in which all the adult members of the village can attend and deliberate on matters concerning the whole community or its members. This institution is a common heritage in most parts of the country. The significant exceptions are Kerala and Tamil Nadu where villages are usually

much bigger than elsewhere and as such the general assembly of the village may become too crowded.

12. For details see Kurien, N.J. (1989).
13. The block set up came into existence in the early fifties with the introduction of Community Development Programme. It consisted of a Block Development Officer, half a dozen Extension Officers and a dozen or so village level workers. Normally the Extension Officers who are the subject-matter specialists were drawn from the line departments like agriculture, animal husbandry, co-operation, etc. This arrangement was alright as long as the BDO had an upper hand in all matters relating to development within the block. However, during the sixties and seventies, when the importance of the block machinery, as the premier developmental instrument, declined and the line departments gained their prominence, many of the EOs reverted back to their parent departments. Also, the introduction of the Training and Visit System for agriculture extension in the seventies further weakened the block machinery. In some of the States, as many as half of the VLWs were withdrawn from the CD set up and attached to the T & V programme. Thus, by the time the IRDP programme was introduced in the late seventies, the block set up was a rather weak and demoralised one. Though there was a specially tailored Centrally-sponsored scheme for the strenghtening of the block machinery during the Sixth Plan the achievement in terms of recruitment and training of personnel was nowhere near the target or requirement.
14. Though there were no fixed target in terms of per centage shares for different sectors during the Sixth Plan, the guidelines indicated that the desired distribution is two-thirds share for primary sector and one-third share for the other two sectors to be shared equally. However, in actual practice the primary sector accounted for 94 per cent in 1980-81 and 83 per cent in 1981-82. This per centage came down to 55 by 1984-85.
15. Though the pre-coded schedule does not permit details of such cases to be recorded in the main body of the schedule, the one page meant for investigator's comments has brought in some interesting observations in this regard. To illustrate, in one particular block of a State, out of the 20 beneficiaries surveyed, 8 were given animal drawn carts as per records. But in reality 4 out of the 8 owned their own animal carts at the time of assistance which they took to the camp where the loan was disbursed. The other four took their neighbour's carts on hire to be presented to the authorities. Obviously the entire money involved was shared by the beneficiaries and the various officials involved.
16. Experience shows that unless the interviewer established excellent report with the beneficiary respondent, he/she will not reveal the details of the bribe payments. Even then, unless the beneficiary is totally alienated from the official functionaries, they will not be bold enough to give the information to the investigator in the presence of the VLW of some other block functionary whose presence at the time of interview, though discouraged, is not unusual. However, it is reported that in some States/regions there are some standard rates of bribes, though informal, which are prevalent. One such case is that of the veterinary doctor's association in one State which advised its members to charge Rs. 50 per certificate for milch animals under the programme as this job does not fall under the normal duties of the government veterinary doctors.
17. Since there is much criticism about the role of the purchase committee in

protecting the interests of the beneficiary, serious consideration is being given to the suggestion to do away with the purchase committees. In fact the experiment of making cash payment directly to the beneficiary for purchase of the asset is currently going on in a set of selected blocks in different States. If the experiment is found successful, it is likely that this practice may be adopted as the standard one.

18. Even if the 'formula' is not equitable to all members of the purchase committee, it is a normal practice that the incidentals of the members of the purchase committee including transport is met by the margins involved in the purchase of the asset.
19. It is in this context that the 'IRDP Cow' is known as 'circulating capital' as it does not stick to a single beneficiary for long. The term 'circulating capital' was first used by V.M. Dandekar in a seminar.
20. Instances of bulk demand have been reported for items like sewing machines, electric pump sets, poultry units, beehives, plough bullocks and animal drawn carts.
21. Not surprisingly, there is hardly an instance where the beneficiary reported that the asset he got was under-priced or was a bargain.
22. To a large measure this propensity or lack of it depends on the income generating ability of the asset, the motivation of the beneficiary to be selfemployed, his entre-preneurial abilities and finally the occurrence of contingencies.
23. To survey has come across a number of instances where the beneficiary was only a frontman or a *benami* owner. The actual custody of the asset was with another person, usually a non-poor benefactor of the poor *benami* owner. One instance was where a well-off farmer acquired a dairy of buffaloes using a number of *benami* beneficiaries who were his attached labourers.
24. For example, RBI study found that 12 per cent assets were missing at the time of the survey.
25. It is worth noting in this connection that not all the 'assets not intact' cases are totally hopeless cases in the sense of generating no income at all. A beneficiary might have received two cows, one of which might have died or he might have sold one. Such a case is reported as 'asset not intact' but the beneficiary may be earning an income from the other cow. Similarly situations have been noticed in the case of many other assets also. In fact, this is one of the reasons for the finding that as against 29 per cent of the sample beneficiaries with "asset not intact' the per centage of cases where no income was generated by the asset was only 24 per cent.
26. Though as per central guidelines, insurance of a perishable IRDP asset is a necessary part of the package of assistance, in actual practice only less than half of all the IRDP assets have been insured (as per concurrent evaluation it was 49 per cent). Even in the case of insured assets the loss does not necessarily lead to replacement of the asset. Even in cases where assets are replaced it is a long drawn and time consuming process.
27. Though the purchase committee normally has an expert to determine the quality of the asset (veterinary doctor in case of animal husbandry units, agricultural expert in case of assistance in agriculture etc.), not infrequently the beneficiary ends up getting an asset which is defective in some respect or other.
28. In actual practice, however, many banks obtain surety (land deeds or personal

surety) even for loan amounts less than Rs. 5,000. Since openly admitting the violation of RBI/NABARD guidelines is difficult, often the bankers explain that they took a surety as the beneficiaries insisted on the same, an incredulous explanation indeed.

29. For example, the credit co-operative are facing a serious situation on account of mounting overdues. During the period 1961-81, while the disbursement of loans increased only 8 times, the overdues increased 24 times. At the end of June 30, 1984, the amount of overdues at the level of primary agricultural credit societies was Rs. 15,65,0 million as against Rs. 9570 million of owned funds.
30. The average IRDP loan amount works out to about Rs. 2,000 per beneficiary. Since the survey was conducted exactly after two years of the loan, the amount of overdues should not normally exceed two-thirds of the loan amount plus interest dues.
31. Though there is hardly any justification for willful default on the part of the borrower, it may be noted in this context that the IRDP borrowers are perhaps the poorest of the lot of all institutional borrowers. And as such a repayment record of IRDP beneficiaries which is not worse than that of other borrowers should be taken as a very encouraging sign.
32. An essential question is whether the default is wilful or not. Though we have not collected information in this respect formally, the evidence as indicated by the comments of the investigators is that, by and large, small amounts of overdues are not deliberate. Among the larger overdues there are two types. The first one is where the beneficiaries got a defective asset or one, which did not generate enough income to make the scheme viable. The other case usually the beneficiary is more articulate, less poor and has the backing of some influential elements in the local community.
33. Same as the last category under note 32.
34. Even a serious study like that of Rath (see note 4 *ante*) which is quite well articulated and well argued otherwise, treated the IRDP assistance to beneficiaries who could not cross the poverty line as a sheer wastage. Of course, crossing poverty line was the avowed objective of IRDP as stated in Sixth Plan. One should not, perhaps, criticise the evaluators if they are faithfully following the stated criterion.
35. Even the calorie requirement which constitutes the basis of the official poverty line has been a matter of 'hot controversy' for the past two decades. Those who believe in 'man lives not by bread alone' want the poverty line to be much more broad-based to include other private consumption as well as public services like health, sanitation, education and other public utilities.
36. For families at the low-end of the poverty spectrum, even a small incremental income may imply a second daily meal or meeting some other pressing family need like urgent medical expenses or enabling a child to attend school rather than earn a supplementary income. At very low levels of incomes the families are usually extremely risk average and as such a steady income from an owned asset will be preferable to a higher but unsteady income from some other source.
37. It is true that most of the IRDP schemes involve rather labour intensive activities. Even then, as against an economy wide ICOR of about 5 for the Sixth Plan, an ICOR of 1.5 for IRDP investment without sufficient empirical basis was too optimistic. And a number of evaluation studies conducted during the Sixth Plan

have confirmed this.

38. Exceptions apart, in most cases the only major change in the economic status of the assisted families is due to the IRDP assets. It is found that the benefits of even the other anti-poverty programmes like NREP and RLEGP go sparingly to IRDP beneficiaries. The empirical findings suggest that the various anti-poverty programmes are of a complementary nature rather than the same group of poor families getting benefits on a supplementary basis.
39. In working out the net increment in family income in relation to pre-assistance level of income, the income from the IRDP asset is estimated after netting the loan repayment.
40. A typical example of such biases in operation is the case of animal husbandry schemes for Scheduled Tribe beneficiaries. It is well known that piggery products constitute an important item in the diets of the ST population in many areas. As such, the ST population generally prefers piggery to dairying. However, under IRDP, it was mostly milch animals rather than piggery units, which were offered to ST beneficiaries.
41. Exclusion of the very poor from the benefits of general development programmes extends even to minimum needs programme (MNP) which included number of social consumption items like primary education, health services, potable drinking water, etc., apart from infrastructural services like rural roads and rural electrification. By and large the benefits of all these facilities and other like subsidised inputs and credit for production purposes are distributed in rural areas in proportion to the existing assets and incomes. And only a residual component of such public goods and services are available for the very poor who do not have any influence over rural institutions and the public functionaries.
42. The implementation of land ceilings laws in various States, over the years has resulted in the distribution of surplus area of only 4.33 million acres (roughly 1.73 million hectares) to 3.38 million beneficiaries. This accounts for a little over one per cent of the net cropped land in the country. For details, see Annual Report, 1985-86, Department of Rural Development, Ministry of Agriculture, Government of India.
43. See, for example, C.T Kurian in Dhatwala *et al* (1986) and Rath (1985).
44. Again, see C.T. Kurian in Dantwala *et al* (1986) for a lucid presentation of this line of argument.
45. According to the guidelines issued in regard to block level planning for IRDP which should include resource survey, resource analysis, family plans, cluster plans, village plans, block plans, annual plans, perspective plans and credit plans, a high level of planning competence is required at the block/district level. Indeed, virtually the services of a mini-Planning Commission are needed at the district level.
46. See G.V.K. Rao Committee Report (1985).

REFERENCES

Bagachee, S. (1987), 'Poverty Alleviation Programme in Seventh Plan An Appraisal', *Economic and Political Weekly*, January 24.

Dandekar, V.M. (1986), 'Agriculture, Employment and Poverty,' *Economic and Political Weekly*, september 20-27.

Dantwala, M.L. (1986), 'Growth and Equity in Agriculture', *Economic Times*, Silver Jubilee Special, December 19.

—— (1985), 'Garibi Hatao: Strategy Options', *Economic and Political Weekly*, March 16.

Dantwala, M.L., Ranjit Gupta and Keith C. D'Souza (1986), (ed) "Asian Seminar on Rural Development — the Indian Experience", Oxford and IBH.

Government of India, Ministry of Agriculture, Dept. of Rural Development, "Annual Reports for 1985-86 and 1986-87".

—— "Concurrent Evaluation of IRDP — The Main Findings of the Survey", various monthly, quarterly, six monthly and yearly reports published between December 1985 to February 1987.

—— (1985), "Report of the Committee to Review the Existing Administrative Arrangements for Rural Development and Poverty Alleviation Programme" (Chairman: GVK Rao), December.

Government of India, Planning Commission, "Sixth Five-Year Plan — Draft 1976-83", Sixth Five Year Plan 1980-85" and "Seventh Five Year Plan", Vol. I and Vol. II, 1985-90.

Guhan, S. (1986), "Reaching out to the Poor" *Economic Times*, Silver Jubilee Special, December 19.

—— (1980), 'Rural Poverty: Policy and Plan Acting', *Economic and Political Weekly*, November 22.

Hirway, Indira (1985), 'Garibi Hatao: Can IRDP Do it? *Economic and Political Weekly*, March 30.

Jodha, N.S. (1986), 'Common Property Resources and Rural Poor in Dry Regions of India', *Economic and Political Weekly*, July 5.

Mukund Kanakalata (1986), 'Bank Credit and IRDP: Madhya Pradesh Experience', *Economic and Political Weekly*, October 11.

Parthasarathy, G. (1985), 'Reorientation of Rural Development Programme — A Note on Some Basic Issues', *Economic and Political Weekly*, November 30.

Rao V.M. (1987), 'Changing Village Structure — Impact of Rural Development Programmes, *Economic and Political Weekly*, Review of Agricultural, March 28.

Rath, N. (1985), 'Garibi Hatao — Can IRDP Do it?' *Economic and Political Weekly*, February 9.

Reserve Bank of India (1981), "Report of the Committee to Review Arrangement for Institutional Credit for Agriculture and Rural Development" (Chairman B. Sivaraman).

Subbarao, K. (1985): 'Regional Variations in the Impact of Anti-Poverty Programme: A Review of Evidence', *Economic and Political Weekly*, October 26.

Sundaram K. and Suresh D. Tendulkar (1983), 'Poverty in the Mid-Term Appraisal', *Economic and Political Weekly*, November 5-12.

Tendulkar, S.D. (1983), 'Rural Institutional Credit and Rural Development: A Review Article', *Indian Economic Review, Vol. XVIII, No. 1, January-June*.

6

PLANNING AND MANAGEMENT OF A RURAL DEVELOPMENT PROGRAMME:

A Study of the Karnali-Bheri Project, Nepal

Dwarika Nath Dhungel and David Ivery Field

1. Introduction

During the earlier period of planned development in Nepal (i.e. from the First Plan 1956-61 to the Fourth Plan 1970-75), trickle down theory was accepted and infrastructure development was considered as a pre-requisite for other development activities. Until the beginning of the Fifth Plan 1975-80, development-oriented efforts were mainly in the field of infrastructure development; during that period, agriculture and rural development did not get much attention. Furthermore, due to the concentration of development activities in and around Kathmandu and in a few pockets in the southern and hilly regions of the country, no substantial improvement took place in the situation of the majority of the population. The fruits of development were not equitably distributed over all the regions of the country. So there was a need to revise the development strategy. At the time when this was being felt by the national policy makers the donors, especially the World Bank, were persuading developing countries to revise their development policies in order to provide a more equitable distribution of the benefits of economic growth.

It was against this backdrop that the Fifth Plan emerged in 1975. In it, "physical infrastructure was de-emphasised for the first time with the agricultural and social sectors receiving first and second priority in investment allocation" (Pradhan, 1985: 3). The Fifth Plan aimed at the implementation of programmes that would increase mass-oriented production, maximise the use of labour resources and promote regional balance and integration. Increasing production and productive employment opportunities and meeting the basic minimum needs of the people were objectives emphasised by the Sixth Plan and reiterated by the current development plan, the Seventh Plan 1985-90.

To achieve these objectives a number of new rural development programmes were initiated in addition to the regular sectoral programmes. They include the Integrated Rural Development Projects (IRDPs), designed to deal with the problems of particular areas, including the problems of small farmers and women; target group oriented programmes, including the Small Farmers Development Programme (SFDP), directed at the problems of specific target groups, and a number of programmes designed and implemented for specific areas of the country.

The Karnali-Bheri Integrated Rural Development Project (K-BIRD) is one of ten IRDPs currently being implemented in the country. It is multi-sectoral in nature, including both programmes designed and implemented for the benefit of target groups – the Small Farmers Development Programme and the Women Development Programme (WDP) – and area-oriented programmes like the agricultural extension, livestock and other programmes, aimed at increasing productivity, providing more employment opportunities and fulfilling the basic needs of residents of the three districts in the project area (Surkhet, Dailekh and Jumla).

The K-BIRD Project is implemented in areas differing widely both climatically and topographically. This makes effective supervision and co-ordination of project activities difficult. Efforts by K-BIRD to provide a sound basis for planning include the collection of background data, the preparation of a Resource Inventory for each panchayat (the lowest unit for planning in the country), inter- and intra-sectoral meetings to bring about greater co-ordination among the participating line agencies, and the development of indicators for monitoring. This paper describes the activities undertaken by the project and discusses the problems identified and efforts made in its planning and management, as well as the lessons learnt in these matters.

2. Background Information

2.1 *Project Area*

The project area includes two districts of the Bheri Zone and one district of the Karnali Zone, all of which are situated in the Mid-Western Region of Nepal[1] (See map Figure 6.1). The total area of the project is 6534 square kilometres; it includes 141 Village Panchayats and a total population of about 450,000.

The terrain is mostly rough, steep and dissected by rivers and streams. Altitudes vary from 500 metres in the south to more than 5000 metres in the north. The climate varies markedly from a humid subtropical environment in the south, with rainfall averaging more than 2000 millimetres, through warm temperate and cold temperate to alpine conditions in the north, were the rainfall is only about 500 millimetres.

The area is relatively inaccessible with only one road linking Nepalgunj in the Terai, on the Indian border, with Birendranagar, the headquarters of Surkhet District in the south of the project area. Access by Twin-Otter aircraft is available from Kathmandu or Nepalgunj to Birendranagar and also to Jumla in the north. Apart from this, travel in the area depends upon trekking. Radio communications are maintained between district headquarters.

People are primarily engaged in agriculture. Farms are small: more than 90 per cent are smaller than 1.5 hectares. The major crops are rice, millet, wheat, maize, potatoes and mustard. Livestock plays an important role, providing milk, meat, eggs, wool, manure, draft power and a means of transport. The forest land also plays an important role in supplying livestock fodder, fuelwood and timber for construction. The land-use and distribution of the livestock are indicated in Table 6.1.

The availability of services in such a harsh environment is limited: health centres are few, the literacy rate is extremely low, potable drinking water supplies are infrequent, electricity is found in only two district headquarters and most people live at or close to the subsistence level.

Pressure on the land varies markedly throughout the project. Population densities range from as low as 4 to more than 500 people per sq. km. In some areas the density of human population exceeds 100 per sq. km, cultivated land per household is less than 1 hectare and forest land per household less than 5 hectares. In their struggle to obtain sufficient food and fuel, people encroach upon forest areas causing severe degradation (desertification) which in turn leads to extensive erosion.

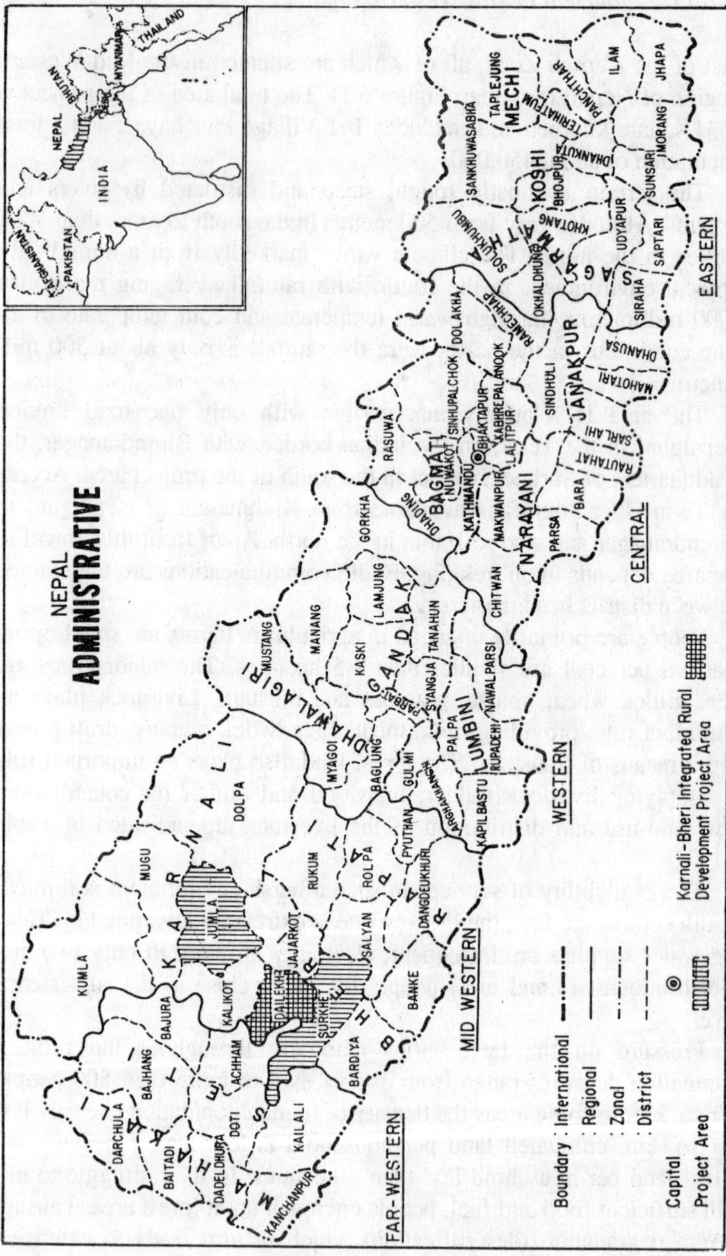

Figure 6. 1 - Location of K-BIRD Project Area

Table 6.1: Basic Project Data

District	Surkhet		Dailekh		Jumla		Total	
Altitude (m)	<1000		1000-2000		2000-3000			
Rainfall (mm)	>2000		2000-1000		<1000			
Population	181666		171736		81422		434824	
Land area (km^2)	2518.2		1472.5		2543.6		6534.3	
Land-use (km^2)		%		%		%		%
Cultivated	525.7	(21)	523.5	(36)	240.6	(9)	11289.8	(20)
Grazing	144.0	(6)	176.5	(12)	662.2	(26)	982.7	(15)
Fragile Forest	588.0	(23)	51.7	(3)	111.8	(4)	751.5	(11)
Other Forest	1214.9	(48)	705.4	(48)	933.9	(37)	2854.2	(44)
Rock/Waste	45.6	(2)	15.5	(1)	595.1	(24)	656.1	(10)
Irrigated	63.4	(3)	17.5	(1)	5.4	(1)	86.3	(1)
Livestock (nos)								
Cattle	89525		106934		61301		257760	
Buffaloes	26425		42873		2142		71440	
Sheep	2008		28752		57048		87808	
Goats	62661		39704		24892		127257	
Pigs	2980		3786		-		6766	
Chickens	146989		55402		1155		203546	
Ducks	2153		-		-		2153	
Total LSU	74873		96216		48431		219520	
Stocking rate (ha/LSU)	3.4		1.5		5.3		3.0	

Note: LSU (Livestock Unit) refers to a mature animal weighing 300 kg and producing 460 litres of milk per year.

Statistics based upon Kenting Earth Sciences, Land Resources Mapping Project (LRMP) 1986, Integrated Survey Section, Survey Department, KTM up-dated by the K-BIRD Panchayat Resource Inventory, 1987.

2.2 *Objectives*

The K-BIRD Project is in the second phase of its implementation. In accordance with the Memorandum of Understanding signed between His Majesty's Government of Nepal (HMG/N) and the Government of Canada (CIDA-HMG/N, 1985), the overall goal of the project is to increase the capacity for self-initiated and sustainable economic, environmental and social improvement in the project area, by assisting HMG/N in accelerating the rate of implementation of its Integrated Rural Development Strategy in the three districts that form the project area. In order to move towards this overall goal, three major avenues are being followed:

(a) the increase of production at a higher rate,
(b) the increase of opportunities for productive employment, and
(c) the fulfilment of the minimum Basic Needs of the people (see paragraph 4 below).

2.3 *Project Activities*

Phase I of the project, implemented between 1982 to 1985, was primarily concerned with the establishment of institutional procedures and the provision of infrastructure. Although these activities have not yet been completed in all parts of the project area; Phase II (1985-90) was designed to concentrate efforts in two main directions: supporting the directly productive sectors of agriculture, livestock, forestry, cottage industries and irrigation, and manpower development activities.

K-BIRD is involved in the following productive sectors:

(a) *Agriculture*: K-BIRD provides financial and technical support to activities in the agricultural sector which include:

(i) extension activities in all three districts, directed mainly towards increased crop production, especially of cereals and vegetables;
(ii) research activities at two agricultural and two horticultural stations, which include the production of seeds and fruit tree seedlings;
(iii) marketing activities in two districts, involving the organisation of groups of producers; and
(iv) training activities aimed at skill development and increased understanding of improved technology, especially at the farmer level.

(b) *Livestock*: K-BIRD similarly provides support for livestock raising activities, including extension, improved breeding, feeding and health control.
(c) *Forestry*: The efforts in forestry are devoted to the community (or social) forestry approach.
(d) *Cottage Industries*: The development of income generating ac-

tivities, especially for women, is the main emphasis of the project's effort in this sector.

(e) *Irrigation and Engineering*: K-BIRD supports a number of engineering activities, including irrigation schemes, drinking water supply projects, track and trail improvements, construction of suspension bridges and rural service centres and development of small-scale industries.

(f) *Credit Facilities*: Various activities in the above productive sectors also receive credit support from the Small Farmers Development Programme, which has recently received financial assistance from K-BIRD.

Manpower development aspects of the project involve a comprehensive training programme at all levels:

(a) At the *grass-roots level* various training programmes are conducted for villagers, some of whom are illiterate:

(i) farmers' tours, discussions, fairs, exhibitions, competitions and meetings in both agriculture and livestock;
(ii) basic training through the outreach programme of the Government Farms and Horticultural Stations;
(iii) skill development through short training courses offered at the Womens Training Centre, attended by both men and women; and
(iv) lead farmer training (for men and women) of Agricultural Assistants and Village Level Animal Health Workers to provide local contacts for improved technology.

(b) At *field technician level* junior technical staff, especially in agriculture, forestry and livestock are provided with in-service training both at home and abroad to complement their original basic training.

(c) At senior technical level, District Officers and other senior technical staff are encouraged to develop skills in specific aspects directly applicable to the increasing demands of rural development. This may involve post-graduate courses.

(d) At management level, management staff have been provided with the opportunity to gain experience from other similar rural development projects.

3. **The Basic Needs Approach and Project Activities**

Like other developing countries, Nepal in earlier periods of its planned development stressed G.N.P. growth and relied on trickle-down to spread its benefits. Infrastructure development was emphasised and a few areas received preference for resource allocation, thereby creating a widening gap between different regions. Large segments of society remained untouched by the development efforts, and people began to migrate to better-off areas. Starting with the Fifth Plan, basic needs – food, shelter, clothing – were given priority in national plans. During the current (seventh) plan, all development programmes are directed towards meeting basic needs.

Following a royal directive, the government outlined programmes to provide all the people with basic minimum needs by the year AD 2000 (HMG/N, 1984). By that date each and every Nepali should have 2250 calories per day and 11 metres of cloth per year, and each family should have 30 square metres of floor-space. Primary health services should be provided in each village by village level health volunteers, and children between 6 and 10 years of age should receive free primary education. Following the publication of this programme, all IRDP activities and/or departmental programmes were to be developed in accordance with the above-quoted targets. Programmes were also expected to indicate which of the basic needs targets were reflected in their activities. K-BIRD's annual programme is also guided by the basic needs policy of HMG/N. Though the health and education sectors do not fall under the purview of K-BIRD, adult literacy programmes, primary health care training, and family planning programmes are supported by the project through the SFDP and WDP. The project also supports irrigation and drinking water schemes. In the years to come, it is intended to intensify those programmes that will enable the minimum basic needs of project area residents to be met.

4. **Administrative Organisation for the Management of K-BIRD**

4.1 *General*

K-BIRD provides funds to the participating agencies to expand and strengthen their activities in the project area. However, apart from managing the foreign training programme for project personnel and hiring consultancy services for project activities, K-BIRD does not implement any separate programmes. Whatever is done in its name is formulated, implemented and monitored by the concerned line agencies as part of their regular programmes.

The institutional framework for the management of K-BIRD is provided by the Decentralisation Act of 1982 (HMG/N, 1982), in accordance with which, in each particular village, the Village Panchayat Secretary (VPS) is responsible for assisting the Village Panchayat (VP) in the preparation, implementation, and monitoring of K-BIRD activities.[2] Public servants posted at the Service Centre Level also provide support to the VPs in managing K-BIRD-funded activities and assist the district level offices in the formulation and implementation of such activities.

At the district level, the District Panchayat Secretariat (DPS), headed by the Local Development Officer (LDO), is responsible for the planning and management of K-BIRD activities.[3] The heads of the concerned sections of the DPS, whose programmes are funded by K-BIRD, assist the District Panchayat and District Assembly in formulating, approving, implementing and monitoring these programmes. They also prepare and submit progress reports to the DP, project office and/or the concerned ministries or departments. It must be stressed that it is the people's representatives themselves who are responsible for the formulation, implementation, monitoring, operation, maintenance and repair of project activities in their areas.

At project level, a Project Co-ordinator's Office (PCO), established as an extended arm of the Co-ordination Division of the Panchayat and Local Development Ministry (MPLD) now known as Ministry of Local Development (MLD) is responsible for helping the DPS to formulate, implement and monitor project activities. The liaison work between the international donor agency (C.I.D.A.) and the participating agencies is also done by this office. The PCO prepares the annual programme and budget of K-BIRD by compiling the District Development Plans approved by the DP/DAs of the Project area. The PCO, headed by the Project Co-ordinator, is located at Birendranagar in Surkhet District.

4.2 *Formulation of Project Activities*

Each section of the DPS prepares an Annual Plan, on the basis of local aspirations expressed by the Village Panchayats, and within the budget forecast and the guidelines provided by the concerned ministry or department. This plan is then submitted to the subject matter committee[4] constituted under the chairmanship of one of the members of the DP. After approval by the respective subject matter committees, the programmes are compiled by the LDO in the form of a DDP and submitted to the DP and DA for approval. They are then submitted to the concerned ministry, department or central level agency for inclusion in the national budget. A diagrammatic representation of the planning process is shown in Fig. 6.2.

4.3 *Implementation and Monitoring of K-BIRD Activities*

The heads of the concerned sections of the DPS are responsible for the implementation of sectoral programmes such as agriculture extension, livestock, etc. However, local development activities such as drinking water schemes, minor irrigation works, community buildings and suspension bridges may be implemented through either contractors or Users' Committees (see section 6.2 below). There is no uniform system in the project area. If the DP decide to constitute a Users' Committee to implement local development activities, the people's representatives then become directly involved in the implementation process, because the Users' Committee constituted by the DP from among the beneficiaries is headed by a member of the Panchayat. In their capacity as chairman and members of a Users' Committee, the members of the Panchayat become involved in managing the construction materials and implementing activities in their area.

The District Supervision Committee (DSC) which includes among others the DP President and Vice-President and the Chief District Officer is the monitoring agency at the district level. Both during their trips to projects in the K-BIRD area and at quarterly review meetings, its members raise various issues and monitor the implementation of K-BIRD activities.

4.4 *Operation, Maintenance and Repair of Completed K-BIRD Activities*

The concerned section of the DPS is responsible for the operation, maintenance and repair of the infrastructure created under K-BIRD. Users' Committees are also entrusted with this task, in relation to the completed local development activities with which they are concerned. In the case of projects completed by contractors, once they are handed over to a Village or District Panchayat, then the panchayat will have to assume responsibility for their operation, maintenance and repair. Users' Committees provide a useful way of achieving these objectives.

FIGURE 6.2: Planning Process of District Development Plan

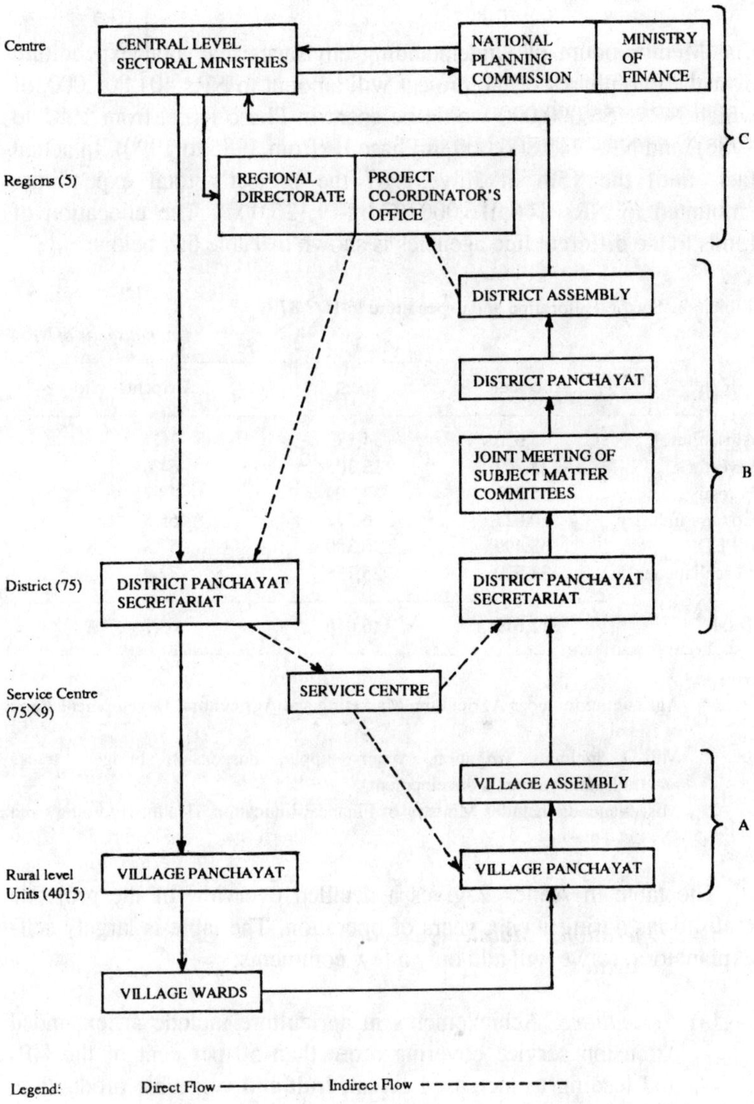

Notes:

(A) Preparation and approval of village level plan and submission of some projects of this plan to the District Panchayat for assistance to implement.

(B) Assimilation of village level projects and preparation of District Development Plan.

(C) Submission of the District Development Plan to the concerned sectoral offices and to the National Planning Commission for inclusion in the national budget.

5. Financial Expenditure and Achievements

The Memorandum of Understanding envisages that total expenditure over the two phases of the project will amount to NRs 401,806,000, of which NRs 156,000,000 would be spent in Phase I (i.e. from 1981 to 1985), and NRs 245,806,000 in Phase II (from 1985 to 1990). In actual fact, until the 15th of July, 1987 the project's total expenditure amounted to NRs 146,016,000 (Cdn$ 9,126,000). The allocation of funds to the different line agencies is shown in Table 6.2, below:

Table 6.2: Sectoral allocation and expenditure to 15/7/87

(in thousands of NRs)

	Allocated	Spent	% Spent
Agriculture*	45,656	34,892	76.4
Livestock	23,707	15,305	64.6
Forestry	35,201	27,709	78.7
Cottage Industry	10,027	6,572	65.5
MPLD+	63,499	36,380	57.3
Miscellaneous++	34,529	25,158	72.9
Total	212,619	146,016	68.7

Note:

* Agriculture includes Agriculture Marketing and Agricultural Development Bank of Nepal.

\+ MPLD includes irrigation, water supply, suspension bridges, tracks and trails, and women's development.

++ Miscellaneous includes Ministry of Finance, Education, Health, Hydrology and District Treasury.

The table in Annex 2 gives a detailed overview of the project's realisations during its six years of operation. The table is largely self-explanatory, so we will add only a few comments:

(a) *Agriculture*: Achievements in agriculture include an expanded extension service covering more than 50 per cent of the VPs and leading to increased cereal, fruit and vegetable production. The supply of inputs such as seeds was also improved.

(b) *Livestock*: Achievements in livestock include the distribution of fodder tree seedlings and improved animals, as well as curative and preventive measures for the protection of animal health.

The mineral block distribution and improved fodder grass production programmes were also supported by K-BIRD.

(c) *Women's Development Services*: Achievements in this sector have included the establishment of offices in the project area, and the involvement of women of project area in various activities to engender confidence, build-up a community awareness, implement self-help projects and generally improve women's ability to participate in village-level planning. Several skill development training programmes were supported to help women raise their incomes.

6. Problems faced by the Project

As was made clear in section 2, the planning and implementation of K-BIRD take place in a harsh physical environment and the local economy is characterised by poverty and under-development. These characteristics create their own constraints for the formulation and implementation of the project. The remoteness of many areas of the project naturally makes transport and communications very difficult. The project has provided wireless facilities in the district headquarters of the project area, but communications within districts and between specific project sites and project headquarters (in Surkhet) remain a problem. Also, because the economy in the rural areas is basically of a subsistence type, there are considerable constraints on what can be done: farms are small, many farmers are in debt and organised credit facilities are only slowly being made available. Alternative income generating activities are limited due mainly to the lack of markets. In addition to these difficulties, there are other problems associated with the planning and implementation of the project. These include scarcity of data, problems of people's participation, and administrative problems.

6.1 *Inadequacy of Available Data*

There has been a marked lack of adequate data at the Village Panchayat level, even though the Decentralisation Act and Regulations required that each VP should prepare a village profile. Similarly, despite the requirement that district profiles be prepared by every DP, the DPs of the project area have failed to prepare and update their district's profiles.

Certain data relevant for rural planning are available in Nepal. However, for various reasons they are inadequate: out of date, inaccurate, incomplete, and generally not detailed below district level. K-BIRD has made a start on the improvement of village level data by breaking down existing district data to the VP level using two main sources: the Land Resources Mapping Project for land-use and land capability and village level data collected by a K-BIRD survey in 1983/84. The data have been compiled into a computer programme entitled *Panchayat Resource Inventory* and includes data on the environment (land-use, altitude, and rainfall); human resources (population, employment and land tenure); livestock resources (livestock numbers, production, health and feed utilisation); and services available such as technical (advisory), financial (credit institutions), support (agricultural inputs, irrigation, water supply) and social services (education, health). Upon completion of the inventory the concerned panchayat would be requested by K-BIRD through the DP to review and up-date the data and then to use it as a basis for planning.

Efforts by K-BIRD to promote improved planning also include the training of VP Secretaries in the use of Village Profiles and the development of improved Village Profiles.

6.2 *Problems of People's Participation*

People's attitudes are a major factor influencing the development process and have a significant impact on both the planning and the implementation stages of the project. Two examples will illustrate the difficulties faced in communicating with the local populations:

(a) Dailekh and Jumla are difficult areas from the point of view of transportation. As a result of this problem and the lack of other facilities, people in these districts live in hardship. For this reason, they consider that the most important project is the construction of a motorable road. Unless this project is undertaken, no matter what has been done in other sectors, the people of Jumla and Dailekh will not feel satisfied with K-BIRD activities. Such a situation gives rise to problems of communication between K-BIRD and its beneficiaries. Similarly, due to a lack of awareness among the local population of problems such as desertification and soil erosion or a lack of appreciation for the appropriate technology, the project has faced difficulties in giving due attention to these matters.

(b) In order to instil a feeling among the people that local development projects have a direct bearing on their lives, they are encouraged to become members of Users' Committees and thus involve themselves in the implementation, operation, maintenance and repair of the activities with which they are concerned. However, on the basis of the number of completed local development projects implemented, during Phase I of K-BIRD, by Users' Committees, it is evident that the local people do not have an active interest in their completion and operation. The quality of construction and the maintenance and repair of activities undertaken by these User Committees also leave much to be desired. Of the total of 79 local development projects funded by the project during that period, 36 were implemented through users' committees. However, by the fiscal year 1985/86 only 11 of these had been completed. Also, among Users' Committees there is a feeling that K-BIRD should provide the funds for the operation and maintenance of completed projects. Thus, instead of fostering self-reliance, government intervention in small projects seems instead to have given rise to a *dependency syndrome*.

6.3 *Administrative Problems*

Problems of a specifically administrative nature faced by K-Bird include the following:

(a) *Lack of co-ordination among sectoral agencies*: the preparation and implementation of development programmes has traditionally been done on sectoral lines. Despite the Decentralisation Act and Regulations, the sectoral agencies, which are supposed to formulate their programmes by taking into account each other's requirements, have not been able to overcome sectoral rivalries. There has been little or no co-ordination or collaboration between sectors. For example, the programmes for irrigation schemes are formulated without taking into account the requirements of the agricultural programmes. When similar programmes are undertaken by different sectoral agencies in the same geographical area, instead of collaborating with the others, each agency is interested only in meeting its own target.

This applies not only inter-ministerially (e.g. between Agriculture and Forestry with regard to livestock feed or Agriculture and MPLD with regard to irrigation projects) but also inter-departmentally (e.g. between Agriculture and Livestock with regard to training programmes or the maintenance of sprayers).

The DP/DA, which are supposed to co-ordinate the different programmes of the DDP, in reality do not take this responsibility seriously enough. The members of DP/DA care more about arguing which local development projects should be implemented in which areas than about ensuring that projects included in the DDP complement each other.

(b) *Ineffectiveness of the Project Co-ordinator's Office*: as mentioned above, the Office of the Project Co-ordinator is primarily concerned with co-ordination and facilitation of the implementation of K-BIRD activities. However, structurally the PCO is placed as an appendage alongside the line agencies and has no implementation role. It is purely advisory in its relations with sectoral line agencies, which are themselves responsible for the formulation and implementation of K-BIRD activities. Since it has no implementation role, the PCO has to rely upon personal or informal relationships to achieve results.

(c) *High Staff Turn-Over*: like other IRD projects, K-BIRD faces a high staff turn-over. Since the beginning of the project in 1982, there have been five Project Co-ordinators, three of whom in the period of one year. One of these co-ordinators held the position for only two months.

This has also been a problem at the level of regional directors, Local Development Officers and other district level officers. From 1981/82 to 1987/88, Surkhet, Dailekh and Jumla each had 4, 3 and 4 different Local Development Officers respectively. Similarly, Surkhet had 2, Dailekh 4 and Jumla 3 different District Technical Officers during the same period.

(d) *Lack of Incentives*: In the management of K-BIRD, two types of personnel are involved: permanent employees of HMG/N and K-BIRD personnel. Even among K-BIRD personnel, some are permanent (for the project period) and others temporary. Most of the officials involved in the project are of these latter two categories. Even in the office of the project co-ordinator only 4 out of 82 sanctioned posts are permanent. In such a situation it is not realistic to expect loyalty and dedication from officials who do not feel any security or commitment beyond the end of the project period. One consequence of this is that, with the exception of permanent staff, K-BIRD personnel tend to think of their posting to K-BIRD as a stop-gap arrangement.

Lack of facilities, including transportation, health care and schooling for children in remote areas, are other factors that affect the working capacity and efficiency of K-BIRD staff. Sometimes it is difficult for the project personnel to obtain foodstuffs in certain areas covered by K-BIRD. For these reasons, most of the project personnel leave their families in their respective home districts. Under such conditions, it is natural for them to think of their families and take advantage of any opportunity to visit them.

(e) *Supply of Construction Materials and Supervision of Projects*: because of the complex tendering procedure, it takes months to arrange for the procurement of construction materials. Transportation of construction materials to Dailekh and Jumla is extremely difficult. Normally it takes ten to fifteen days to get a bag of cement (50 kg) from Birendranagar to Jumla. The transportation of construction materials from district headquarters to the project site is yet another problem and materials supplied for one project are often used in another one. There is also a problem of loss of quantity during transportation.

In addition to this, effective supervision of construction activities has yet to be achieved. Due to the difficulty to travelling within the project area, K-BIRD has not been able to supervise construction activities effectively.

7. Efforts made to deal with the Problems and Constraints

In addition to the attempt, already mentioned, to improve the data base for planning, the project has taken a number of measures to minimise the problems that have faced it. These include:

(a) *Human Resource Development*: training has played a major role in K-BIRD activities not only at the level of skill development but also at the managerial level. Considerable emphasis has been laid upon training village level workers, both male and female, especially at the level of Agricultural Assistants (lead farmers) and Village Level Animal Health Workers; district and regional level personnel have also received appropriate training.

(b) *Co-ordination*: it is no easy task to bring together line agencies which have traditionally been rivals. Through personal contact, seminars and meetings, efforts have been made to obtain collaboration on related activities. As an example, organisations such as the Women Training Centre, Cottage Industries Development Board and Appropriate Technology Unit have been brought together to discuss possible expansion of the bee-keeping programme.

Co-ordination is required both between different line agencies working in the same field and between different line agencies working in related fields (e.g. livestock and fodder trees). To help the line agencies to co-ordinate their activities, K-BIRD has organised inter-agency meetings of related agencies. At the annual planning meeting organised at the national and regional level, agencies are requested to consider each others requirements.

(c) *Monitoring Indicators*: in order to utilise monitoring and evaluation information fully, it is essentially to select carefully the projects and measurable objectives. There are a total of 706 projects in 41 sectoral agencies; out of these 137 (19%) were selected for monitoring. The following is an example of the indicators selected for monitoring a rice production programme:

(i) location and area of programme;
(ii) inputs (seed, fertiliser, irrigation, chemicals);
(iii) personnel involved (implementation, supervisory);
(iv) funds spent;
(v) outputs (yield per ha, comments of farmers).

8. Lessons from K-BIRD experience

Below we present a number of lessons from our experience with the planning and implementation of K-BIRD.

(a) *Project Area*: if the transportation network is good, it may not matter whether the project area is large. On the other hand, where transportation is a serious problem, it is desirable from the point of view of management to have a small (one or two districts) and geographically continuous area. If the project area corresponds to an administrative area (i.e. a district, zone or region), it is easier to deal with project issues. Since K-BIRD straddles zonal boundaries, project management has to deal with two zonal administrators, which is not always easy.

(b) *Formulation of Project Activities*: where project implementation is traditionally based on a sectoral approach, it is not easy for all the agencies involved in an IRD programme to think of co-ordinating with each other. In such cases, instead of attempting to have a large number of components within the programme of an IRDP, it may be preferable to have only a few, selected on the basis of the priority needs of the area. This will normally make the project much easier to manage.

(c) *Implementation*: for successful implementation the beneficiaries must be involved from the planning stage through to the operation, maintenance and repair of completed projects, especially construction projects. It is essential that the necessary inputs are in place to enable implementation to proceed. These include not only basic inputs but also a sufficient number of trained people, dedicated to the work in the project area. To have the necessary commitment from the project personnel it is desirable to have permanent employees, especially at the officer level, posted to the project. Greater opportunities for training should also be provided. A further measure which could reduce the effects associated with hardship posts would be the systematic rotation of officers from hardship areas to more congenial locations, after a certain period of duty.

(d) *Monitoring and evaluation*: this is closely linked to plan preparation, since specific measurable objectives must be incorporated into the original plan proposals. In order to assess the progress of a project, indicators are required. However, even a hundred per cent achievement of a given project within a particular sectoral programme may not necessarily indicate conclusive progress towards achieving the Basic Needs objectives. The need to carry out periodic impact evaluation studies must be emphasised since only then can a true picture of the overall trend be obtained.

(e) *Construction Projects*: in order to improve the performance with regard to construction projects three main avenues need to be explored:

(i) increasing the use of locally available materials and involvement of real beneficiaries in the construction, maintenance and repair of projects;
(ii) creating storage facilities within the K-BIRD area nearer to sites where supplies are needed; and
(iii) tightening construction contracts and carrying out regular supervision and monitoring.

(f) *Project Management*: The district being the focal point for K-BIRD activities, the Local Development Officer has played the role of coordinator. From the point of view of project sustainability, however, experience shows that this is not the proper mechanism for project management. A possible alternative arrangement (unless, that is, the project is managed through an NGO) would entrust this responsibility to the field officer of the lead agency located at the regional level (department or regional directorate). However, while facilitating coordination, institutional arrangements at the project level must avoid giving the other agencies involved the feeling that a super-ministry is emerging.

9. Concluding Remarks

It could not reasonably be expected that K-BIRD would solve all the problems of its beneficiaries in a period of seven or eight years. Rural development is a long-term process which demands continuous efforts and readjustment of programmes taking into account the needs and requirements of project beneficiaries.

In K-BIRD's earlier phase, the area development approach was emphasised and its activities were formulated and implemented accordingly. It is, however, now being realised that if the project is to help certain target groups, for example small farmers and women, to improve their conditions, specific programmes for those target groups need to be implemented. This is why the Women Development Programme hitherto implemented in two districts only has been expanded to the third district. Similarly, from the fiscal year 1987/88, the Small Farmer Development Programme is being implemented as a K-BIRD activity. In years to come these programmes will hopefully receive preference in resource allocation and be further expanded. It can be seen from this that K-BIRD is trying to tackle development problems using both the target group and area development approaches. Studies are to be funded to establish the impact of K-BIRD activities on different aspects of the project beneficiaries' living conditions.

Postscript (June 1990)

The recent popular movement has swept away the panchayat system and ushered in an era of multi-party system. The political structure, including the local units of panchayat – village and District panchayat was abolished. The village and district panchayat have, as an interim arrangement, been replaced by the village committee and District development committee which for the time being, would consist of the district as well as village level functionaries of the government. Thus the district development planning process indicated in figure 6.2 and the role of the District Panchayat/District Assembly and District Supervision Committee in the planning as well as management of the K-BIRD project activities no longer hold true. Until the future shape of local government becomes clear and its role in the management of integrated rural development projects is identified, the district level agencies of the participating agencies will manage the K-BIRD activities for which assistance and support are to be provided by the office of the project coordinator. But to ensure the people's participation in the construction activities, the system of users' committee which, unlike in the past, will consist of the real beneficiaries, has been retained.

With the changes in the political system there will be changes in rural development policy; institutional arrangements and the planning process for the development programmes in general and rural development programmes in particular are going to be affected. However the development of rural areas through the regular departmental and special programmes will have to be continued. Also due to the inter related nature of rural life, it will remain preferable to deal with all the problems of villagers in a holistic manner. From this perspective, the retionale on which the IRDP was initiated is still valid. But based on the lessons learned from the K-BIRD and other projects, the IRDP will have to be designed in such a way as to be easier to manage; it will have a direct impact on the life of the rural people in general and the poor in particular, and the real beneficiaries, rather than only the elected officials, will have a say in the planning and management of project activities. With the termination of the present phase in July '92 these facts will have to be considered by both the donor and HMG/N while designing the next phase of the K-BIRD project.

NOTES

1. The Kingdom of Nepal is divided into five development regions, fourteen zones and seventy-five administrative districts.
2. The Village Panchayat or Town Panchayat is the lowest level elected institution. It consists of one ward member, the Chairman and Vice-Chairman and the six presidents of the grass-roots level units of government-sponsored class organisations (i.e. Organisations of Women, Youth, Peasants, Elders, Ex-Servicemen, and Labour). The period of office of ward members, VP Chairman and Vice-Chairman is five years. The presidents of class organisations mentioned above are ex-officio members. The members of the VP and four other elected members for each ward constitute the Village or Town Assembly. The period of office for these members is also five years. The Village or Town Assembly is the final approving authority of Village Level or Town Level activities and it supervises the implementation of these activities. Therefore, the annual programme approved by the Village or Town Panchayat is reviewed or revised and its implementation is monitored by the Village or Town Assembly. There are 4015 Village Panchayats and 33 Town Panchayats in the country.
3. In each of the seventy-five districts there is a District Panchayat (DP) which consists of President, Vice-President, the district level presidents of the six class organisations and nine other members. The President and Vice-President are elected by an Electoral College consisting of the representatives of the Village and Town Panchayats. In each of the nine areas into which districts are divided one member is elected by the representatives of the Village and Town Panchayat in the area. The term of office for elected DP members is five years. At the district level there is also a larger body called District Assembly (DA). It consists of the DP members and representatives of the Village and Town Panchayats. After approval by the DP, the DDP needs to be finally approved by the DA for implementation. Implementation of the DDP is supervised by the DA. Final decisions regarding the mobilisation of resources (both human and fiscal) are made by the District Assembly.
4. The following Subject Matter Committees are constituted at the district level:

   (i). Forestry, Soil conservation and Watershed Management and Industry;
   (ii). Maintenance and Repairs;
   (iii). Agriculture and Irrigation;
   (iv). Health and Population ; and
   (v). Education and Culture

REFERENCES

CIDA-HMG/N (1985), "Memorandum of Understanding between HMG/N and the

Government of Canada for the K-BIRD Project, Phase II".

His Majesty's Government of Nepal (1982), *Decentralisation Act 1982*, Ministry of Panchayat and Local Development, Kathmandu.

HMG/N (1984), *Programme for Fulfilment of Basic Needs (1985-2000)*, National Planning Commission, Kathmandu (1984).

Pradhan, B. B. (1985), "Integrated Rural Development Projects in Nepal, A Review" ICIMOD, Kathmandu (Occasional Paper No. 2).

APPENDIX 1

LIST OF DISTRICT LEVEL OFFICES INCLUDED IN THE DISTRICT PANCHAYAT SECRETARIATE

1. Education and Culture-related Office
2. Health and Population-related Office
3. Agriculture and Irrigation-related Office
4. Works and Transportation-related Office
5. Drinking Water and Water Power-related Office
6. Forest, Soil Conservation and Environment-related Office
7. Industry Commerce and Tourism-related Office
8. Fuel-related Office
9. Local Development and Social Welfare-related Office
10. Sajha and Cooperative-related Office
11. Other Development-related Office

The Local Development Officer is the head of the District Panchayat Secretariat and administrative head of the offices mentioned above.

APPENDIX 2

K-BIRD's ACHIEVEMENTS (1981-JULY 15, 1987)

1. *Agriculture*
   Extension Activities (Area coverage)
   - Cereals 30,000 ha
   - Fruit trees 305 ha
   - Vegetables 250 ha

   Distribution of inputs
   - Cereals 80 Mt.
   - Vegetables 8 Mt.
   - Fruit trees 30,000 Saplings/year
   - Fertilisers 306 Mt./year
2. *Livestock*
   Distribution of Improved Stock
   - Bulls 56
   - Buffalo bulls 58
   - Bucks 120
   - Rams 204
   - Boars 28
   - Asses 12
   - Yaks 6
   - Chickens 16,006
   - Fodder tree seedlings distribution 40,000 per year
   - Improved grass fodder production 22 ha per year
   - Prevention of diseases by vaccination 50,000 per year
   - Parasite control 190,000 per year
3. *Forestry and Soil Conservation*
   - Establishment of nurseries 36 + 24
   - Production of Seedlings 840,500
   - Plantation 337 + 156 ha
   - Gully control 13 sites
4. *Cottage Industry*
   Establishment of businesses
   - Hosiery 5
   - Textile 22
   - Paper Making 2

- Carpentry 25
- Leather works 2
- Tailoring 15
- Carpet making 6
- Mechanics 1
- Training 1,000

5. *Appropriate Technology*

Installation

- Power pumps 8
- Water turbine 2
- Rural electrification 2

Distribution

- Smokeless ovens 16
- Seed bins 5
- Beehives 38

6. *Infrastructures*

- Rural Service Centres 7
- District-level training centres 3
- Drinking water schemes 14
- Irrigation 14
- Tracks and trails 3

7. *Human Resource Development Training Programmes related to: Agriculture*

- Farmers 1,441
- Technicians 502

Livestock

- Farmers 1,079

Technicians

- Forestry 79
- Soil conservation 50

Skill Development

- Masons 151

Special programmes for women

- Bee-keeping 1,231
- Rabbit rearing 86
- Income generation 145
- Nutrition & grain preservation 58
- Smokeless ovens 15
- Refreshers 59

Source: K-BIRD Project Co-ordinator's Office, Birendranagar, Surkhet.

7

THE INTEGRATED RURAL DEVELOPMENT PROJECT OF RATNAPURA IN SRI LANKA: Lessons from Experience

Manel Jayamanne

1. Introduction

The purpose of this paper is to present the experience of the author with the Integrated Rural Development Project (IRDP) of Ratnapura in Sri Lanka. The paper presents the approach adopted in IRDP Ratnapura (IRDP-R), stressing some of its differences from earlier approaches, and discusses the lessons that may be learnt from its experience for improving the design and formulation of future IRD programmes.

The IRD programme in Sri Lanka is described first, together with some of the most salient criticisms to which it has been subjected. This is followed by a brief characterisation of the Ratnapura district and of the approach and methodology adopted in the planning and implementation of IRDP-R. Next the implementation of the IRDP during the past four years is described, together with the changes introduced during implementation and some observations on the performance of the project. Finally, a number of lessons that may be derived from this experience are enumerated and discussed.

1.1 *The Integrated Rural Development Programme Lanka*

The district-based Integrated Rural Development Programme (IRDPP) was initiated in Sri Lanka towards the late 1970s, as a public sector investment strategy. Its main objective was to improve the living conditions of the rural population in those districts that do not benefit directly from large, high priority projects such as the Mahaweli Project (Irrigation, Hydro-Electricity and Settlement), Urban Development Programme, Free Trade Zone or National Housing Development Programme. "The IRDPP as conceptualised in Sri Lanka is not the only instrument through which rural development is undertaken" (Morapaya, 1986); rather, it is viewed as a supplementary programme designed to accelerate rural development, which is carried out in addition to the on-going efforts of all other agencies operating in rural areas.

Since its inception in 1979, IRDPP expanded to cover 14 administrative districts in Sri Lanka, out of a total of 24. All the IRD Projects rely on foreign funding, bilateral or multilateral. This has led to a diversity of planning approaches, which may broadly be classified into two main types:

(a) the 'blueprint' or 'programme' approach, adopted in the projects sponsored by multilateral agencies such as IBRD/IDA or IFAD, and
(b) the 'annual planning', 'rolling plan' or 'process' approach, adopted in the projects financed by bilateral agencies like SIDA, NORAD, and The Netherlands Programme of International Co-operation.

The rather experimental way in which IRDPP started in Sri Lanka required a great deal of flexibility, diversity and innovation. The guiding principles formulated at the outset stressed the importance of adapting the design of each IRD project to the needs and resources of the specific district in which it was to be implemented. The experience during this period also indicated the need for a national rural development policy. The guidelines for such a policy are currently being formulated by the Ministry of Plan Implementation (MPI), which is responsible for the planning and implementation of the IRDPP.

IRDPP in Sri Lanka is today a well-established rural development programme, which enjoys considerable popularity and support among district political leaders, the government, the external donor agencies and the population at large. Several factors have contributed to this success, foremost among which are the priority assigned to rural development, both nationally and internationally, the trend towards decentralisation in Sri Lanka and the flexibility of the planning process, which allows district planners to take fully into account the economic, social and political realities of their districts (Perera, 1985).

Ratnapura District was included in the National IRDP Programme in 1984, with financial support from the Government of the Netherlands, as the 11th district in which IRDP was introduced.

1.2 *The Debate on IRDP*

Among the arguments which have been adduced in favour of adopting IRDP as an approach to rural development the following may be mentioned:

(i) A multi-sectoral approach is more suitable to the interdependent nature of problems of rural development.
(ii) The integration of activities in time, in space and in relation to the beneficiaries allows a more effective solution of the problems of rural development.
(iii) The flexibility built into the design of IRD projects enables planners to incorporate lessons learnt during implementation in order to correct errors and adverse effects when they are discovered.
(iv) IRDP creates opportunities for local talent to initiate and develop innovative organisational structures.
(v) The mechanisms for popular participation included in the IRDP planning and implementation processes provide an opportunity for the poor to voice their needs, which can then be taken into account in the formulation of development objectives and policies.
(vi) The improved co-ordination among existing government agencies brought about by IRD projects facilitates their effective implementation and also their continuing operation and maintenance, even after the projects are wound up.
(vii) IRD projects have made noteworthy efforts to address the problem of poverty and to promote income-generating activities aimed at reducing inequality.

However, the IRDP approach has also been frequently criticised. The most important criticisms may be summed up as follows:

(a) *Objectives and composition of IRDP investment packages*:

The objectives generally included in IRDP are to raise income levels, to reach the poorest of the poor, to pay special attention to women and less privileged target groups, to maintain the ecological balance and to stimulate popular participation in the planning process. These objectives are often criticised for being vague, unrealistic and at times contradictory. Because of the overload in terms of objectives, projects often lack a clear direction and fail to reach integration of the multi-sectoral activities. In fact, IRDP is often criticised for the limited degree of integration effectively achieved. This is attributable to the scattered nature of the projects implemented, especially when investment is relatively small (e.g. the same families may not receive benefits of *both* a latrine construction programme *and* a drinking water supply scheme, if the size of the programme is small in relation to the population).

(b) *Management and organisational problems*: The management and organisational aspects of IRDPP have received great attention. The requirements for successful management of IRD projects do not match the bureaucratic and political context in which they are implemented. The success of any development project depends largely on its environment (Wiggins, 1985). The multi-sectoral nature of IRDP activities implies that the physical and organisational environment in which the projects need to be managed is both broad and complex, which in turn weakens management control.

(c) *Implementation capacity and efficiency*: Three different studies of project implementation have estimated that more than 50% of the factors causing serious problems or failures in development projects are beyond the control of project management (Bowden, 1986). On the other hand, the tasks of project management demand specific and far-reaching skills from the managers, which range from knowledge of the sectors covered by their projects to the bargaining and negotiating skills necessary to reconcile conflicting interests and demands and to maintain harmonious relations with implementing agencies. The organisational structure of the IRDP has been criticised as ill-adapted to the requirements of effective management. The implementation capacity and efficiency of the implementing agencies have also been criticised. This has turned co-ordination into a critical issue.

(d) *Sustainability*: Limited capacity and efficiency have led critics to question the sustainability of activities undertaken, once the particular project under which they have been carried out is wound up. The doubts raised in this regard are strengthened by the lack of resources within the government to operate and maintain the assets created by IRDP, once the donors withdraw.

(e) *Influence of foreign financing*: Finally, donor financing results in a tendency to meet donor priorities rather than those of the government or intended beneficiaries. In fact, donor preference is a decisive factor in determining investment levels and directions. This may result in excessive emphasis on financial and technical aspects and neglect of important social, cultural and political factors.

2. **IRDP in Ratnapura District**

2.1 *The district*

Ratnapura District is situated at the southern wall of the central hills of Sri Lanka. The total land area of the district is 3275 sq. km. Two main rivers (the Walawe and the Kalu Ganga) and a large number of tributaries flow through the district.

The elevation of the area ranges from 72 m to about 900 m above sea level. The district can be divided into three distinct climatic zones, namely wet, intermediate and dry. The dry and intermediate zones receive rain during the North-west monsoon period (December to February) and the intermonsoonal period (March to April and October to November). The wet zone area receives rain from the North-west monsoon as well as the South-east monsoon period of May to July. In addition, intermonsoonal rain also occurs on the wet part of the district. Temperature ranges between 23 and 32 degrees Celsius in the lower areas and between 18 and 22 degrees Celsius in the higher elevations.

The 1981 Census gives a figure of 797,087 for the population of the district, an increase of 18.4 per cent over the 1971 figure. The average annual growth rate for the period was two per cent, which is slightly higher than the national average of 1.7 per cent. The average density in the district is 246 persons per sq. km. However, the density falls as low as 100 persons per sq. km in some areas in the intermediate and dry zones and rises to 300-400 persons per sq. km along the main trunk road which runs from the western to the southern border of the district. The urban population in the district was only 7.4 per cent of the total in 1981.

The majority of the people speak Sinhalese and are Buddhists. Hindu Tamils who are concentrated mainly in large plantations and some Muslims live mainly in and around townships, where they form a significant part of the business community.

Ratnapura district is divided into 15 Assistant Government Agent (A.G.A.) Divisions, which are further disaggregated into 165 smaller *Grama Sevaka* (G.S.) Divisions. There are in the district eight electoral constituencies for the National Assembly. The organisation of local government is presently undergoing several fundamental changes.

2.2 *Objectives of the IRDP-Ratnapura*

At the time of formalisation of the agreement concerning Dutch funding for IRDP-Ratnapura (IRDP-R), neither Sri Lanka nor The Netherlands had a clear idea concerning the approach or the contents of the programme. However, the following broad objectives were agreed upon:

(a) To enhance development in backward areas and target groups in the district through an integrated and multi-sectoral package of investments designed to provide basic needs and to promote income generating activities.

(b) To reinstate the lost ecological balance within the district especially in hydrological catchment areas and in areas where soil erosion is significant.

(c) To further the decentralisation of the planning process in order to encourage popular participation in each of its steps.

These objectives are not very specific to the IRDP-R. The provision of basic needs through multi-sectoral investment activities is common to all IRDPP. However, the emphasis here is on spatially selected areas and on the people who live in those areas.

2.3 *The Planning Approach*

The planning approach adopted was based on the principle of reducing the planning effort, by limiting the area upon which IRDP-R would concentrate its activities. An attempt was made to combine boundaries of hydrological catchment areas with existing administrative boundaries. This resulted in demarcating a number of so called "Key Areas" for intervention. The key areas may be interpreted as relatively homogeneous sub-regions of the district. Key areas normally consist of between two and five G.S. Divisions, with a total surface of 10 to 30 sq. km. Populations range from to 2000 to 4500 people.

Initially, seventeen key areas were demarcated. Given the limited capacity of the project, however, it was decided to start work on only three key areas, in order to test the appropriateness and replicability of the approach. Each of the areas selected was located in one of the three climatic zones in which the district is divided. The limitation of the number of areas to three created some political problems because of pressure for inclusion of other areas, irrespective of the results of the pilot projects undertaken. On the other hand, it allowed the project to move quickly from data-gathering and planning to implementation.

2.4 *Planning Methodology*

Data on the pilot key areas were initially collected, in a very short time, from secondary sources, such as the AGA Office, Statistical Office of the District, G.S. and people's organisations. The development needs of the areas were further assessed with the following categories of people:

(a) *Beneficiaries*: Group discussions were held within each key area with people and their organisations in order to assess their views on development needs.

(b) *Government Officials*: Formal discussions were held with government officials in the areas to assess needs and the technical feasibility of proposals.

(c) *Political Leaders*: Politicians were consulted to obtain their points of view on the needs of the people. IRDP-R actively sought the support of the politicians, who play a significant role in every aspect of development in Sri Lanka.

The IRDP-R intervention in the key areas was planned on the basis of the information gathered in this way. For each area, a multi-sectoral package of projects was designed to address its development needs. An example of such a package is given in Annex 1. The sectors included in the packages are the same for all key areas, but the scale of investments and the relative importance of the sectors vary according to perceived problems and needs.

The composition of the package was intensely debated, especially by politicians. Investment on roads and education was the hottest issue. The main argument in this case was the need to have these facilities in all key areas equally. Sectors with little symbolic value or where returns can be exacted only in the long-term were not as vigorously demanded by the politicians.

The IRDP-R took the initiative of giving responsibility for the local planning process to an existing Government functionary who had not been fully utilised until then, namely the AGA. A 'planning cell' (PC) was created to carry out decentralised planning functions. The PC is headed by the AGA and consists of the Development Officer (DO), Statistical Officer (SO), Rural Development Officer (RDO) and *Grama Sevaka* (GS). The Secretary of the PC is the Development Officer, who is directly linked with the IRDP-R as he is an officer from the Ministry of Plan Implementation (M/PI). The responsibilities of the PC include data collection, identification of needs and assignation of priorities and project formulation, monitoring and review. The capacity of the PCs is still being strengthened in order to utilise available skills to a maximum.

One important element in the case of IRDP-R is the role of the annual review mission: under the aid agreement, the project activities are reviewed every year by a joint mission which consists of a consultant from The Netherlands and a counterpart official from the M/PI. The investment directions, ceilings, etc. are determined by this mission who submits recommendations for further improvements. These recommendations are decisive.

3. Implementation

The investment programme for the project is an annual programme, which is formulated in the framework of the above recommendations and the guidelines of the M/PI. The size of the total investment depends on the achievements in the previous year and on the budgetary allocations of the Central Government. Component projects are usually small in terms of investments and coverage, and designed to be completed in one year.

Implementation is generally carried out by existing government departments, statutory boards and government corporations. However, certain constraints and limitations of these organisations led IRDP-R to find alternative agencies, especially non-governmental organisations (NGOs), to handle implementation. This by-pass was inevitable, given the types of projects, time period available, size of the investment and especially the emphasis on popular participation.

The IRDP activities undertaken by various implementing agencies are co-ordinated by a Project Office (PO), headed by a Project Director under the general supervision of the Government Agent (G.A.), who is the chief administrative officer of the district. The responsibilities of the Project Director include:

(a) Formulation, implementation and monitoring of IRDP activities.

(c) Management of financial resources in order to achieve the main objectives of IRDP.

(d) Reviewing progress at regular time intervals and resolving implementation bottlenecks, so as to ensure smooth and timely implementation.

(e) Representation of IRDP-R at the district and national levels.

(f) Co-ordination with the Donor Agency at project level.

Co-ordination is strengthened at the district level by the District Co-ordinating Committee (DCC), consisting of the district heads of the line agencies and chaired by the District Minister, which meets quarterly to discuss and resolve bottlenecks, review progress and settle priority conflicts at the district level. Finally, there are National Level Steering Committees for the multilaterally-funded and bilaterally-funded IRD Programmes. Monitoring is handled at the National Level by the Monitoring and Evaluation Unit (MEU) under the Director, Regional Development.

4. Experience with the IRDP-R

The relatively short period of operation of the IRDP-R has already yielded useful lessons, many of which are relevant for the IRDP in general. They may be discussed under the following three main headings:

(i) Planning with IRDP-R
(ii) Implementation and
(iii) Impact on rural development.

4.1 *Planning in the IRDP-R*

The planning approach adopted by IRDP-R reflects experience with other approaches adopted in IRDP projects, and is an attempt to improve on them. The important feature of the planning approach of the IRDP-R is the emphasis on space and the attempt to reduce the area of intervention to a manageable size, in order to reduce the planning effort while increasing effectiveness. The selection of key areas is based on rational criteria of homogeneity, administrative unity and relative backwardness in terms of access to public facilities, urban centres, life style, income level. Key areas are also of a manageable size.

The first key areas selected were only higher elevations, where rivers and waterways commence. The project is currently expanding to the G.S. adjoining the present key areas. This will result in project activities starting from the top hills and gradually spreading to the valley bottoms. The concept of a key area can easily be understood by the people, politicians and administrators, given the administrative identity of the areas (G.S. Divisions).

By starting on a small scale, planners need not spend long periods of time in data collection, information gathering, problem analyses, project identification, etc., as happens for instance in World Bank-funded IRD projects. The subjective judgement of the planner can be supported by data quickly collected from secondary sources. Similarly, household-specific data, needed to identify needs and formulate projects, can easily be obtained by carrying out simple house-to-house surveys.

The small size of the area facilitates the direct consultation of people. Group discussions have been organised in each key area, in order to get an impression people's needs, aspirations and suggestions. This has given local people the opportunity to express their own ideas about their problems and ways to solve them. The village elites rarely dominate these meetings, especially because the villagers are capable of raising their own voices. At the same time, the presence of planners with a fairly broad knowledge and experience on the power structure can influence the situation and use the existing power structure for the benefit of the majority. One need not be too radical about de-linking the poor from the elite in Sri Lankan villages. The social situation in rural Sri Lanka is somewhat different from what development planners have experienced in other less developed countries. The national policies on Education, Health, and franchise, even prior to independence, have made people aware of their own environment. The literacy rate and election turn-outs in Sri Lanka are the highest in this region, mass media are relatively developed and the indicators of physical quality of life are very positive. The small size of key areas also facilitates the formulation of integrated investment packages, which are included into an investment programme per key area. The composition of this programme has to respect the sectoral ceilings set by the Annual Review Mission each year. At the same time, however, the investment package proposed for each key area is carefully designed to achieve integration, at least within the IRDP investment.

Key area planning in the IRDP-R does not require the same level of highly specialised skills and expert contributions as World Bank-funded projects. Planners need simple techniques to handle their task and a great deal of understanding of the needs, environment and culture of the people. They must also be able to organise people, seek their views and mobilise the resources available. The planning capacity of the present staff of the IRDP-R ideally matches the needs in the key areas. Furthermore, the task of the planning cells, which include officials who do not belong to the Ministry in charge of IRDP, is also facilitated by the small size of the areas.

The flexibility built into the planning procedures of IRDP-R allows the continuous updating of annual plans, the correction of errors and the incorporation of lessons from experience. Some sectoral projects which did not develop satisfactorily (e.g. land development) were deleted during the implementation period and later dropped from the plans, while sectors where satisfactory results were achieved (e.g. forestry and agriculture) are retained and reinforced.

The key area approach thus seems an appropriate response to the specific requirements and constraints facing IRDP-R. The approach does, however, have a few drawbacks that should be mentioned. A first difficulty relates to the intra-regional imbalance created by this approach. In the first four years of implementation IRDP-R could only cover 27 G.S. Divisions grouped in 8 key areas, which account for only 15 per cent of the land area and 10 per cent of the people in the district. Hence, inequality has increased as a result of the project's intervention.

Co-ordination of implementing agencies at the district level in the stage of plan formulation is somewhat difficult, partly because key areas form only a small part of the district. The formulation of the key area investment programmes is done by staff of the IRDP-R in consultation with the people and the local level representatives of the implementing agencies. However, it is sometimes difficult to convince district heads of the implementing agencies of the needs of the key areas, and this makes co-ordination a time-consuming exercise. An attempt has been made to improve this situation by inviting district level organisations to draw up sectoral plans for investment in the district. This would allow key area-based PC to operate within the framework of a district-based plan and thus make their task easier. This has been achieved so far for Education, Health, Forestry and part of Rural Credit.

4.2 *Implementation*

A first problem in the implementation of IRDP-R concerns the attitude of the line agencies and difficulties in the relations with them. In spite of the decentralisation of 1972, which has to a certain extent brought line agencies together at the district level, horizontal communication and co-operation between line agencies is almost non-existent. In fact, horizontal communication and dialogue is feasible mainly at the personal rather than the functional level. Each Government agency has its normal functions, and prevailing attitudes are such that whatever else is required of such an agency is regarded as an "outside" or "additional" activity and often remains undone. This attitude is very clearly expressed in relation to the question of funding. At the beginning of the IRDP in Sri Lanka, it was assumed that capital was in short supply, as a result of which there was surplus capacity within the existing line agencies. IRDP funds were regarded as a *supplementary* source of finance for capital investment. At the operational level, however, the reality is different. The line agencies have a tendency to treat IRDP as an outside agency, as a result of which the work planned under IRDP – which they see as "outside" work – can only be carried out if additional funds are provided.

Secondly, the co-ordination with other sources of financing in the district, such as the Decentralised Capital Budget (DCB), District Development Council (DDC) funds and line agencies hardly takes place. In brief, this means that at the district level there is no mechanism to integrate or co-ordinate the use of funds coming to the district for capital investment. This may result in waste of resources due to duplication of activities.

A third source of difficulty concerns the implementing capacity of line agencies. There is no single way to assess the capacity of a line agency. However, it is generally recognised that implementing capacity is limited. This has even been proved in certain sectors – e.g. roads – where set targets were not completed. Because of the limited time horizon of the project and of the strategic importance of certain sectors, this led to an alternative way of implementing project activities where IRDP-R by-passed the line agencies and took direct responsibility for the implementation of certain activities, such as roads, water supply scheme, community reafforestation, etc. This required substantial involvement on the part of project staff and the recruitment of specialised staff, e.g. Civil Engineers and Technical staff to design and to supervise construction of roads. This overloaded IRDP-R as an implementing agency. In addition, such a practice may create problems in connection with handing over the maintenance of the assets created.

In the direct implementation of certain projects, the participation of the local population was stimulated, with very positive results. Firstly, local level organisations, such as rural development societies and Thrift and Credit Co-operative Societies (TCCS), were strengthened and involved into implementation These societies operate within the area where project activities are implemented. The work is handled by those of their members who live in the area and who will certainly be beneficiaries of the project. Hence, there is a feeling of involvement and of responsibility for the project. The work done was satisfactory in terms of quality and cost effectiveness.

4.3 *Impact on Rural Development*

The IRDP-R has yet to undertake a proper impact evaluation after four years of operation. However, the IRDP-R has had a significant impact on the areas where it is presently in operation. Rural areas which were isolated have been or are being linked with urban or semi-urban centres. The access of people who live in backward areas to public facilities such as education and health has been improved. The development of infrastructural facilities such as roads, markets, service centres, etc. has created opportunities for income generation. The quality of life has improved. For instance, every village in the key areas now has a water sealed toilet and safe drinking water closer to the villagers' homes.

Implementation through the village level organisation has created employment opportunities for the rural labour force. For instance, Medagonoya village with 95 families was an isolated hamlet between a hill range and a river. The IRDP-R commenced integrated investment in this area in 1984 first with water supply, sanitation, community centre and school building. Secondly, the reafforestation of the hill range, which was fully denuded, was undertaken. Next was the construction of the road connecting the village to the market and urban centres. The village people participated in the implementation of all these activities. As a result, the village has experienced considerable and positive change. Almost all the houses which were only wattle and daub prior to IRDP-R involvement are now constructed with bricks. Every member has a savings account with the TCCS. The participation of the beneficiaries has also facilitated the handling and maintenance of assets after completion. For instance, people have organised themselves into groups to maintain the water supply scheme constructed.

On the other hand, it must be admitted that, within the key areas, IRDP-R was unable to address all the development issues. The investment undertaken so far in the key areas has not had equal results in all of them. As an impact evaluation has not been done so far, it is difficult to quantify the situation. The change in the situation in some of the key areas over the past four years is tremendous. In certain other areas, the results achieved are marginal. This difference in achievement, even among the key areas, is due to the different conditions in each key area. Areas where the changes are most important are the areas with greater development potential.

5. Conclusions

On the basis of my experience with the IRDP in Ratnapura District, I would like to present the following conclusions for discussion in this seminar:

5.1 *Planning Approach*

I strongly maintain the key area approach is ideally suited for rural development, provided that the following conditions are fulfilled:

(a) The planning effort should be entirely in the hands of local planners. The inputs of expatriates should be limited to observations and support to the development of the capacity of local planners through training.

(c) Multi-sectoral investment packages should be designed on the basis of an in-depth analysis of the nature, causes and interrelations of development issues in the area.

(d) The planning effort should be a *continuous process* where understanding is increased over time, vague perceptions are cleared and conclusions revised in the light of new knowledge and of changing conditions. It should certainly not be a "once and for all" planning effort.

(e) A strong effort should be made to institutionalise the local capacity for planning. Even without an IRDP there should be an institution to handle planning functions at the local level.

(f) Planning efforts must be directed towards selecting and designing activities which together contribute to solve a particular problem or problems. Integration implies functional relationships between various activities and presupposes the co-ordination of activities in time, in space, and also in relation to the beneficiaries.

(g) Learning by doing, learning from errors, adjustment to changing conditions, gradual improvement of activities in a desired direction rather than pre-determined targets should be built into the planning approach.

(h) A coherent policy on Integrated Rural Development which is consistent with other national policies should be adopted.

5.2 *Implementation*

The performance of the IRDP-Ratnapura suggests the following conclusions:

(a) The IRDP management should be handled by experienced and capable generalists and not by specialists.

(b) Implementation should not always be carried out directly, bypassing line agencies, unless short-term project output is considered more important than sustainability.

(c) High priority should be given to strengthening existing local institutions, rather than building new ones.

(d) Executive agencies must be made aware of how much can be gained, at little cost, by subordinating implementation to a co-ordinated plan that takes into account rural development needs and requirements.

Finally, my experience suggests that although IRDP is not the perfect solution to the development issues in rural areas, it may be regarded as a "Second Best" solution. IRDP as a rural development strategy has proven successful, due to its capacity to address the interdependencies and complementarities which exist in rural areas in most LDCs. The effectiveness of this strategy depends on the way it is handled by the decision-makers, managers and foreign donors, whose support is often crucial.

REFERENCES

Birgegard, L.E., 1987, "A Review of Experience with Integrated Rural Development (IRD)", mimeo, Uppsala.

Boarden, P., 1986, "Problems of Implementation", *Public Administration & Development*, Vol. 6, No. 1.

Morapaya, R.B., 1986, "State of the Art, Report on Integrated Rural Development Programme of Sri Lanka", CIRDAP – 1986.

Perera, K.P.G.M., 1985, "District IRD Programme, HIRDEP and Local Level Planning", in W.M. Leelasena and K.A.S. Wickrama, eds, *Proceedings of the Workshop on Local Level Planning & Implementation.*

Wiggins, S., 1985, "The Planning & Management of Integrated Rural Development in Dry Lands: Early Lessons from Kenya's Arid and Semi Arid Lands Programme", *Public Administration & Development*, Vol. 5, No. 2.

ANNEX 1

Targets and Achievements – IRDP Ratnapura 1984-87
Sectoral Classification of Annual Investment Programme

Sector	1984			1985			1986			1987			Total		
	Target	Expenditure	%	Target	Expenditure	%	Target	Expenditure	%	Target	Expenditure	%	Target	Expenditure	%
1. Rural Roads	2,076,000	916,883	44	9,021,000	5,320,156	59	9,740,000	7,474,298	77	8,800,000	5,323,820	60	29,637,000	19,035,157	56
2. Rural Water Supply	860,000	587,509	67	1,785,000	839,655	47	3,410,000	748,122	22	1,807,000	1,513,030	83	7,862,000	3,688,316	47
3. Latrine Construction	-	-	-	605,000	577,963	95	2,070,000	1,950,000	94	2,701,000	2,581,897	95	5,376,000	5,110,228	95
4. Soils Agriculture	1,200,600	348,230	29	4,876,000	1,776,969	35	3,730,000	1,360,189	79	1,350,000	787,857	58	11,156,600	4,213,245	38
5. Education	-	-	-	1,960,000	240,996	12	1,485,000	605,432	41	4,510,000	2,374,400	53	7,955,000	3,220,828	40
6. Health	-	-	-	3,495,000	56,789	1.6	3,980,000	3,039,659	76	4,050,000	1,099,395	27	11,525,000	4,195,843	36
7. Energy	-	-	-	4,130,000	3,599,063	87	3,190,000	5,440,570	100	1,800,000	1,750,760	97	9,120,000	10,790,893	100
8. Animal Husbandry	-	-	-	150,000	159,317	100	520,000	277,935	53	450,000	47,510	10	1,120,000	484,762	43
9. Off-Farm Employment	-	-	-	-	-	-	750,000	-	-	570,000	197,333	35	1,320,000	197,333	15
10. Estate Housing	387,000	326,997	84	1,734,000	939,031	54	2,850,000	1,959,273	69	3,150,000	1,162,175	37	8,121,000	4,387,476	54
11. Reafforestation	419,600	187,275	44	4,133,000	3,176,460	77	5,595,000	3,880,089	69	5,163,000	3,967,941	77	15,310,600	11,202,765	73

Contd.

Annex 1 *Contd.*

Sector	1984			1985			1986			1987			Total		
	Target	Expenditure	%	Target	Expenditure	%	Target	Expenditure	%	Target	Expenditure	%	Target	Expenditure	%
12. Buildings	511,000	102,117	19	1,895,000	964,320	81	2,110,000	982,877	46	1,350,000	1,541,244	100	5,866,000	3,590,558	61
13. Training	-	-	-	-	-	-	345,000	153,910	44	900,000	251,181	28	1,245,000	450,091	32
14. Irrigation	235,000	79,819	33	247,000	191,297	77	925,000	150,961	46	2,270,000	556,669	24	3,077,000	978,746	32
15. Local Level Organization	-	-	-	447,000	179,558	40	275,000	198,713	72	900,000	507,089	56	1,622,000	885,360	55
16. Surveys & Studies	-	-	-	2,625,000	25,198	-	725,000	126,452	17	900,000	55,070	16	4,250,000	206,720	4
17. Special Provision	-	-	-	-	-	-	500,000	96,469	11	450,000	234,856	52	950,000	291,325	30
18. Overheads	1,196,000	150,366	12	3,994,000	1,116,959	27	3,500,000	1,697,544	48	3,900,000	2,774,898	71	12,590,000	5,739,767	45
19. Women Activities	-	-	-	-	-	-	-	-	-	450,000	154,783	34	450,000	154,781	34
20. Land Development	-	-	-	750,000	-	-	-	-	-	450,000	134,082	30	1,200,000	134,082	11
21. Miscellaneous	-	-	-	-	-	-	-	-	-	2,500,000	1,538,140	61	2,500,000	1,538,140	61
Total	6,885,200	2,699,196	39	41,847,000	19,094,728	46	45,100,000	30,102,861	67	48,421,000	28,554,130	59	142,253,200	80,450,915	56.5

Source: IRDP-Ratnapura.

8

INTEGRATED RURAL DEVELOPMENT IN INDONESIA: Problems and Prospects

Moeljarto Tjokrowinoto

1. Context

The New Order Government of Indonesia came into existence out of the economic shambles of 1966. In 1965 the inflation rate reached 1,500 per cent (Greenville, 1982: 140). The consumption of rice per capita fell from 86 kg in 1964 to 81 kg in 1966, while steadily increasing imports of rice drained scarce foreign currency reserves (Hansen, 1973: 5). The average annual rate of growth of the GDP between 1960 and 1965 was only 2.0 per cent, the lowest growth in the history of the nation. Under these conditions, the margin of error that the Government could afford in its policies was very narrow. A policy miscalculation would be unbearable.

Economic consolidation, rehabilitation and stabilisation policies and programmes were adopted and implemented to overcome the economic decay. The emphasis on growth and modernisation was inevitable, in a situation where the nation was at the brink of economic collapse. The new economic system adopted was based on incentives rather than on distribution or on planned allocation of resources. Price mechanisms, monetary and credit policies and budgetary policies were designed to stimulate entrepreneurs to invest, innovate and engage in economic activities.

The policy choices at the national level had their repercussions on rural development. Rural development strategies were influenced by the orientation towards growth and modernisation. Modern, capital-intensive private production units were "planted" into a traditional labour-intensive sector with the hope that new job opportunities would be created by a trickle-down effect and the diffusion of new agricultural technology was stimulated in order to eliminate rural underdevelopment (Hannig, 1986: 1).

The economic results of this policy were indeed impressive. Hyper-inflation was brought under control: the inflation rate went down to about 17 per cent within two to three years. The annual rate of economic growth averaged 7.35 per cent between 1970 and 1980, with its highest value at 9.87 per cent in 1980. From being the largest rice-importing country, Indonesia became self-sufficient in rice.

However, the high rate of economic growth was accompanied by growing inequality in the distribution of income. The coefficient of regional inequality increased from 0.362 in 1969 to 0.572 in 1976 (Sjafrizal, 1987: 421). The Gini index in major cities went up beyond 0.45. The Government was aware of these unintended consequences of economic growth. Corrective measures were taken in 1978 by adopting the Eightfold Path of Equitable Distribution Policy, encompassing:

(i) equal access to human needs, particularly to clothing and shelter;
(ii) equal opportunity of education;
(iii) equal distribution of income;
(iv) equal opportunity of employment;
(v) equal opportunity to engage in business;
(vi) equal opportunity to participate in development, particularly for women and youths;
(vii) equal distribution of development throughout the country; and
(viii) equal access to justice.

Policies and programmes intended to attack poverty directly at the grass-roots level were adopted, such as small credit programmes, village cooperatives, rice-price policy, nutrition improvement, rural education, small-scale industries, etc.

New administrative arrangements were added to the existing structure, to ensure better distribution of development outputs. *Unit Daerah Kerja Pembangunan* (UDKP), which literally means "Development Working Area Unit" and *Program Pengembangan Wilayah Propinsi* (PPWP), or "Provincial Development Programme" (PDP), within which the Integrated Rural Development (IRD) Strategy was implemented, were institutionalised. Although in reality growth and modernisation were still the predominant development orientation, the long-term perspective seemed to underline the importance of equity-oriented and capacity building strategies, including IRD.

The deterioration of the international economy started to affect the Indonesian economy when the oil price fell from its peak of US $35 to a low of less than US $10 in 1981/1982. The rate of economic growth soon dropped to 2.24 per cent (Sundrum, 1986: 42). This revealed the vulnerability of the Indonesian economy to the international market situation. The dramatic decline of the rate of economic growth in 1982 proved that former impressive growth rates were not primarily a result of the enhancement of the capacities of the national system, but were due to rapidly increasing exploitation of oil and gas resources in a period of high prices of oil and gas (Hannig, 1986: 5), and to foreign assistance. More inward-looking strategies aiming at the enhancement of national capacities through, among other things, the adoption of a better thought-out IRD strategy, became seen as a *conditio sine qua non* of sustained development.

The adoption of this inward-looking strategy side by side with the strategy presently carried out to enhance the competitiveness of export commodities in the international market will become more relevant in the future, if the international market situation, as hypothesised by Peter Drucker (1986), is not merely a conjunctural phenomenon, but an indication of structural change known as "uncoupling", i.e. the absence of relationship between the economic growth of Western industrial countries and the demand for primary export commodities of the LDCs.

This paper deals with the lessons from experience with the implementation of Integrated Rural Development in Indonesia in the context described above.

2. The Genesis

As is probably the case with many developing countries, Integrated Rural Development was unknown to Indonesian bureaucrats up to the 1970s. The basic assumption commonly held by bureaucrats was that rural development was basically agricultural development, and that the underdevelopment of rural Indonesia was the underdevelopment of its agriculture (Loekman Soetrisno and Mubyarto, 1987: 53). Consequently, the Ministry of Agriculture became the core ministry for rural development.

Early attempts at rural development were reflected in what was known as the "Kasimo Welfare Plan", announced in 1952. Kasimo was then the Minister of Agriculture. The plan followed the Dutch colonial *olie vlek* or "oil stain" strategy, by which good farming techniques were demonstrated at critical locations in the countryside and were expected to spread gradually from there (Timmer, 1974: 209). In spite of the plan's name, socio-economic welfare of the peasantry was not the sole objective of rural development as perceived by the government at that time. Perpetual shortages of foreign exchange to import rice and the government's commitment to rice distribution to civil servants and the military led the government to turn to the peasantry for food supply.

Major organisational changes occurred during the Old Order Government's "Cabinet of 100 Ministers". Rural development was assigned to a newly-formed department, the Department of Transmigration, Co-operatives and Rural Development. This reflected the broader perspective in the government's perception of rural development. Meanwhile other departments were also involved in rural development. The Department of Education, for instance, was interested in literacy programmes and other non-formal education; the Department of Social Affairs focused its activities on mobilising community participation, self-help and co-operation among peasants through the 'Village Social Institution' (*Lembaga Sosial Desa*). As the economic capacity of the nation grew stronger, government rural development programmes involving various departments also grew. The Directorate General of Rural Development of the Department of Home Affairs became the new focal point of the national machinery dealing with rural development.

The adoption, described above, of the Eightfold Path of Equitable Distribution in 1978, implied a political commitment to a shift from the growth-first model to more integrated approaches to development. Alternative or complementary administrative arrangements needed to be established to facilitate better distribution of the fruits of development. The Integrated Rural Development strategy was considered as one of the most suitable means to achieve this goal. It was not a coincidence that the government adopted the mechanisms of UDKP and PDP. While the UDKP has been under the authority of the Directorate General of Rural Development and the PDP under the jurisdiction of the Directorate General of Regional Development, both of the Department of Home Affairs, both have been engaged in Integrated Rural

Development for slightly different purposes and using different approaches, although both of them are committed to the same basic objective of eradication of rural poverty and inequality. Integrated Rural Development as has been carried out through the UDKP and the PDP is an integral part of the process of implementing the policy of the Eightfold Path of Equitable Distribution. An analysis and comparison of Integrated Rural Development as carried out through the two mechanisms will hopefully reveal the strengths and weaknesses of the two approaches.

3. **Integrated Rural Development in the Context of UDKP**

3.1 *The Impetus*

The Government of Indonesia classifies the 60,645 villages of the country, according to their levels of development, into three categories: *desa swadaya* or traditional village; *desa swakarya* or transitional village; and *desa swasembada* or modern village. The classification is based on seven criteria for each of which a village gets one, two or three points according to its situation.

These criteria comprise:

(1) source of income (primary, secondary and tertiary);
(2) village output or yield, i.e. total products and services of a village within a year;
(3) degree of adherence to custom or tradition;
(4) village institutions;
(5) levels of education;
(6) mutual help, and
(7) village infrastructure.

Villages having a score of 7 to 11 are classified as traditional; 12 to 16, transitional; and 17 to 21, modern. This classification helps the government to monitor achievement in turning traditional villages into modern villages. The Five Year Plan set the target of bringing all traditional villages to the transitional level, and the transitional to modern. The achievements of the plan between 1971/72 and 1975/76 are indicated in Table 8.1.

Table 8.1: Rate of Achievement in Bringing Swakarya Villages to the Level of Swasembada Village

Year	Swasembada Village (%)	Growth (%)
1971/1972	1,5	-
1972/1973	2,0	0,5
1973/1974	3,0	1,0
1974/1975	4,5	1,5
1975/1976	6,5	1,9

Source: Directorate General of Rural Development, UDKP, Jakarta, 1977.

The rate of growth of *Desa Swasembada* was far below the value necessary to ensure the conversion of all the villages to the level of *Desa Swasembada* within five Five-Year Development Plans, i.e. in 25 years. To achieve the necessary average annual rate of change of *Desa Swadaya* and *Desa Swakarya* into *Desa Swasembada* within five Five-Year Development Plans, a new administrative arrangement called *Unit Daerah Kerja Pembangunan* (UDKP) or "Development Working Area Unit", was created. The new arrangement incorporated the concept of Integrated Rural Development in the system.

3.2 *The Nature of the UDKP System*

As commonly understood, one of the basic assumptions of Integrated Rural Development is that rural poverty is a multi-dimensional phenomenon and consequently, it will not be possible to alleviate rural poverty through uni-sectoral or fragmentary approaches. Aware of that, the proponents of Integrated Rural Development believe that a consistent and harmonious set of policies and programmes has a much better chance of achieving good results. The government has a strategic role to play in the formulation of this harmonious and consistent set of policies through, among other things, promoting decentralised administration with people's participation and orchestrating the various programmes so that a balanced growth can take place through involvement of both the public and private sectors (CIRDAP, 1987: 8).

It was precisely these basic ideas which inspired the establishment of the UDKP. Although Law No. 5/1974 designates the provincial Governor as the sole government official responsible for co-ordinating development activities in the province, and the *Bupati* (District Head) as the single government official responsible for co-ordinating development activities in the *Kabupaten* (District); in reality their authority is not too effective, primarily because sectoral departments and other governmental agencies in Indonesia have a long tradition of pursuing sectoral approaches. They plan, implement and evaluate their own programmes and formulate their own budget. Normatively speaking, at the provincial and district level, the planning process should be co-ordinated by the respective Provincial and District Planning Agencies. However, since the Planning Board lacks resources and means of co-ordination, sectoral approaches seem to prevail over an integrated approach.

The UDKP system shifts the emphasis to the process of converting traditional and transitional villages into modern ones by developing villages within the respective sub-districts (*kecamatan*) in an integrated and comprehensive manner, under the co-ordination of the *Camat* (Sub-district Head). Its main attributes are:

(i) Comprehensive and integrated planning at the sub-district level involving the sub-district administrative apparatus, field offices of the central agencies in the sub-district, and the people concerned through the *Lembaga Ketahanan Masyarakat Desa* or Village Resilience Institution; the Village Resilience Institution involves villagers in the formulation of village development plans under the chairmanship of a village head.

(ii) The planning and implementation of the development plan of the sub-district is co-ordinated by *Camat* or Sub-district Head, who is the only government official in charge of co-ordinating all development activities in the Sub-district.

(iii) In the process of developing traditional and transitional villages into modern ones, the *Pattern of Village Order* (*Pola Tata Desa*), formulated by the Department of Home Affairs, is used as the reference.

(iv) All development agents mentioned in point (i) above should identify the potential as well as actual resources in the villages within the sub-district, the problems faced by the villagers and also the plans proposed by the villages; based upon these, they formulate a development plan for the sub-district.

(v) Cadre forming is an integral part of the system.

(vi) Infrastructure building and the use of appropriate technologies, both endogenous and newly developed, are also characteristic of the UDKP system.

The UDKP system replaces the Bupati (District Head) with the Camat (Sub-district Head) as the integrated agent of rural development. Sub-districts are considered closer to the villages and so are thought to be in a better position to solve village problems than higher administrative units, economically more viable than villages, small enough to meet the requirements of eco-development, and administratively more effective and efficient.

The idea of integration in the UDKP system covers horizontal as well as vertical integration. Horizontal integration involves the integration of the activities of field offices and the sub-district apparatus, taking into account the eco-system, social system, village potentialities of the various sub-districts and the pattern of village order formulated by the Minister of Home Affairs. Vertical integration involves integration between the UDKP sub-district and both lower (i.e.village level) and higher level development areas. These horizontal and vertical linkages are expected to generate synergistic effects which will accelerate the transition to modern villages.

4. Integrated Rural Development in the Context of PDP

4.1 *Impetus*

Provincial Development Programmes came into existence as a result of three major factors:

(a) The political decision of the government to take corrective measures to eliminate the inegalitarian consequences of the growth-first model of development by adopting the policy of the Eightfold Path of Equitable Distribution and by reversing the priority of the "Development Trilogy" to income distribution, economic growth and political stability in 1978.

(b) The will to activate newly created Provincial Planning Agencies and District Planning Agencies by allocating funds to trigger their activities.

(c) The provision of soft loans and technical assistance from USAID, the Federal Republic of Germany and the World Bank.

These factors led a key group of civil servants in the National Planning Agencies, the Department of Home Affairs, the Department of Finance and the Department of Public Works, to design a programme which would on the one hand promote equality through attacking poverty directly at the grassroots level and on the other develop the capacity of provincial and local bureaucracies to identify the problems of poverty in their areas of jurisdiction, formulate plans to tackle it, mobilise various resources, implement the plans and monitor and evaluate the development projects.

Out of 27 provinces in Indonesia, only 11 are involved in the PDP, namely Aceh, Bengkulu, West Java, Central Java, East Java, South Kalimantan, East Nusa Tenggara and West Nusa Tenggara, funded by USAID; West Sumatra and East Kalimantan, funded by the Federal Republic of Germany; and Yogyakarta Special Province, funded by the World Bank.

4.2 *The Objective of the PDP*

Although the PDP has been in operation in Aceh and Central Java since 1977-1978, it was not until 1980 that it was formally regulated. In 1980, the Minister of Home Affairs issued Instruction No. 19/1980 establishing two major objectives for the PDP:

(a) to increase the incomes and enhance the welfare of low income villagers living in critical areas; and

(b) to increase the administrative capability of the PDP-related field officers of the Central Government and local bureaucrats and in particular to promote the capability of Provincial Planning Agencies (Bappeda Tingkat I) and District Planning Agencies (Bappeda Tingkat II) in planning and implementation, project management and evaluation, and reporting.

To achieve the first objective, the aforementioned Instruction of the Minister of Home Affairs set up some criteria for project selection. According to these, the projects that deserve local development assistance of the PDP are those which:

(a) directly raise the incomes of villagers whose productivity is low;

(b) yield the quickest possible output;

(c) fit into regional and district development planning frameworks;
(d) are simple and small in scale;
(e) create and broaden employment opportunities;
(f) stimulate and promote local activities;
(g) are supportive of other local development programmes, such as the INPRES (Presidential Instructions) programmes; and
(h) are feasible from the technical, economic, financial, social and environmental point of view.

In the case of credits channelled directly to the people via banking and formal credit institutions in the respective villages, projects should meet the following criteria:

(a) be supportive of other local activities;
(b) raise income and fit the following specifications:

- involvement of small sums;
- administrative simplicity;
- simplicity in lending technicalities;
- the lowest possible rate of interest; and
- lasting effects.

4.3 *The Organisational Set-up*

The PDP develops, strengthens, and uses the existing institutional structure at the provincial and sub-provincial levels, rather than creating an *ad hoc* system of its own. Although some *ad hoc* committees are created at the central level to decide on the overall policy direction of the PDP, there seems to be no fundamental structural change at the provincial, district, and sub-district levels.

There is a rather top-heavy structure of committees dealing with the PDP at the central government level. Overall policy direction is given by the *Panitia Pembina* (Foreign Aid Steering Committee), whose membership consists of seven senior officials representing the Department of Home Affairs, the National Planning Agency, the Department of Finance, the Department of Public Works, and the Department of Agriculture. This committee constitutes the co-ordinating body of the PDP. In addition, there is a *Panitia Teknis* (Foreign Aid Technical Committee) consisting of sixteen officials from the above departments who hold the rank of Director or its equivalent. However, in reality, the committee plays a largely formal role in the process of programme review. The actual day-to-day decisions are made by the technical staff, consisting of eighteen junior officials from the same departments.

The executive agency for the implementation of the programme is in the Department of Home Affairs, in particular the Directorate General of Regional Development, which has direct lines of command to various levels of local government. The Directorate General bears the responsibility for reviewing and evaluating all PDP programmes submitted by the provincial governments before they are submitted to the National Planning Agency. The National Planning Agency plays a significant role in *ex-ante* programme evaluation. In its day-to-day operation, the Directorate General works closely with foreign donors who support the programme. There are three donor project officers and two consultant officers at the central government level.

The governor has the responsibility for planning, implementing, supervising, and reporting on the utilisation of local level development assistance. In this, he is assisted by: (1) Provincial *Bappeda*, or Planning Agency, which is responsible for planning and co-ordinating the central government field offices and district governmental units and for supervising programme or project implementation; (2) the provincial governmental units, central government field offices, and other provincial agencies which are responsible for carrying out the programmes or projects in their respective fields; (3) the district heads or *Bupati* who, with the assistance of the district *Bappeda*, district governmental units, central government field offices at the district level and other technical implementing units, are responsible for project planning and implementation in their respective jurisdictions; and (4) government credit institutions which are responsible for managing and disbursing credits. Two foreign consultants are provided for each PDP province whose main role is to help the local government build up administrative capacity as well as technical skills.

Administrative support for the programme is reflected in the delegation of the major planning and co-ordinating role to the Planning Agencies at the provincial and district levels; in the growing attention to cross-sectoral co-ordinating mechanisms in programme planning and implementation; in the provision of greater opportunities for sub-district and district chiefs to influence significantly local development strategies; and in the greater allocation of time devoted to the PDP, which exceeds the proportion of the entire development budget which is allocated to the PDP.

4.4 *The PDP Philosophy and Integrated Rural Development*

IRD as implemented within the context of the PDP can only be understood if we understand the basic philosophy of the PDP. The PDP is governed by Law No 5/1974 on government in the Regions, which sets down three major principles of central-local relations, namely (i) the principle of "real and responsible autonomy and decentralisation", (ii) the principle of "deconcentration" and (iii) the principle of *medebewing* (i.e., the right and obligation of regional government to help in the implementation of central government functions in its own region). The PDP has, however, some distinctive characteristics of its own which influence the implementation of IRD. The basic philosophy of the PDP can be summarised as follows:

(a) The PDP is characterised by its strong commitment to a regional rather than a sectoral approach.
(b) Contrary to the common practice of central government where financial support to sub-national governmental levels is allocated through Presidential Instructions where sectoral utilisation is rigidly specified, central government support to the PDP constitutes a "block grant" that can be disbursed more freely to meet specific needs of the regions, subject to a number of limitations described in paragraph 4.2 above. Consequently, the IRD project mix varies widely between PDP Provinces or Districts. In Madura, East Java, for instance, the project mix consists of small village credit programmes, cattle fattening, poor family assistance and reafforestation. In other provinces in Central Java, on the other hand, the project mix consists of poor family assistance, home gardening intensification, small industries and land fisheries.
(c) Unlike conventional stereotypical and uniform approaches to rural development, PDP projects are adaptable to socio-cultural variations. This enables the PDP to mobilise socio-cultural resources to support its development programmes.
(d) The flexibility of the PDP encourages local bureaucrats and project beneficiaries to carry out innovative activities through social or policy experiments (Rondinelli, 1983) or social learning (Korten, 1980). The experiment of the Small Village

Credit Programme in Madura, East Java, to let borrowers' groups guarantee the repayment of loans instead of asking for collateral, is an example.

(e) Being an experiment in building a self-sustaining capacity for integrated poverty-focused rural development activity, the PDP inc orporates the following features (Honadle, 1979):

- it is experimental;
- it is capacity building (in institutions and for beneficiaries);
- it promotes integrated rural development;
- it promotes poverty-focused rural development and
- it aims to promote institutional capacity for integrated poverty-focused rural development that is self-sustaining and thus capable of continuing beyond the inputs of project funds and technical assistance.

This philosophy gives considerable latitude to individual provinces to set priorities for beneficiary selection and sub-project mixes that fit the specific problems, needs and aspirations of the regions (Schiller, 1988: 19). The PDP philosophy encourages provinces and districts to engage in institutional learning in the process of priority and standard setting to enable them to justify their priorities and standards.

It is precisely this flexibility which makes it difficult to describe the implementation of the Integrated Rural Development strategy. IRD is location-specific and varies from one province to another, from one district to another. However, it is possible to mention some major features of the IRD as implemented within the context of the PDP.

(a) It gives equal status to economic and social development as is manifested in its effort to raise the incomes of the rural poor and to increase the capacity of local institutions and beneficiaries to identify development opportunities and efficiently plan and manage development programmes for the poor.

(b) It is designed to integrate the rural poor in the process of social change by encouraging them to participate in development activities. Networking between local bureaucrats, cooperatives and other social institutions and the people creates a participatory environment.

(c) It is based on community-based resource management. The project inputs such as seed money, technical assistance, and training are intended to trigger the dynamics of development activities. However, the projects are expected to revolve and self-sustain beyond the project inputs.

(d) Cultural compatibility and the mobilisation of socio-cultural resources is the common strategy used in this IRD. The involvement of *niknik-mamak* (highly respected elders) and ulama (religious leaders) in West Sumatra in the process of rural development has been very successful. The manipulation of "shame-culture" in East Java to generate social control within borrowers' groups for credit repayment is another example.

(e) The adoption of an incremental rather than a blue-print approach gives room for social experiments. The errors made in the process of social experimentation become inputs for policy and programme reformulation. Since projects are location-specific and small in scale, it won't be difficult to make corrective measures. The failed *in natura* credit programme in East Nusa Tenggara, for instance, was easily transformed into other types of credit institutions.

(f) The multi-faceted causal complex of rural poverty calls for an integrated approach involving inter-sectoral linkages. The rehabilitation of critical land in Yogyakarta Special Province, for instance, is linked with programmes of reafforestation, income generation and preservation of water resources. The District Planning Agency is responsible for the process of integration.

(g) The IRD strategy as implemented in the context of the PDP also involves a process of bottom-up planning which starts with deliberations in the Village Resilience Institution. It is the villagers who identify their problems and needs, define the target groups, formulate the project proposals, identify and mobilise local resources to match the seed money allocated from above.

The manifestation of those principles may vary between PDP provinces and districts. In general terms it may be said that the implementation of IRD under the PDP is considered as an experiment in decentralisation amidst strong centralising tendencies. It provided district government officials with the resources and skills needed to plan and manage rural development in co-operation with the beneficiaries, focusing on increasing the income and productivity of those in the lowest stratum of the social pyramid.

5. Comparative Analysis

Two different variations of Integrated Rural Development have been presented above, one in the context of UDKP (Development Working Area Unit) and the other in the context of Provincial Development Programmes. They are based on different philosophies, goals and methods. Integrated Rural Development in the context of the UDKP aims at accelerating the process of transformation from traditional and transitional to modern villages by manipulating factors which influence source of income, village outputs, tradition, village institutions, level of education, mutual-help and village infrastructure. Integrated Rural Development in the context of Provincial Development Programmes aims at alleviating rural poverty through enhancing institutional capacity of local bureaucrats and the beneficiaries.

The differences in objectives between the two programmes led to differences in their approaches. The UDKP tends to rely on a stereotypical and uniform blueprint approach oriented towards the Pola Tata Desa (Pattern of Village Order) imposed from above, leaving little room for local variations. The PDP is based on social experimentation and institutional learning, trying to achieve its goals incrementally. It is quite adaptable to local socio- cultural environment and gives room for embracing error in the process of institutional learning.

While the expected results of IRD within the context of PDP are increased standards of living for the rural poor and increased local rural development planning and management capacity, as measured by such indicators as improved performance, increased capacity for decentralisation, institutional learning and institutional innovation (Schiller, 1988: 43), the result of the IRD within the context of UDKP seems to be ritualisation of organisational behaviour imposed from above.

The position of "integrating agent" is another striking difference between the two. The *Kecamatan* or sub-district is an administrative rather than an autonomous unit of government. Consequently, the *Camat* (Sub-district Head) does not control resources as well as other means of co-ordination. Therefore, he tends to perform his integrating ineffectively. The agents of the PDP in the districts and provinces are the District and Provincial Planning Agencies. Formally speaking, they have the authority to help the Governor or the *Bupati* to draw up and implement integrated plans. The main problem is to strengthen their authority *vis-a-vis* sectoral departments. They will then be in a better position to integrate development activities, horizontally and vertically.

In conclusion, the PDP type of Integrated Rural Development seems more likely to contribute effectively to the effort of strengthening national resilience in the context of unstable international economic conditions. The PDP philosophy, goals and methods should be adopted as a national pattern for the management of regional and rural development beyond the present 11 PDP Provinces.

REFERENCES

CIRDAP (1987) *State of the Art: Integrated Rural Development in Asia-Pacific*, Dhaka, Bangladesh: CIRDAP.

Drucker, Peter (1986) "The Changed World Economy" in *Foreign Affairs*, Spring.

Greenville, Stephen (1981) "Kebijaksanaan Moneter dan Sektor Keuangan Formal" ("Monetary Policy and Formal Financial Sector") in Anne Booth and Peter McCawley (eds), *Ekonomi Orde Baru (The New Order Economy)*, Jakarta: LPBES, pp. 132-165.

Hanning, Wolfgang (1986) *Towards a Blue Revolution*, Bielefeld, University of Bielefeld.

Hansen, Gary E. (1978) The Politics and Administrative of Rural Development in *Indonesia: The Case of Agriculture*, Berkeley, California Center for South and Southeast Asia Studies.

Honadle, George (1974) "Institution Building in the PDP Context", mimeo.

Korten, David (1980) "Community Organization and Rural Development: A Learning Process Approach". *Public Administration Review*, 5 (40), pp. 480-511.

Mubyarto & Loekman Soetrisno (1987) "Indonesia, in CIRDAP, op. cit., pp. 53-55.

Rondinelli, Denis (1983) *Development Projects as Policy Experiments*, London and New York; Methuen.

Schiller, J. (1988) "Learning from PDP: Evaluating the Provincial Development Programme", paper presented in the National Conference on Area Development Programme, held by Ditjen Bangda Depdagri-P3PK UGM-USAID, Yogyakarta, 12-15 April 1988.

Sjahrizal (1987) "Pengelolaan Kegiatan Pembangunan di Indonesia" ("The Management of Development Activities in Indonesia"), *Ekonomi dan Keuangan Indonesia*, Vol. XXXV, No. 4, pp. 415-436.

Sundrum, R.M. (1986) "Indonesia's Rapid Economic Growth 1968-1981, *Bulletin of Indonesia Economic Studies*, Vol. XXIII, No. 3, December.

Tunner, Peter C. (1975) "The Political Economy of Indonesia", *Food Research Institute Studies*, Vol. XIV, No. 3, pp. 197-231.

9

INTEGRATED RURAL DEVELOPMENT: The Philippine Experience

Pulcra M. Nietes

1. Introduction

Among the various approaches to rural development that emerged at the start of the 1970s, the Philippines adopted integrated area development (IAD), which provided a strong focus on spatial integration and geographic boundaries as determinants of the scale, components and management requirements of IRD projects. This approach provided the basic justification for massive public investments in well-defined geographic areas that were classified as depressed or lagging, and whose development would substantially affect the economic growth of the broader region where they were located.

A double objective underlay IAD projects: to accelerate economic growth in depressed areas in order to correct regional disparities, and to shift benefits in favour of the marginalised poor, thereby achieving social equity. The overriding criteria in area selection were the magnitude of the natural resource base and population size, together with socio-economic criteria such as low income, inadequate social services and high incidence of tenancy and landlessness.

From 1973 to 1980 a total of around P9 Billion were invested in eight large-scale projects; these funds originated from loans and grants from bilateral sources and international lending institutions, as well as government counterpart funds. Their beneficiary areas included 20 provinces with a combined population of more than seven million people.

In the 1980s, the Philippines was caught in the general concern among the development community with the search for effectiveness in dealing with the problem of mass poverty in the third world. Because of the dependence of the country on external financial and technical assistance in developing its IAD programmes, its own experience was subjected to the same "deconstruction" that preoccupied the experts and to the search for new directions.

Criticism of the foreign-assisted IAD projects has been varied. At one extreme it was claimed that IAD projects merely made the poor poorer as the benefits from the projects were virtually all appropriated by the middle income sector and failed to reach their intended beneficiaries. More moderate critics recognised the difficulty of implementing complex multi-sectoral projects and the failure of existing bureaucratic structures to adapt to the management requirements of IAD projects. The apologists, on the other hand, claimed that more time was needed to generate the socio-economic impact expected from these interventions but that such impact was inevitable.

On the whole, the criticism was healthy and constructive, and sharpened the analysis of the complex problems of rural development, which include such areas as the structure of power and wealth (politico-economic), accessibility (spatial), knowledge and values (socio-technical) and public investment control (governmental). With increasing awareness that poverty and oppression were directly related to the insurgency problem, another dimension was added to the complexities of rural development: internal security.

For most advocates of IAD in the 70s, IAD was a humbling experience. The first lesson they learnt was that it was inappropriate to seek absolute solutions for rural development problems in the physico-economic models brought in by foreign technical consultants and massive external funding. In the formulation of George Honadle, IAD projects could not provide the engine of growth; at best they merely served as the starter motor. A second lesson was that it was not possible to cope with the complexities of rural development through even the most rational blueprint, but only through a rigorous learning process in which beneficiaries should play the key roles. The third and most important lesson was that, in spite of strong policy pronouncements supporting IAD, its radical innovations could not prevail against the highly centralised systems of control which greatly diminished the effectiveness of IAD projects.

The present paper aims at summing up the lessons from more than a decade of planning and implementing IAD projects. It discusses the overall IAD experience, focusing on historical background, conceptual framework, problems of implementation, impact evaluation and future direction. It traces the evolution of IAD projects from their original (pre-1980) to their current (post-1980) form, which was motivated by the aim to correct the identified drawbacks and shortfalls of the traditional models. In its last sections, the paper focuses on the experience with a specific IAD project, namely the Palawan IAD Project Phase I, which was planned in 1978-80 and implemented in 1981-88. This was a transitional project and represented in many ways the new IAD as distinct from those started in the mid-70s, at the same time that it retained many features of the earlier IAD approach. It ushered in a new wave which is today reflected in the newly funded Aurora IAD and the pipeline projects of NACIAD including Palawan IAD Project, Phase II.

2. Historical Background

IRD in the Philippines spans three decades of experimentation with approaches that were "in style" among the international development community at the time they were adopted. The experiments were generally accompanied by the creation of governmental bodies concerned with their implementation. These organisations have undergone changes in their structures and their powers and effectiveness have diminished overtime. Many of their basic concepts have since been incorporated in subsequent approaches.

2.1 *The Community Development (CD) Programme*

The Community Development Programme, which was started in the 1950s under President Ramon Magsaysay, was the first systematic nation-wide effort to integrate all rural development activities at the *barrio* or village level. The programme, which received massive support from the US Government, operated along the concept of self-help and self-reliance and sought to strengthen the newly-organised Barrio Councils as the institutional channel for horizontal and vertical communication. For the first time a mechanism for both political and developmental access between the grassroots and the national government was made possible.

The merits of the CD programme were mostly in its effectiveness in political integration. It provided concrete contact points between village people and government and exposed leaderships at all levels to the problems of the rural sector. However, as a mechanism for integrating national and local resources for increased productivity and livelihood, the programme was hampered by the generally low level of productive technology, particularly in agriculture, around which community development programmes were organised. The research centres and other institutions that were needed to backstop the CD programme were actually developed later and only after the acute deficiency in rural technologies had substantially weakened the programme.

The CD programme was implemented directly from the Office of the President by the Presidential Assistant on Community Development (PACD). From 1955 to 1973 it had a massive organisation that covered all the villages of the country. When the government was reorganised in 1973, PACD was transformed into the Bureau of Community Development of the new Ministry of Local Government. With the shift in emphasis to general assistance in local government administration, CD as a distinct programme was slowly phased out.

2.2 *Decentralisation and Regional Development*

The general governmental reorganisation that was decreed by President Marcos in 1973 was preceded by several studies conducted by the newly organised National Economic and Development Authority (NEDA). The studies included several alternative regional delineations of the country based on the balancing of geographic, economic, demographic and ethnic-cultural factors. Accompanying the alternative regional delineations was the designation of potential regional capitals that could serve as sites for the decentralised operation of sectoral departments and other major services of the national government. The regionalisation scheme that was officially adopted provided for twelve planning and administrative regions outside the greater Manila area which, covering five cities and 12 municipalities, itself constituted the National Capital Region.

An important part of the regionalisation scheme was the creation of the Regional Development Council (RDC) which was composed of the governors and the mayors of the provinces and cities of the region and the regional directors of the national government agencies. In a later mandate, the people's representatives to the National Congress also became members of the RDC. The NEDA Regional Office provided the technical secretariat to the RDC.

Rural development dominated the policy agenda of the RDC and became the overriding goal of the 5-year comprehensive regional development plans and the Regional Development Investment Programmes (RDIP) prepared by the regions since 1973. Emphasis was placed on spatial integration which would hopefully improve the functional linkages between the region's population centres and their hinterlands and the promotion of employment in farm and non-farm sectors. A bottom-up planning system was adopted in the preparation of the RDIP, starting with the formulation of the Municipal Development Investment Programmes (MDIP), which were subsequently consolidated and augmented to form the Provincial Development Investment Programme (PDIP). The PDIP provided the substantive inputs into the RDIP.

Several regions adopted the IAD approach in sub-regional planning, using spatial integration and market linkages as its basic rationale. IAD provided the framework for the planning of clusters of municipalities which possessed a major market and urban services centre. Large provinces were subdivided into several IAD planning areas. Sectoral projects designed to contribute to the development of both the centre and its hinterlands were then programmed for implementation within a target time frame. The investment requirements of all these projects were then consolidated to form the PDIP. The funding structure was, however, still not integrated under the PDIP and RDIP.

2.3 *Integrated Area Development Projects under the National Council on Integrated Area Development*

To many observers, IAD appears as a revitalised and broadened (functional and geographic) community development model. The ideological and policy rationale of social justice, equity and self-reliance is embodied in both CD and IAD. The main difference is that IAD emphasises the spatial integration of broad economic resource regions and not merely of politico-sociological communities. Within this broad framework, it works beyond mere "areas of interest" to "areas of effectiveness" as it seeks to correct the socio-economic imbalance between urban and rural areas and between rich and poor regions.

IAD was developed as a reaction to the highly sectoralised approaches which had dominated development programming since independence. The lop-sided economic growth which merely widened regional and social disparities was attributed to the investments in infrastructure and services that favoured the growth of Metropolitan Manila and the regions and agricultural areas that were already relatively productive. It was primarily to complement regional development efforts that the Government identified several resource regions in the early 70s as recipients of integrated funding packages to cover costs of basic infrastructure, agricultural development and social services. Funding sources included the USAID, WB and ADB. The Government also created a Cabinet Co-ordinating Committee for Integrated Rural Development Projects (CCC-RDP) to co-ordinate the IAD projects.

In 1978, a permanent institution, the National Council on Integrated Area Development, was created which took over the functions of the CCC-IRDP. In addition to its having jurisdiction over the on-going foreign-assisted projects, NACIAD enjoyed support at the highest policy level with the President, and later the Prime Minister, as Chairperson.

Policy support to IAD as a project development and management concept has continued through the 70s and 80s with NACIAD providing its key organisational inputs such as planning, co-ordination, monitoring and evaluation. A set-back in policy development was experienced after the Office of the Prime Minister was abolished in 1986. However, the Technical Secretariat has sustained its previous level of operation and its continuing work program. At present, NACIAD is temporarily attached to the NEDA while a study on its appropriate placement in the bureaucratic system is being conducted.

3. Summary of Major Foreign-assisted Projects

A total of nine projects, of which three have been completed, were implemented from 1975 to 1988. The first of these is the Mindoro Integrated Rural Development Project covering two provinces in Mindoro Island off the southern coast of Luzon Island. Project components include roads, ports, irrigation, agricultural support services, watershed protection, schistosomiasis control and assistance to tribal communities. Funding for Phases I and II totals P1.435 B, mostly World Bank loans. The project will be completed at the end of 1988.

The second IAD project is the Bicol River Basin Development Project, covering the provinces of Camarines Sur and Albay. Massive capital investment goes to irrigation and flood control and roads. The non-infrastructure projects include health, nutrition and population control, fisheries and agricultural support and watershed development. Total cost reached P1.85 B by 1987 with the USAID, Asian Development Bank (ADB) and EEC as major sources of funding.

The third IAD project is located in Cagayan Province which is a sub-basin of the huge Cagayan River Basin. It is primarily an integrated agricultural development project supported by the Japanese Government. Its primary component, irrigating and flood control, was completed in 1984.

Another large-scale IAD project is located in Samar Island; it has funding from the World Bank and the Australian Government. Major components include roads and ports, irrigation, water supply, power, agricultural development and schistosomiasis control. Total project cost is P2.179 B.

Palawan is the 5th major IAD project; it is funded with a loan from ADB and a grant from the EEC. Total cost for Phase I is P954 M which is mainly spent on roads, irrigation and flood control, agricultural support, water supply, malaria control and environmental protection.

The Zamboanga del Sur Development Project was actually the Second Phase of a bilateral assistance project started by the Australian Development Assistance Bureau (ADAB). Its components, which included road development, irrigation, water supply, agricultural support, health and local government institutional development, ran to a total cost of P329 M at the time of completion in 1986.

The island of Bohol in the central Philippines is the recipient of a Japanese loan and grant assistance for irrigation development and agricultural support amounting to P623 M.

Two other World Bank assisted rural development projects which were not full scale IAD packages were placed under the NACIAD monitoring umbrella. These were the Philippine Rural Infrastructure Projects for six depressed provinces and three land settlement projects for land reform beneficiaries. Major components included roads and ports, irrigation, water supply and health and social services. The combined cost of the projects amounted to P955 M. Both were completed in 1985.

A summary of the major foreign-assisted projects is presented in Tables 9.1 and 9.2.

Table 9.1: Major Foreign Assisted Projects

Project	Area Coverage	Implementation Period	Funding Sources
1. Mindoro IRD Project	Mindoro Island		
Phase I		1975-1983	WB*
Phase II		1979-1988	WB
2. Bicol River Basin Dev't. Programme	Camarines Sur, Albay, Sorsogon		
USAID funded		1975-1986	USAID*
BRBIDP		1980-1988	ADB/EEC
3. Cagayan IAD Project	Cagayan Province	1977-1988	JICA* OECF GOJ
4. Samar IRD Project	Samar Island		
WB-funded		1980-1986	WB
NSIRDP Phase I		1979-1983	ADAB*
NSIRDP Phase II		1984-1988	ADAB
Western Samar Master Plan Study		1987-1988	JICA
5. Palawan IAD Project	Palawan	1982-1989	ADB
6. Zamboanga del Sur Dev't. Project—Phase II	Zamboanga del Sur	1982-1989	ADAB*
7. Agusan, Bukidnon, Capiz - Land Settlement Project	Settlements in Agusan del Sur, Bukidnon and Capiz	1978-1985	WB*
8. Philippine Rural Infrastructure Project	Abra, Aklan, Antique, Capiz, Kalinga-Apayao, Bohol	1978-1986	WB*
9. Bohol IAD Project	Bohol	1982-1991	JICA OECF Government of the Netherlands Government of New Zealand

*Completed

Table 9.2: Summary of NACIAD Ongoing Projects (*in million pesos*)

Project/Component			Transport Dev't	Irrigation Flood Control	Water Supply	Agri'l Support & Com. Dev't	Health and Social Services	Environmental/ Watershed Protection	Electrification	Local Gov't Support	Total
Mindoro	Phase I	1975-83	304	171		9	13	10			507
	Phase II	1979-88	525	397	6						928
Bicol		1975-87	508	1,128	37	98	60	21			1,550
Cagayan		1977-88		560		86			31		677
Samar		1979-88	1,691	41	87	241	71		47	1	2,179
Palawan		1982-89	442	116	38	277	21	60			954
Zamboanga D.S.		1981-85	196	27	29	46	10			21	328
Agusan, Bukidnon, Capiz		1978-85	270	5	3	21	6				305
PRIP		1978-86	530	88	26		6				650
Bohol		1982-91		521		102					623
Total			4,464	3,054	226	880	187	91	78	22	9,002

Notes: For ongoing projects, the estimates were taken from the original project documents.
The total of P9.002 B includes foreign assistance. The cost of studies, Project Offices operation and maintenance of Project Offices, which is estimated at P7.47 M, are not included.

4. The Conceptual Framework of IAD Projects

The standard IAD model generally starts with the formulation of a problem structure showing the interrelationships of negative factors identified as the root causes of rural poverty. This structure is commonly referred to as the "vicious circle" of poverty. The dynamic model derived from a systems analysis of such a structure was based on the assumption that development objectives are the inverse of the problems and that the vicious circle can be transformed into a growth cycle through a concerted attack on the interacting elements causing the problems. The integrated attack combines physical, institutional and social structural interventions intended to promote economic well-being, attitudinal changes and institutional capabilities for self-sustaining growth. Together, these interventions constitute the IAD strategy.

An IAD project is necessarily multi-functional and multi-sectoral. The problems it seeks to solve within a temporal frame reflect the multiple facets of poverty such as low income, malnutrition, lack of access to social services, lack of productive assets, ignorance, etc. Their solution requires the co-ordinated efforts of various disciplines and sectoral agencies.

Secondly, an IAD project focuses on a defined geographic area where the problems can be viewed in their interrelationships. This makes possible the systematic structuring of the required interventions which should be mutually enhancing in their impact on the life of the rural poor.

Thirdly, IAD builds on the people's accumulated experience with socio-technical change and must therefore utilise participation techniques in planning, implementing and monitoring development projects. Full participation of local government, implementing agencies and beneficiary communities in various aspects of IAD ensures sustainability of development benefits after the completion of project assistance.

From this general framework are derived the complementary objectives of the IAD projects:

- Increase the productivity of land and water resources.
- Improve the quality of labour through manpower development.
- Generate employment opportunities in both farm and non-farm sectors.

– Improve social services.
– Provide for local participation in development.

The complementation of sectoral components and the timing of their inputs into the implementation programme are the two most critical elements in the IAD scheme. The complementation itself has a strategic importance as it is linked to the strategic objectives of spatial integration and de-marginalisation of the masses of the poor. The right timing of inputs, on the other hand, has implications for the efficiency and cost-effectiveness of IAD projects, since it can determine substantial savings in time and cost.

4.1 *Spatial Integration*

The use of the IAD strategy to create functional linkages between resource regions on the one hand and market and urban centres on the other, or between areas of production and areas of consumption, is reflected in the emphasis placed on transport and communications in IAD projects. For projects approved in the 1970s, the percentage of total project cost going into roads and ports and communications amounted to 50% or more (Table 9.2).

The concept of "farm-to-market" roads was developed quite extensively in the USAID-funded Bicol River Basin Development Programme. It refers to the combination of farm feeder roads and secondary roads connecting them to the main national highways and thence to the market towns. The Bicol project put emphasis on farm-to-market roads because the major trunk lines, namely the South Philippine-Japan Highway and the South Line of the Philippine National Railways, had already been built.

In areas as Mindoro and Samar Islands, where even the main national highways were not yet in place, the World Bank identified as the major component the improvement of the circumferential highway and the major seaports through which the islands' products are shipped to other parts of the country. It is for this reason that transport and communications infrastructure accounted for much of the cost of these island IADs.

Another aspect of spatial integration strategies relates to the strengthening of the role of town centres and middle range cities in providing urban services and higher level social facilities for the region. These basic considerations are not overlooked in IAD planning.

However, direct investment in urban facilities is generally not included in IAD packages. It is presumed that Government efforts would be exerted to promote complementary programmes through both public and private initiatives to address this end of the IAD spectrum. Examples of these complementary programmes are the Regional Cities Development Programme and the Programme for Essential Municipal Infrastructures, Utilities, Maintenance for Engineering Development.

4.2 *De-linking the Poor*

The process of de-linking of the poor from their economic and political shackles comes under such labels as "emancipation", de-marginalisation", "empowerment" and "participation". Emancipation is an old concept that developed alongside the agrarian reform movement and meant the severance of the dependency links that characterised landlord-tenant relations in the Philippines. De-marginalisation, which appeared in development literature in the 70s, refers to the conscious process of moving the poor masses of population away from the non-benefited margins into the mainstream of economic and political development. Empowerment is the self-directed capacity building of community groups so that they can gain access to democratic political processes as well as economic space. Empowerment means more than having your voice heard, it means sharing in the ownership of assets and in the distribution of economic gains.

The active process involved in all these concepts is people's participation, which must be translated into systematic procedures for planning, managing and sustaining development programmes by the beneficiaries themselves. The chances involved in this process are all-encompassing: institutional development, technical skills build-up, attitudinal changes, asset formation and decision-making. The final end are self-reliant communities that are able to sustain a progressive rate of socio-economic development.

De-linking takes project activities to the grassroots and utilises micro-analysis in contrast to the macro-framework of spatial integration. The concept is operationalised in NACIAD's small-scale high impact projects (SSHIPs) which were started in pipeline areas in the early 1980s. SSHIPs represented a shift in the concept of IAD toward small-scale community based rural projects with a high level of people's participation. They emphasise indigenous resource management and community organisation. Generally, income-generating activities managed by beneficiary associations serve as the entry points in these projects.

Participatory strategies cover such areas as local level planning, project development and management and community organisation. In all phases, field agencies of the national government and local government staff provide the technical and institutional inputs into community development. GO-NGO collaboration is likewise promoted. The role of NGOs is centred on community organising activities.

4.3 *Decentralised Organisational Structure*

A unique feature of IAD projects is the simultaneous operation of sector-specific management structures corresponding to the components of the IAD package. Depending on its degree of autonomy from the central ministry or department, sectoral management takes place either in the special projects office (SPO) mode or through normal agency (routine) channels. The SPO mode is generally used by infrastructure agencies such as the Department of Public Works and Highways and the National Irrigation Administration. A Field Management Office under a project manager is established to administer all aspects of implementation from design to construction and operation. The SPO operates independently of the hierarchical structure of the national agency and reports directly to a highly placed official in the central office/national headquarters.

In the case of project managers operating in the routine mode, top-down control and vertical reporting go through the hierarchical structure of the line department. This means that project operation is controlled at the regional level. Sectors operating in this mode include agriculture and fisheries, health, social services and natural resources and environment.

The IAD Project Office co-ordinates all the multi-sectoral components of the IAD package. It is established by law as a semi-autonomous body operating with its own budgetary allocation. NACIAD has limited control over its operations: it merely reviews its annual budget requests and carries out financial and performance monitoring and evaluation of the project as as a whole.

Being located at the project site, the IAD Project Office has to work closely with the local government institutions, non-governmental organisations and community groups. Its effectiveness in inter-sectoral co-ordination depends on its use use of formal and informal structures at the local level. The personal leadership and management skills of the Project Director are critical since he has a wide ranging field for decisions affecting the IAD project.

IAD works best with sectoral agencies that are highly decentralised and with active local government participation. For highly centralised agencies, *ad hoc* co-ordination mechanisms have to be established. Examples are the Project Co-ordinating Committees at the provincial and regional levels and the old practice of designating a cabinet co-ordinator to help remove constraints emanating from control departments like budget and audit departments, and sometimes lending institutions.

Past attempts to have a fully decentralised management structure and funding scheme for IAD projects have failed except for the EEC-funded Aurora IAD project which started implementation in 1988. The major constraint on an integrated budgetary system managed on-site by the IAD project office was the reluctance of sectoral departments to relinquish financial control over their components. Of late, however, the departments of health and agriculture have regionalised financial decision-making with regard to their respective components of IAD projects. Such a development will facilitate action, because important decisions can be made by the regional level directors without having to seek approval from the central bureaucracy.

5. Problems in Implementing Old Projects

The first five years of operation of IAD projects in the Philippines (1975-1979) were a critical period of testing planning and management methodologies. This was also the period of development of national capabilities so that local staff working as counterparts to expatriate consultants began to provide more substantial inputs into the project development process. It was, after all, the Filipino managers and technical staff who had to confront the problems of implementation after most of the foreign experts had gone. In the same way, the agencies concerned with the implementation of project components had to bear the brunt of criticisms of project deficiencies, regardless of whether these stemmed from ineffectiveness of staff, organisational shortcomings or constraints emanating from the terms of loan and grant agreements or imposed by national government control agencies.

Many of the problems of the early IAD projects can be traced back to the planning process, to methodological deficiencies and to the design of the organisation and management structure of the IAD project. These problems may be summarised as follows:

1. *Overemphasis on infrastructure*: This can be seen in the apportioning of IAD project funds (80% on the average) and in the role that infrastructure is assumed to play in the development process: that of a first level input that would spur the process of socio-economic development. Conversely, non-infrastructure development, including direct support to the productive sectors, service delivery systems for credit, inputs, market and institutional development and social services, were given secondary importance.
2. *Special projects mode of implementation for large components*: The major drawback of this mode was the gap it created in terms of operational capabilities between the special project management unit (PMU) and the regular agencies that would maintain continuing operations after the end of the project. As a result, completed projects could not be properly maintained by their inheriting institutions which had a lower level of technical and financial capabilities.
3. *Limited development capability build-up*: A corollary to the dependence on PMUs for project implementation was the lack of provisions for sustainability through the building up of the planning and management capabilities of inheriting institutions. Institutional strengthening covers such processes as the transfer of responsibility for planning, construction and maintenance; management responsibilities including co-ordination, monitoring and evaluation, training and community organizing when necessary. This was one of the most serious weaknesses of first-generation IAD projects.
4. *Failure to conduct immediate baseline studies*: The final test of an IAD project is the degree to which it achieves its growth and equity objectives. It can set realistic targets only if it possesses accurate benchmarks or starting points. Unfortunately, most of the first IAD projects started their operations without adequate area and group-specific socio-economic profiles of intended beneficiaries. This resulted in the inability to measure project impacts accurately.
5. *Failure to define effective mechanisms for people's participation*: At best, participation appears to have been an

"afterthought" in the early projects, resorted to only as a remedial measure to ease problems of project sustainability and in response to heightened awareness by beneficiary groups of their potential role in their development. Given the large-scale character of the old projects, with their emphasis on spatial integration at regional level, people's participation did not appear as integral to the concept of IAD but merely an appendage composed of discrete grass-roots "experiments" in institution building and human resource development. The Ministry of Agrarian Reform and the National Irrigation Authority have provided the success stories of people's participation in the Bicol River Basin Development Programme before 1980. These agencies organised beneficiary groups and involved them in planning and design, canal construction and operation of communal irrigation systems.

Another set of problems encountered in earlier IAD projects related to implementation and was mainly due to constraints posed by the existing national administrative and budgetary systems. Effective implementation of IAD was premised on decentralised decision-making and management of funds, and on integrated budgeting for its multisectoral components. This concept was in direct conflict with the highly sectoral bureaucratic and budgetary structure. The problems engendered by this conflict include the following:

1. *Organisation and management*: To adapt to the highly centralised bureaucracies of sectoral ministries who had a direct hand in executing the various components of the IAD projects, these projects had to assume a very complex organisational and management matrix that spread out horizontally across various national field agencies and local governments and vertically through the administrative tiers to the national centres for policy and decision-making. The IAD project office, with the mandate to co-ordinate but without the authority to implement works and services, or even control financial resources, was by itself never strong enough to prevail against the centralised executive authority of sectoral ministries or even local governments and regional bodies. Co-operation could be gained only through a formal multiple agency agreement or through informal methods such as *ad hoc* consultative committees. Also helpful was the

secondment of personnel from co-operating agencies and the designation of a major implementing agency to coordinate all the associated activities of other co-operating agencies (the lead agency concept). A most useful practice has been to assign a cabinet member to act as co-ordinator at the highest policy and administrative level; such co-ordinators normally used their personal influence to get co-operation from the concerned ministers.

2. *Budgetary procedures and funds flow*: Associated with the constraints of centralised sectoral authority was the highly sectoral budget process. As a rule, budgetary allotments were released to the central offices of the various ministries, which in turn channelled the funds to their implementing offices. As is often the case, this procedure lost sight of the need to synchronise the execution of complementary sectoral activities which which were co-ordinated by the IAD project office. In case sectoral priorities prevailed the central ministry might choose to defer the release of funds for the IAD project. Delays in implementation due to budget release delays by 18 to 20 months affected practically all IAD components.

   The lack of capability in the field of programming and budgeting on the part of project managers may have contributed to delays in fund releases. Where the agency concerned failed to follow the budgetary guidelines of the office of Budget and Management, a mispriority might be committed leading to the loss of support to a component for a whole budget year.

3. *Inter-agency co-ordination*. As most of the executing agencies of IAD projects had centralised structures, co-ordination had to be done at various levels from project site operations to provincial/district office to regional office and finally at the national level. It was the practice of the government to establish project co-ordinating committees (PCCs), where the field level offices and local government were represented, and Regional Co-ordinating Committees (RCC) where the super-ordinate offices of these agencies were in turn represented. This multi-level co-ordination structure is quite complex and conflicts would arise from differences in sectoral orientation and views on development, and sometimes also from leadership and personality differences.

   Experience has taught that effective co-ordination was possible if the co-ordinating agency was vested with authority from some higher office or if it had control over resources to be used to the benefit of co-operating agencies. In this case co-ordination had both a horizontal and a hierarchical structure. Where the local government executive, for instance, used his authority to bring together field agencies of the national government assigned in his jurisdiction, co-ordination was easier to accomplish. It was therefore to the advantage of the IAD projects office to work closely with local authorities in carrying out its co-ordinating function. Thus, the Provincial Governor served as chairman of the RCC in IAD projects in the provinces of Palawan, Aurora, and Zamboanga del Sur.

Co-ordination became more complex and informal as project management dealt with non-government sectors such as business groups, private voluntary organisations and beneficiary groups. Its effectiveness in these cases was highly dependent on the leadership, skills and personality of the Project Director. The choice of this officer was therefore a critical factor in IAD management.

A third set of problems related to the monitoring and particularly evaluation of IAD projects. Monitoring project performance, both physically and financially, posed little problem. It was in the area of impact evaluation that methodologies were less well developed. The most common problems included the inadequacy of baseline socio-economic data and the difficulty in determining what changes could be realistically attributed to the IAD project. It was also recognised that some important changes were not measurable or tangible.

6. **Impact of Completed Projects**

Attempts to evaluate the socio-economic and environmental impact of IRD projects have ranged from the impressionistic journalistic account to the systematic scientific analysis. Defective methodology seems to be the obvious problem and some questions have remained unsolved. Are the benchmark data used to measure change adequate and accurate enough? To what extent can the observed changes be attributed to the IAD project? Should non-quantifiable indicators be accepted?

While all completed projects were subjected to a thorough performance and accomplishment evaluation in terms of achieving their physical and financial targets, they were not assessed in terms of their impact on their beneficiaries and the resource base of the area. On the other hand, the on-going Bicol River Basin Development Programme did attempt to make such an assessment in 1985, 10 years after its inception.

The methodology used for the BRBDP impact evaluation assumed three levels of impact areas: specific project site, programme area and whole region. The findings of the study definitely showed significant positive changes in socio-economic indicators at every level. Its most important lesson, however, was the decreasing confidence in attributing changes to the IAD project as one moves from the site level toward the broader region. To begin with, it is extremely difficult to determine the proportion that the IAD package represents of total interventions in the area, including both public and private initiatives. If, for this reason, the impact of IAD projects at the regional level cannot be measured, then how can such projects be evaluated as regional development projects?

The impact of IAD projects on the programme area is likewise indirect and difficult to measure, except for components of spatial integration like roads, communications and power supply, or institutional development projects addressing management capabilities at this level. Thus, if the flow of goods and services along these circuits has increased over the years, costs have gone down and returns increased, a major role in causing such changes can be confidently attributed to the IAD project as a whole. Nevertheless this cannot be expressed in quantitative terms.

With regard to the direct impact within the project site, studies have shown that IAD projects had considerable impact on the socio-economic situation of their target beneficiaries. Specific interventions, affecting productive activities or health, are implemented together with monitoring schemes that give periodic impact evaluation during the lifetime of IAD assistance. Systems development, monitoring and evaluation have also progressed, resulting in better data, greater speed in their generation and improved cost effectiveness, as new management information systems are installed in IAD agencies.

A very important impact that is often downplayed in evaluating IAD projects is the improvement in the general level of skill and commitment of field manpower of government agencies, in technical fields, community organising and institutional development, and general administration and management. Also important is the imparting of the same skills to the beneficiaries themselves through participatory techniques in planning and project management. Local leadership has been sought out and developed, thereby shortening the period needed for developing self-reliance in community undertakings.

In the infrastructure sectors, such as irrigation and road development, a new community development orientation has been introduced as more participatory approaches are applied and beneficiary organisations are developed to take over post construction management. Perhaps the most complete shift in orientation from physical to social infrastructure is the case of rural water supply. What used to be the domain of the engineering offices has become the concern of the neighbourhood user group in terms of choice of location, design, and cost sharing in construction and maintenance of completed works.

7. Second Generation, New and Pipeline Projects

IAD projects planned after 1979, including the second phases of earlier IAD projects, reflect the conceptual and methodological changes that took place in rural development planning, not only in the Philippines but also in other developing countries. They were also attempts to correct the observed shortfalls of the old projects. This was to be expected since the first IAD projects were experimental in many ways. In general, the shift was toward a stronger socio-economic, environmental and institutional development orientation, away from the techno-physical and economic emphasis of earlier projects.

The most decisive changes in the configuration of IAD projects were in the components themselves. The new projects placed more emphasis on upland technology development, environmental protection, rural industries, local government capability build up, nutrition and agricultural credit.

Thus, they were definitely software-oriented and placed investment in technology, institutions and human resource ahead of infrastructural investment. Upland and rainfed communities and areas which were left out of the first IAD projects now received greater emphasis. Relatively more attention was also directed at human resource development through improved health, nutrition, manpower training and other social services.

The new configuration of IAD projects substantially affected the procedures involved in project planning and management. It also led to changes in the key role players in the rural development process. In the broadest terms, the traditional hierarchical flow of decision from top to bottom had to be replaced by bottom-up flows as more participatory approaches were being adopted, particularly for components that were highly localised and dependent on the co-operation of community groups and local institutions. The new procedures implied a reversal of roles between central agencies and their offices in the field and between central institutions and local-based bodies, including local government, local business, non-governmental institutions and beneficiary groups.

7.1 *Selection of IAD Project Areas*

The integration of the development process for broad geographical areas like a province or group of provinces requires macro-level analysis. The selection of priority areas for IAD is a central government function and is based primarily on inter-regional comparisons of levels of development and the seriousness of the poverty situation. The assumption inherent in this process is that household-level poverty is correlated with economic indicators for the area as a whole. Macro-analysis relied mostly on secondary statistics and official documents. The problem structure derived from this exercise was highly sectoral, which explains the tendency to equate rural development with the development of agriculture and its supportive infrastructure. The traditional IAD projects were strongly influenced by this perspective.

For new and pipeline projects, economic resources development was strongly complemented by a social orientation. The basic assumption is that improving the condition of poor households on an aggregate scale will create equitable regional development. Hence, integration should focus on the provision of household needs on a sustained basis. Both the selection of project areas and the components of the project take primary cognizance of the integrated needs of poor households. The definition of poverty under this concept applies primarily to the capabilities of households and communities to control their environment, inclusive of economic, social, political and ecological factors. Hence, the spread of components is necessarily wider for new and pipeline areas.

The criteria for area selection applied for old projects and those developed in 1981 by the NACIAD reflect the radical shift from broad economic considerations to household and community-level indicators (Table 9.3). It is obvious that the new criteria are no longer biased towards regional growth *per se* but rather towards the achievement of social equity objectives.

The 1973 criteria were used to identify only the initial IRD projects: Mindoro, Bicol, Cagayan and Samar. The 1981 criteria were developed by the NACIAD and used to identify the planning areas for the period 1983-87. Areas planned between 1979-82, including Palawan, Bohol and Zamboanga del Sur were selected by special nomination and approved by the NACIAD Council. However, their designation as areas deserving IAD was later validated by the 1981 criteria.

7.2 *Planning and Project Development*

The strategic shift associated with the new IAD orientation affected not only the components of the projects but the very process of planning itself. The foremost effect was increased local participation in all phases of planning, from setting strategic objectives to operational planning. Problem and project analysis now brings the planner all the way to the grass-roots through village-level consultation workshops, which involve the village population, local government representatives, national line agencies and community development agents of all kinds. Village workshops are conducted in sample villages representing topographic-economic zones so that the overall findings can be safely generalised to the level of the zone.

Plan formulation is likewise a participatory process, involving the planning officers of line agencies, the local governments and representatives of private organisations. The agenda of planning workshops includes the verification of secondary socio-economic information, problem identification, setting of goals and objectives, formulation of strategies, sectoral programming and costing, and choice of implementing strategies.

7.3 *Small Scale High Impact Projects (SSHIPs)*

An offshoot of local participation is the concept of small-scale high impact projects, which also emerged at the beginning of the 1980s. SSHIPs represent a shift of the concept of IAD toward small-scale community-based rural projects implemented by the beneficiaries themselves with technical and financial assistance from various national and local agencies. Its emphasis is on local resource management with national government support to accelerate the rural development process.

Table 9.3: Criteria for Area Selection, 1973 and 1981

1973 Criteria	1981 Criteria
- Areas with high tenancy rates	A. Economic
	1. Per Capita Household Income
- Relatively underdeveloped areas with development potentials in more than one section of the economy (crop production, livestock, fisheries, forestry, mining, industry, others) measured by certain indicators.	2. Employment Rate 3. Level of Industrial Activities a. no establishment b. % of labour force in manufacturing
- Areas whose inhabitants have income within lowest income bracket-average annual family income below P2, 500.00	B. Social 1. Health Status a. Morbidity rate b. Infant mortality
- Areas with potential for swift development	c. % of malnutrition among children
- Areas requiring relatively small incremental investments to generate high benefits	2. Educational Studies a. Literacy rate b. % of age 6-14 in school c. % of age 15-25 in school
	3. Housing Facilities a. % of dwelling units with toilets b. % of dwelling units with potable water supply
	4. Transportation/Communications Facilities a. km of roads/sq.km of arable land b. % of households with radio sets c. Newspaper/1000 population d. No. of telephones/1000 population e. No. of ports f. No. of commercial and municipal fish landing ports.

Three entry points are used in SSHIPs: (1) planning at the village level resulting in project prioritisation based on needs; (2) project development assistance and (3) community organisation. SSHIPs are highly dependent on close inter-agency linkages at the field level and, when necessary, on sharing the costs of the input requirements of the projects. In terms of the projects themselves, priority is given to income-generating projects, although community-run social services such as health, sanitation and child care may also receive priority. In recent years efforts have been made to promote government/non-government collaboration in these projects. Experience has shown that NGOs have been very effective in handling the community organising aspects of SSHIPs.

As the agency mandated to pursue IAD strategies, the NACIAD assumes an important role in SSHIPs. Foremost is the task of developing methodologies for local-level planning and of training local government staff to help beneficiary groups develop their SSHIPs. Attendant to this is the development of effective monitoring and evaluation systems for SSHIPs in order to improve their operation. Local agencies involved in SSHIPs also have to be trained in using the management information system developed by NACIAD. It is also NACIAD's task to develop the necessary linkages between beneficiaries, implementing agencies, local government and NGOs. The catalytic role of NACIAD has been effective in spreading SSHIPs to all provinces. At the last count, there were around 100 prototype projects implemented in more than 150 locations. They show the potential of a fully decentralised community-based planning and management system, with strong support from government agencies.

8. **Case Study: The Palawan IAD Project**

8.1 *General*

In order to illustrate the new approach to IAD developed by the NACIAD, some salient characteristics of the Palawan IAD Project (PIADP) will be briefly presented here. The Palawan Integrated Area Development Project (PIADP) was approved in 1979 and implemented from 1982 onwards. Palawan Island was selected because of the following reasons:

(a) its wealth of natural resources and high potential for economic development;

(b) a marked deficiency in social facilities;
(c) the low income level of a majority of its population, which was growing very rapidly due to immigration from other parts of the country; and
(d) the rapid degradation of its land resources due to overexploitation of its forests and unsuitable farming practices of upland dwellers.

The PIADP was a significant deviation from the earlier IAD projects. It was the first project to provide a programme of environmental protection and management with emphasis on the conservation of upland soils, forest and fishery protection and assistance to upland settlements. It included a strong drive to eradicate malaria and to improve the general health of the inhabitants. PIADP also became the first project to integrate nutrition considerations in the process of planning and project preparation. The Nutrition-Oriented Development Plan provided a methodology of situational analysis and planning which could be conducted in parallel, and interlocking at critical points, with the analysis and planning of the nutrition-relevant components of PIADP. A third important innovation in IAD planning introduced by PIADP was the institution of a hierarchical structure for local development management, with the participation of the provincial, municipal and village governments. Called Area Development Management Programme (ADMAP), this institutional development programme was also designed for the political, economic and social integration of the various communities in the project area.

8.2 *The Project Area*

The province of Palawan is an archipelago with a large elongated mainland and more than 1,500 islands (see map in Fig. 9.1). It extends over 600 kilometres across the South China Sea towards Sarawak. Its total land area is almost 1.5 million hectares. The mainland is mountainous with narrow strips of coastal plains mostly on the western side. At mid-section of the mainland is the city of Puerto Princesa, the capital of the province.

Around 58 per cent of the land is forested, and a major portion of this is occupied by concessions to private logging and mining companies. Pastures occupy 14 per cent, and the remaining 28 per cent are suitable for agriculture. However, upland agricultural and deforested areas have been occupied in increasing numbers by *kaingineros* or slash-and-burn farmers. Only about 16 per cent of the agricultural land is irrigated. There is a predominance of rainfed rice and corn, coconut and other tree crops. Lack of irrigation combined with low technology levels results in low yields. A serious problem is the increasing threat to the ecological balance of the province due to intensive logging and mining operations and to soil degradation caused by kaingin farming.

Fig. 9.1: Map of Palawan

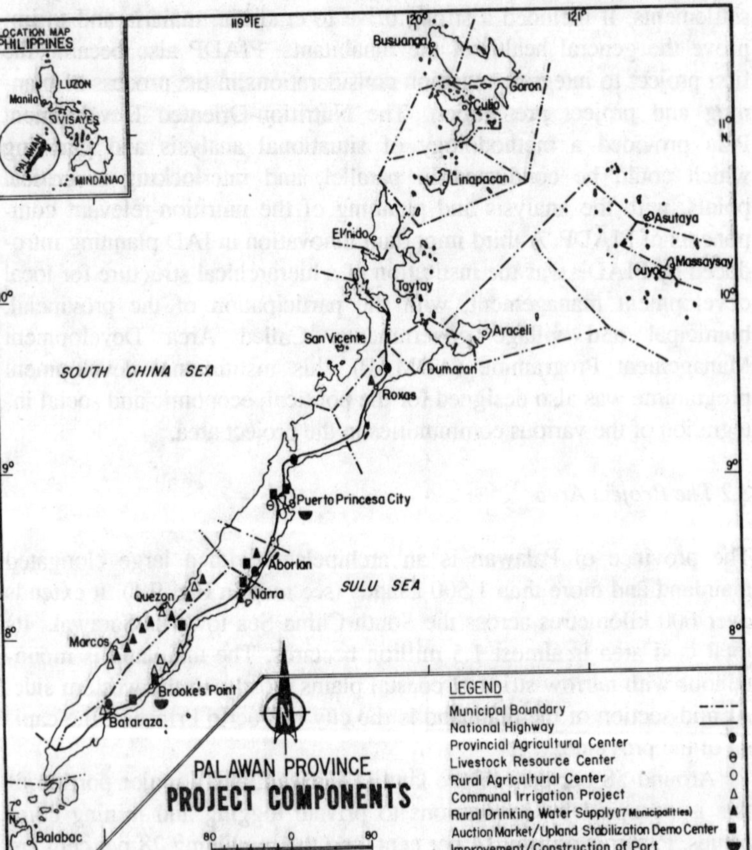

Another major economic resource of the province are its coastal and nearshore fisheries. At present, the industry is limited to small-scale producers and fish products consist mainly of dried fish which is exported to Metro Manila and other parts of Luzon. Commercial fish catches in the offshore areas are landed directly in the Iloilo and Manila fishing ports.

Palawan has approximately 500,000 inhabitants, of which 75 per cent live in Puerto Princesa and in the Southern portion of the island Average density is only 35 persons per square kilometre, way below the national average of 186 persons per square kilometre. A majority of the population are first- to third-generation migrants, mostly from Luzon and the Visayas. The aboriginal population have been pushed into the mountainous interior and remote islands. The population growth rate is very high due to continuing immigration.

The socio-economic situation of a majority of households is sub-marginal, with a median family income that is only 58 per cent of the national figure. Eighty percent of the households depend on subsistence farming and fishing for their livelihood. Ethnic minority groups, which constitute 20 per cent of the population, are semi-nomadic, depending on shifting cultivation in public lands, hunting and gathering for their subsistence.

Basic infrastructure, including transportation, communications, irrigation and water supply as well as health and education facilities, is inadequate and is concentrated mostly in the proximity of Puerto Princesa. Malaria is endemic in many parts of the province. Other prevalent diseases include respiratory, gastro-intestinal infections and other associated with poor sanitation, environmental condition, lack of primary health care and poor nutrition. Lack of potable water supply is a common problem.

Government programmes for the improvement of rural life are inadequate and uncoordinated primarily due to lack of financial resources, weak management structure, low level of technical capability and poor communications facilities. Government services are hardly available in the more remote rural villages and daily life is governed by informal socio-religious institutions and structures.

8.3 *General Concept and Objectives*

The interaction of physical and socio-economic conditions that negatively affect the environment in Palawan became the basis for a development concept that was long-range and comprehensive and laid strong emphasis on environmental management and conservation. At the same time it defined critical combinations of poverty and environmental stabilisation that needed to be immediately addressed. The resulting project was a package of selected concrete actions constituting the initial phase of a strategic long-term development plan for the island.

The project has two principal objectives:

(a) to raise the level of production in agriculture, fisheries and agro-industries in order to increase rural household income and productivity;
(b) to achieve a balanced use of resources in order to protect the ecosystem of the Province and to sustain a long term high productivity of agriculture, forestry, fisheries and rural industry.

8.4 *Development Problems*

These objectives were derived from an analysis of the island's economic and social situation which revealed the following major weaknesses:

1. In the lowlands, agriculture has a low productivity; the agricultural practices used in the uplands are dangerous for environmental balance and soil fertility.
2. Livestock activities are underdeveloped and insufficient.
3. Coastal fishery development is hampered by the limited market and the lack of up to date technology.
4. Forests are of low quality and inadequately exploited.
5. The mining sector is not oriented towards the internal development of the province and is of almost no benefit to the population.
6. Cottage and rural industries are undercapitalised and weakly connected with other productive sectors.
7. There is practically no industry to support agricultural production, livestock and forest production, upstream or downstream.

Analysis of these problems and their causes revealed the following bottlenecks:

1. *Insufficient Infrastructure*: Lowland and upland agriculture, fishery and rural industry development are hampered by the lack of infrastructure which would allow a full development of the existing potentialities. Deficiencies in roads and ports lead to difficulties in the distribution of agricultural inputs, high cost of transportation of products, isolation of local market, and difficulties in technology transfers. Irrigation schemes are insufficiently developed and the existing irrigation network is underutilised because of poor maintenance and lack of manpower. Except for Puerto Princesa, there is no source of reasonably priced power. Coastal fisheries are not supported by the necessary infrastructure, especially for marketing.
2. *Uncertainty of Land tenure*: The absence of a clear system of land appropriation and the slow progress of land tenure improvement programmes, particularly cadastral surveys and titling, hamper private investments in agriculture and favour short-term crop production in fragile upland areas. In addition, uncontrolled mining and forestry activities threaten the environmental balance.
3. *Lack of Complementary Industries*: Lack of industries to complement agricultural production leads to limited input use and processing of available raw materials.
4. *Poor Health Situation*: Productive potentials of the population and the land are greatly hampered by poor sanitation, malnutrition and widespread malaria.
5. *Weak Rural Institutions*: Co-operative and other farming and fishing organisations are not developed, leading to inadequate access to inputs and markets.
6. *Weak Credit System*: Medium-and long-term credit are inadequate.
7. *Management*: National and provincial organisations responsible for development activities do not have enough qualified staff and are not coordinated in their field operations.

8.5 *Project Components*

The components of the project reflect the priority intervention sectors, which take into account the main problems to be solved and the most important bottlenecks identified in the analysis of these problems.

8.5.1 *Agricultural Development*

(a) *Irrigation*: Rehabilitation of existing communal irrigation systems and construction of new ones; strengthening support services to improve water management and irrigation practices.
(b) *Agricultural Intensification and Diversification*: Establishment of agricultural centres for the development of appropriate farming technologies, extension and training and other support services.
(c) *Livestock development*: Establishment of a livestock resource centre to produce improved stocks of cattle and goats for dispersal to smallholders.
(d) *Agricultural Credit*: Improvement of existing credit delivery systems and provision of credit.
(e) *Upland Stabilisation Programme*: Development of an integrated programme to control shifting cultivation and assist tribal communities in developing environmentally sound technologies.

8.5.2 *Transport Development*

(a) *Roads*: Construction/improvement of main roads and village access roads roads, and providing for their maintenance by the Provincial Engineer's Office.
(b) *Ports*: Improvement of port facilities in Puerto Princesa and construction of port facilities in Brookes Point.

8.5.3 *Health Facilities and Services*

(a) *Malaria Control*: Strengthening of Malaria Eradication Services throughout the Province through the Department of Health's Provincial Office.
(b) *Rural Drinking Water Supply*: Rehabilitation/construction of water supply sources and formation of Rural Waterworks and Sanitation Associations; provision of sanitary latrines.

8.5.4 *Land Classification and Titling*

(a) *Land Classification*: Completion of the Government programme to classify 700,000 hectares of public lands.
(b) *Land Survey and Titling*: Support for the government's program to survey alienable and disposable land and process land ownership titles.

8.5.5 *Environmental and Project Benefit Monitoring and Evaluation*

(a) Formulation of a monitoring and evaluation system to keep track of problems, improve project implementation and measure socio-economic impact.
(b) *Integrated Environmental Programme*: Formulation of an environmental regulations plan and a long-range utilisation and monitoring scheme of the province's resources while preserving its ecological balance.

8.5.6 *Project Management*

Establishment of a Project Office to coordinate and monitor project implementation as well as plan subsequent phases of the project.

8.6 *Spatial Integration*

A unique decision factor in the Palawan IAD that influenced strongly the specific location of project components was the existence of a provincial road network which was not utilised fully.

The decisions on the location of basic infrastructure were primarily aimed at maximising the advantages derived from their mutual interconnection and establishing forward and backward linkages with agricultural production. In order to provide a more efficient delivery system for agricultural, social and governmental services, several major settlements were identified as the location of collective infrastructures servicing the farming population around these settlements. Services specified for development in these centres include veterinary services, auction market and slaughter houses for livestock, distribution of inputs and chemicals, machine shops, training and research, storage and warehouse, seed dispersal for agriculture, fish landing marketing and processing facilities for marine fishery and workshops for rural industry.

Where development interventions need to be integrated by a transport network, the provision of roads and bridges and port facilities would naturally constitute a critical factor. In PIADP this is reflected in the rather large percentage (46.3%) of total project cost to cover these infrastructure components, mostly new construction. The figure for new construction of feeder roads in agricultural development areas on both sides of southern Palawan ran to 144 kilometres and rehabilitation of feeder roads in these areas ran to 47 kilometres.

8.7 *De-linking the Poor*

The poverty orientation of PIADP is manifested in the priority given to areas where the majority of the population is below the poverty line. As mentioned earlier, an innovative planning methodology was adopted whereby the prioritisation of areas for specific components was influenced by the level of nutrition of specific target groups. The integration of nutrition considerations in project component planning was premised on the assumption that nutrition by itself can stand as an indicator of poverty and that the health conditions of poverty groups can be greatly improved by supporting food production whether as a primary or a secondary agricultural activity. Direct intervention to improve health and sanitation through water supply and sanitary latrines, malaria control and the fielding of nutrition workers was also identified as a special project component.

The most depressed households and communities are to be found in the forested hinterlands where they practise slash-and-burn agriculture. The project focuses on these areas not only as a strategy to assist these poverty groups but also to stabilise the upland environment thereby protecting agricultural lands in the lower slopes and plains areas. The upland stabilisation programme was designed as a fully participatory strategy where settlers are trained to develop a resource management consciousness and a capacity to assume responsibility for resource conservation in the areas they presently occupy.

With regard to lowland settlers, a critical concern of the project was the insecurity of tenure of small farmers in the absence of ownership titles on the land they tilled. As a result it was decided that the speeding up of survey and documentation to effect land transfer to legitimate occupants should be a component of the PIADP. The ownership of land and consequent security of tenure is a key element in the de-linking strategy of poverty-oriented projects such as PIADP. The possession of land enables the farmer to undertake longer range planning for his livelihood and improves his access to institutional support, particularly credit.

Finally, the provision of infrastructure support, particularly irrigation, in lowland farming was necessary to raise the production level of grain farmers, particularly those with small landholdings. As such projects are generally accompanied by the development of users' associations, they raise the level of consciousness of project beneficiaries of their own capabilities, which is an essential element of the delinking process.

9. Conclusion

The persistent problem of mass poverty in the rural areas continues to challenge policy-makers and development planners. The widening impacts of poverty today include critical environmental concerns and the socio-political problems of insurgency and rebellion. Almost two decades of experience with integrated rural development programmes have heightened the perception of these problems. This has in turn led to a recognition of the integrated approach and the need to sustain and strengthen efforts to alleviate the problem from an immediate and a long-term perspective.

Systematic efforts have been made to improve the conceptual framework, the planning process and management strategies in the search for effectiveness in dealing with the problems of rural development. The changes in the configuration of IAD projects from the first to the second generation and to new and pipeline projects demonstrate how the accumulated knowledge has been put to use in providing a clearer focus on the problems and defining more effective solutions.

10

INTEGRATED RURAL DEVELOPMENT. Lessons from Philippine Experience

Manuel P. Garcia Jr.

1. Introduction

Of the many issues in rural development administration, the question of the sectoral-functional as against the areal-spatial approach causes the most concern. Because of the view that the conventional government delivery system for various development services does not lead to a unified result due to its fragmented sectoral orientation, the need for an integrated approach to rural development has been recognised.

Many Third World countries have been implementing Integrated Rural Development (IRD) programmes as a way of accepting the challenge arising from the advantages of integration over sectoralisation, yet these IRD programmes are as difficult as any change-oriented innovation. In the two decades since the IRD approach has entered the rural development scene, numerous problems have been experienced in its operationalisation. Consequently, some analysts begin to question the viability of IRD as a development approach. A growing cynicism about IRD is illustrated by the comment of Koppel *et al.* (1985):

> Integrated rural development, integrated area development — these have acquired some notoriety in development circles. The glow has certainly dimmed. We can't be certain that the complexities these strategies seem to require are efficient, effective, or even feasible. There is widening suspicion that we really haven't yet seen an integrated development programme — at least not in terms of what we expected to see. It may also reflect a type of cynicism that integrated development simply cannot be done. Probably, where we really are is that we are uncertain whether the knife is dull or the

steak is tough — we just know we're having a hard time slicing through it.

On the other hand, we could conceivably still move towards a more meaningful development via the IRD approach, if problems such as the managerial implications of integration, target group identification, vertical-horizontal and areal-sectoral co-ordination, and grass-roots participation were to be effectively resolved.

This paper means to clarify some questions surrounding IRD by analysing the Philippine experience and drawing lessons from it. It mainly deals with major IRD/IAD projects under the auspices of the National Council on Integrated Area Development (NACIAD). For the purposes of this paper, no distinction is made between IRD and IAD: the two terms are used interchangeably. The ensuing sections of the paper present a brief overview, a critical analysis, and a discussion of the prospects of Philippine IRD.

2. An Overview of IRD in the Philippines

The formal recognition of the need for integrating the sectoral-oriented delivery mechanisms for rural development dates, in the Philippines, from 1973, when the Presidential Letter of Instruction 99 adopted the integrated area development (IAD) approach, and designated the Cabinet Co-ordinating Committee on Integrated Rural Development Projects (CCC-IRDP) the overseeing government entity. Attached to the National Economic and Development Authority (NEDA), the CCC-IRDP was authorised by the government to choose IAD sites and prepare and implement projects in these sites with funding from local and foreign sources. The IAD in Bicol Basin became the pilot IRD in the Philippines.

In May 1978, the CCC-IRDP was replaced by the National Council on Integrated Area Development (NACIAD) and, in October 1982, NACIAD membership was expanded to include the whole Cabinet. The NACIAD, as the supra agency for all IADs/IRDs, was established in order to integrate multi-sectoral activities and resources of the government rural development delivery system, which operates through the line departments. Administratively based at the Ministry of Agriculture during its formative period, the NACIAD was later given an autonomous status as IRD national co-ordinating agency under the Office of the Prime Minister, with the Cabinet Co-ordinators overseeing the IAD operations in major regional sites. Under the present government, the NACIAD was placed under the supervision of NEDA in July 1987.

Structurally, from the mid-fifties to the early seventies, the region had been the locus of administrative decentralisation. Following its adoption by the government, the IAD/IRD approach was made the rural development strategy and administrative mechanism for decentralised planning and implementation of area-oriented projects and programmes. At the same time, the region remained the geographical setting for administrative decentralisation for the sectoral line agencies whose activities are co-ordinated and synchronised through the integrated approach.

The Philippine IRD approach aims to accelerate growth in depressed areas in a region by integrating various sectoral programmes, projects and activities, increasing local participation in development planning and implementation, and distributing equitably economic gains through public investments in marginal and lagging sectors, so that these sectors can catch up with regional growth. It has six innovative features, namely: (1) defined geographical unit; (2) multi-sectoral operation; (3) spatial integration; (4) grassroots participation; (5) political commitment and (6) administrative organisational integration. Implemented in a sub-region within a "rural region", the IRD scheme uses both the politico-administrative boundaries and the ecological factors, i.e., river basin, island, to integrate "politico-economic administration with resource-based environmental/ecosystem management".

In an IRD area, the activities of the various government line agencies are co-ordinated to produce complementary effects on the beneficiaries. IRD spatial integration aims to connect the rural farming areas with urbanising town (market) centres. The participatory design of IRD integrates the grassroots' needs into government development plans through meaningful participation of the local people in the planning and decision-making process, and in the implementation of the various programmes and projects. The political commitment to IRD is facilitated through the designation of a Cabinet Co-ordinator in every major IAD project. The programme/project office (PO) is established with co-ordinating authority and jurisdiction over the multi-sectoral activities included in IRD plans and programmes (Limcaoco, 1984: 17-18).

A typical IRD package includes the following components: (1)

agricultural development, comprising pilot demonstration farms, extension, and irrigation; (2) infrastructures such as farm-to-market roads, flood control, bridges, and ports; (3) social services like nutrition, health, and environmental sanitation; (4) rural industries; and (5) local-level development planning. To operationalise the IRD strategy, programmes and projects are guided by the following objectives: (1) increased economic productivity; (2) greater employment opportunities; (3) more equitable distribution of wealth; (4) effective delivery of social services; and (5) increased political and administrative capacity. As the overall administrator of IRD, the NACIAD anchors its operation on the following: (1) institutionalisation of the implementing mechanisms for IAD through formal planning, monitoring and budgetary controls; (2) formulation of an integrated framework plan to guide the development of the depressed areas; (3) rationalisation of the participation of the rural people through their local government in development planning and implementation; (4) initiation of small-scale and high-impact projects utilising available indigenous resources; (5) efficient mobilisation and channelling of multi-sectoral resources into integrated rural development activities; and (6) generation of private sector participation in IAD projects and establishment of the appropriate mechanism for it (NACIAD, 1986: 10-16).

Since 1973 the NACIAD has undertaken nine major IAD projects (see section 2 of Chapter 9 by Nietes, in this volume– Eds.). Most of these have already ended or are about to end. Only two of the nine will continue until 1989. Presently, the NACIAD has identified a number of potential IADs called "planning areas" where technical assistance in integrated plan formulation has been extended and some initial foreign grants have been provided. The more visible co-operating government agencies are the Department of Public Works and Highways (DPWH), National Irrigation Administration (NIA), Department of Agriculture (DA), Department of Agrarian Reform (DAR), Department of Health (DOH), Department of Environment and Natural Resources (DENR), Philippine Ports Authority (PPA), Central Bank (CB), National Manpower and Youth Council (NMYC), National Electrification Administration (NEA), and Philippine Coconut Authority (PCA).

The NACIAD, as the national administering and co-ordinating body for major IAD projects, has a multi-tiered set-up comprising of the Council Proper, the Programme Co-ordinating Committee (PROCOM), the Technical Secretariat, and the Project Offices (POs) (Fig. 10.1). The prominent members of the Council Proper are the secretaries of DPWH, DA, DAR, Department of Finance (DF), DENR, Department of National Defence (DND), DOH, Department of Local Governments (DLG), Department of Budget and Management (DBM), and Department of Trade and Industry (DTI); the Director-General of NEDA; and the Executive Director of NACIAD. By virtue of Executive Order 230, which transfers NACIAD to NEDA, the NEDA Director-General takes the leadership of the Council Proper at the moment. The NACIAD Executive Director assumes the leadership of the Technical Secretariat and chairs the PROCOM which is composed of Duty/Assistant Secretaries of the Council members, and the heads of the Presidential Management Staff (PMS) and the NIA.

The PROCOM assists the Council Proper in ensuring commitments of the co-operating member agencies to IAD projects. On the other hand, the Technical Secretariat (TS) extends staff support to the Council Proper. The TS is composed of the Project Planning and Development Department (PPDD), Policy Research and Development Department (PRDD), Programme Management Department (PMD), and Finance and Administrative Office (FAO). The PPDD prepares IAD plans for identified areas, while the PMD monitors and evaluates major IAD projects. The PRDD conducts policy research on IAD operation and formulates policy recommendations and guidelines needed in NACIAD decision-making. At the IAD sites, POs are established to perform the decentralised function of administrative co-ordination of the inter-agency planning and implementation of IAD project components.

Each of the major IAD projects has its own Project Office, which normally has a Manila liaison unit and which consists of: project planning (for plan preparation and project development), project implementation management (for inter-agency co-ordination, monitoring and evaluation), and finance and administration (for budgeting, accounting and personnel management) (Fig. 10.2). NACIAD (1986: 20) indicates that some POs have directly implemented some IAD components, although the usual arrangement is for the co-operating line agencies to implement these components. A few, like PIADP and BRBDP, have established institutional development structures for target group participation and for serving as conduits of assistance from national development programmes. The POs in Bicol and Palawan have established localised feedback mechanisms from the provincial down to the village level to encourage the participation of beneficiaries in project planning and implementation. On the other hand, POs in

Samar, Cagayan, Palawan, Bohol and Bicol have implemented project components directly, in co-ordination with the technical agencies.

As Table 10.1 shows, while all the major IAD projects have similar internal core structures, they differ somewhat in their inter-agency co-ordinating structures as well as in the number and nature of project components established. In every PO, there is at least one inter-agency executive and/or advisory committee helping the PO director implement the IAD programmes, projects and activities.

Concerning manpower, on average the number of PO personnel per IAD project is 92; however the variance is considerable with a high of 169 in the SIRDP Office and a low of 18 in the BIADP Office. The majority of the PO personnel are specially hired staff with much higher salaries than those of regular government officials. Meanwhile, more than 5,000 seconded staff from co-operating line agencies (i.e. nearly 13% of the total government field staff) have been deployed to the various IAD projects.

Table 10.1: Comparative Features of IAD Project Organisations

Project	Core structure (internal)			Co-ordinating structure (inter-agency)	
	Project Planning & Development	Project Implementation Management	Finance & Administration	Project Executive/ Advisory Committee	Major Project Components
MIRDP(1)	v	v	v	2	6
BRBDP(2)	v	v	v	2	6
CIADP	v	v	v	1	2
SIRDP	v	v	v	3	2
PIADP(3)	v	v	v	1	6
ZDSDP	v	v	v	3	5
ABC-LSP	v	v	v	1	3
PRIP	v	v	v	1	5
BIADP	v	v	v	2	3

Notes: (1) With two parallel provincial POs.
(2) With three inter-agency provincial management committees and 20 sub-provincial integrated development areas (IDAs).
(3) With institutional development unit.

Fig. 10.1: Organisational Structure

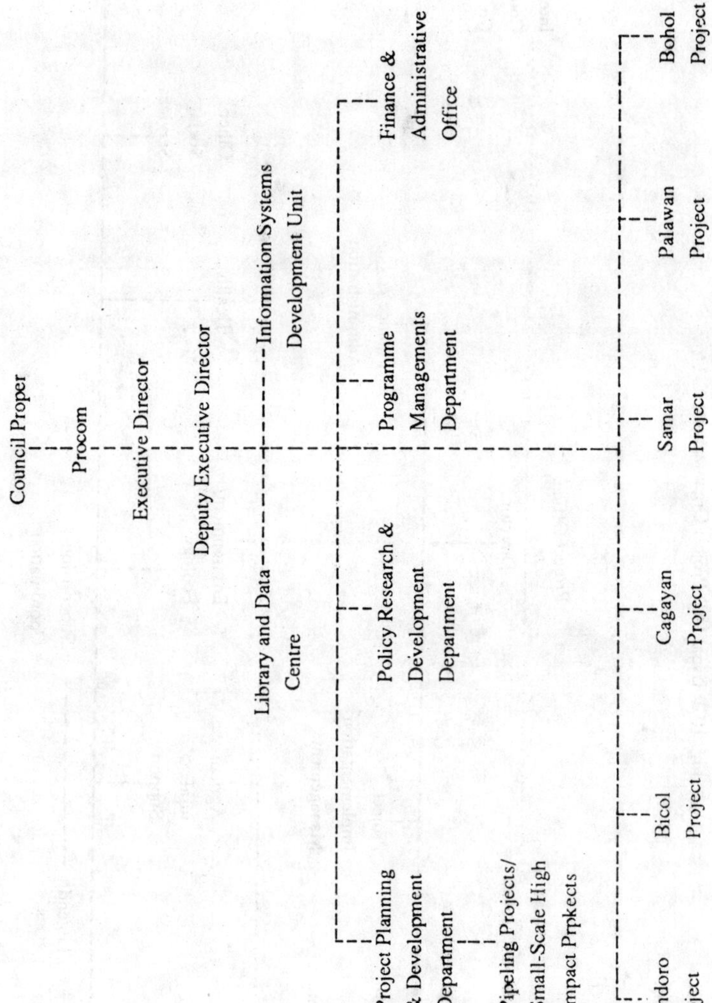

Fig. 10.2: Usual IAD Project Organization

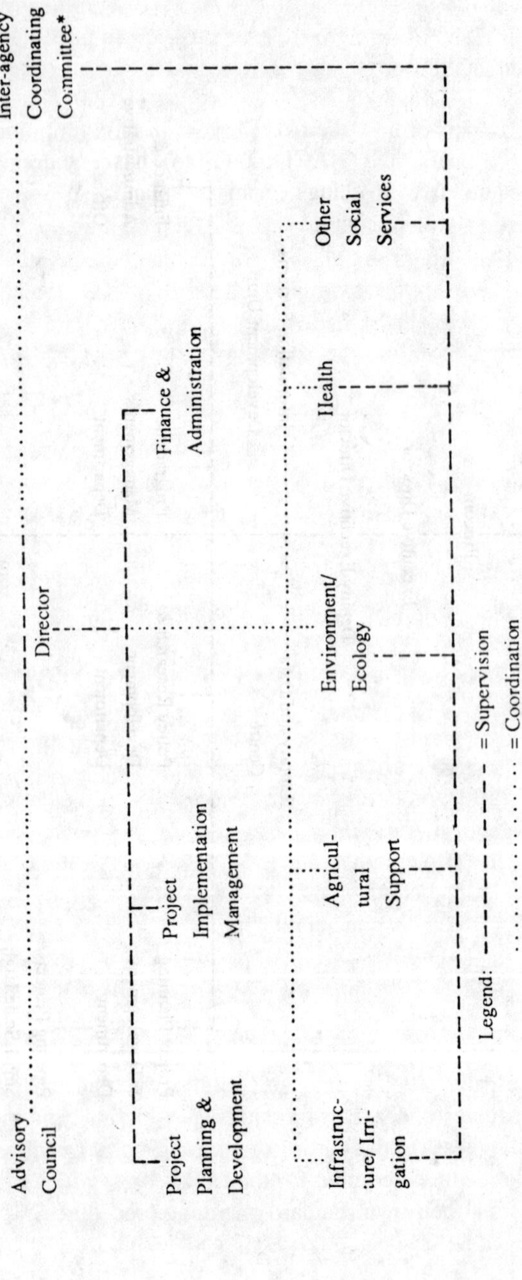

* Each head of a cooperating line agency is supervising his own component manager.

With regard to funding, at the end of 1985 the total IRD budget reached US$784 million. The shares of the Government of the Philippines (GOP), and of foreign assistance vary from project to project; for instance, in ZDSDP these shares are equal, while the GOP share is 71 per cent for CIADP and only 29 per cent for BIADP.

In its analysis of how the IRD projects in the Philippines fared over the past 15 years, the NACIAD (1986) has categorised the IAD problems into five headings, namely: planning; organization and management; implementation; monitoring and evaluation; and sustainability. The major drawbacks in IAD planning are attributed to five factors: (1) overemphasis on infrastructure; (2) difficulty of the special project mode to lead eventually to full integration of activities into the regular functions of the co-operating government line agencies after the project phase-out; (3) absence of an explicit provision for building the administrative/institutional capability of the co-operating line agencies and local authorities to sustain post-project operations (except for ZDSDP, which was effective in transferring IAD resources and responsibilities to the Provincial Government due to a systemic institutionalisation process); (4) failure to conduct reliable base-line studies before the start of the project; and (5) failure to define effective and workable mechanisms for target beneficiaries' participation.

Problems of organisation and management relate to the co-ordinating and *ad hoc* (matrix) nature of the IAD POs and the ultimate reversion of the IAD special project phase-out. This complicated *ad hoc* arrangement has induced organisational conflicts resulting from divergent sectoral orientations of personnel, divided loyalties of seconded staff (mother agency *versus* IAD PO, and personal jealousies due to different salaries than the PO staff).

In project implementation, despite the IAD special mode which eliminates bureaucratic delays, the implementing (co-operating) agencies still tend to concentrate more on their regular programmes than on their IAD contributions through the project components. The failure of a single component to be implemented due to "budgetary mispriority" reduces the integrated impact. Inter-agency co-ordination in IAD project implementation is stalled by the natural resistance of central line agencies to relinquish control over funds allocated for sectoral components under their functional jurisdiction" and the "difficulty and unwillingness on the part of sectoral agencies to adjust to the systems and procedures required for the IAD project which may be highly divergent from their own standard operating procedures".

Moreover, the NACIAD examines the monitoring and evaluation problems as arising from inadequate baseline socio-economic data, the difficulty of attribution of socio-economic changes, and "immeasurables", considering that the IAD has "more intangible than tangible or measurable impact". Lastly, the problem of sustaining the IAD organisation is not felt so much at the level of NACIAD as at that of the PO, with its limited lifespan, and at the grassroots level where the established organisations of the beneficiaries may disintegrate due to inadequate institutionalisation.

In fairness to NACIAD, it is worth mentioning that some structural problems identified during the Phase I period were given solutions on a case-to-case basis. For example, the problem of responsibility transfer was solved by the ZDSDP in its Phase II when a systematic institutionalisation process was implemented. However, the other IADS were not as effective. While in the earlier IADs, the POs were staff-heavy, latter IADs, i.e., BIADP, ZDSP Phase II, had smaller staffs. Attempts to improve the monitoring and evaluation system through computer-based data handling were made. Lastly, the designation of Cabinet Co-ordinators (now Cabinet Officers for Regional Development or CORDs), and the transfer of NACIAD to NEDA, consolidate the IADs into a unified Cabinet-level system with the central planning body as the overall supervising agency.

3. A Critical Analysis of Philippine IRD

The NACIAD has admitted that while the IRD concept has been recognised as sound, it is by its translation into how IAD planning is effectively done, how the implementation of multi-sectoral activities is managed and co-ordinated, and how the target beneficiaries participate in and benefit from the process, that it should be evaluated. The performance of IAD in the Philippines will be analysed below, from the points of view of integration, decentralisation, and economic empowerment and genuine development of the rural poor.

3.1 *Strategy of Spatial-Functional Integration*

The spatial or areal dimension of IRD makes it highly innovative, in contrast with the sectoral-functional nature of the conventional government service delivery system. The first mechanism for spatial-functional integration is through infrastructure, where the goal is to achieve the geographical integration of farming and other production areas with urbanising town centres serving as tradeposts for the rural sector. These town centres also serve to define government functional areas for the delivery of services in health, nutrition, agricultural extension, social services, political affairs, local governance, etc., to their rural hinterlands. The high percentage (70% to 80%) of IRD fund allocation to infrastructure such as roads and bridges could attest to this.

While infrastructure could be instrumental in areal integration of various development functions such as production and marketing, it could also result in enclave economies where the rural poor are at a disadvantage because infrastructures are veered to serve the rural elite. For instance, in CIADP, a national highway leading to Port Irene in the far north was built despite the absence of human settlements along the way, according to a former employee. The same employee added that the former Cabinet Co-ordinator, who was also concessionaire, allegedly acceded to the construction of this highway in order to facilitate the transports from the concession site to the seaport. There are other unreported cases where the national highway had to be re-routed to accommodate "political demands" of regional politicians.

In Antique Province, one of the NACIAD planning areas (potential IADS after Phase II), the U.N. Economic and Social Commission for Asia and the Pacific (ESCAP), through its Inter-agency Committee on Integrated Rural Development, allocated 45 per cent of its project budget to livelihood support services (e.g., demonstration farms, nurseries, farm mechanisation, livestock breeding centres, and cottage industries) and 30 per cent to training and organization development, while only 25 per cent went to infrastructures such as irrigation and roads (RD No. 9 1987). According to ESCAP, this reversal in IAD strategy from "hardware" (i.e. infrastructure) to "software", i.e., institutional development, was done because of the inability of infrastructure to facilitate "physical integration" for rural development.

The second integrating mechanism is organisational/institutional co-ordination among the co-operating agencies. Spatial-functional integration could be enhanced through administrative organisational matricing, where the IRD would serve as the "connective tissue" that links two sets of delivery organisations — the sectoral-functional line agencies organised hierarchically from the national down to the municipal level on the one hand, and geographically-oriented local government units (LGUs) based in the provinces, cities, and municipalities on the other.

With its own national budget allocation, the programme/project office (PO) of Philippine IRD is given co-ordinating authority over the various IRD components, e.g., agriculture, physical infrastructure, health and nutrition, and other social services, contributed by co-operating line agencies. The PO serves as field secretariat and co-ordinating body, while the project staff to work on the various components are provided by the co-operating line agencies as seconded staff. There is also an inter-agency executive co-ordinating committee or council, composed of the heads of the co-operating line agencies and the LGUs. The resulting administrative organisational structure is an *ad hoc* one featuring a matrix set-up.

In other words, with regard to the activities performed by the co-operating line agencies, the PO or integrated area manager serves as IRD project co-ordinator, as per inter-agency agreement, although the inter-agency personnel seconded to the project are obliged to follow his instructions ("supervision") in connection with the master IAD plan, and to submit regular progress reports in order to achieve co-ordination and complementation in the delivery of the various components. In effect, the personnel of the co-operating line agencies have two bosses — their own agency superiors at the provincial/regional level, and the IAD manager/director.

The NACIAD admits that the IRD POs, being merely co-ordinating bodies, have no authority or control over the execution of IRD components and activities, which are done by the co-operating line agencies. Moreover, the IRDs have to deal with the centralised and sectoralised national budgetary system, where the funds for the various IRD components are separately released to and controlled by the respective executing line agencies — the process called "routine mode of implementation". Although the "special project mode of implementation" has been allowed to some degree with regard to IRD operation, including a special instance of permitting direct release of funds to the Regional Project Office (as in the NEDA-administered Central Visayas Rural Projects), which then allocated the funds to the executing line agencies, the routine mode of project implementation remains the dominant procedure. Consequently, the "mandate to coordinate cannot prevail against the centralised executive authority of line agencies and sometimes that of the local governments and co-existing regional bodies". Furthermore, "co-ordination is particularly difficult for project components that are implemented through routine mode where activities to support IAD are integrated into the agency's regular work programme and use personnel who are not fully released from their regular functions. Under this set-up, in the event of resource constraints, or during peak periods in the activity system, the agency usually would give higher priority to its own regular function rather than its commitment to the IAD project." (NACIAD, 1986).

3.2 *Strategy of Expansion of the Economic Base of the Rural Sector*

In the Philippine context, small islands are relatively poorer than the larger ones. For example, in one region — Region IV or Southern Tagalog — where provinces are classified as "mainland" and "island", the island provinces have lower per capita income and greater incidence of poverty. The government ascribes the underdevelopment of many island provinces, including the IAD islands such as Mindoro, Samar, Palawan and Bohol, to physical constraints mainly due to lack of infrastructure. Thus, Phase I of IRDs in the Philippines was basically infrastructural, while Phase II continues the infrastructural thrust of Phase I while complementing it with institutional development for both the participating line agencies and the target beneficiary groups.

The IRD rationale for overemphasis on infrastructural development in Phase I is the role of infrastructure in stimulating socio-economic growth. The problem of regional economic imbalance or disparity is addressed through the construction of physical infrastructure such as roads and irrigation systems in the lagging regions. Development planners believe that to connect the many poorer towns with the few richer ones in the island-province is to spur rural development in the area. Whatever growth is generated in this way is expected to trickle down to benefit the rural poor. If irrigation increases farm production and roads facilitate trade, then the small farmers may be able to sell their surplus agricultural produce more conveniently to the urbanising town centres.

Other IRD mechanisms for expanding the economic base of the rural sector especially in depressed regions include agricultural development packages, small-scale high impact projects, rural industrialisation, appropriate technology and human resources development, and mobilisation and utilisation of local or indigenous resources. These have been continuing from Phase I to the end of Phase II. The remaining regular IADs, such as those in Bohol and Palawan, and the post-Phase II planning areas which have foreign financial support in the form of grants, will be guided by a strategy shift from infrastructure to livelihood support services (i.e., software projects and medium-scale investment planning) where the participation of the private sector (business groups, non-government organisations) is encouraged.

It is somewhat paradoxical that despite the various attempts to uplift the economic situation of the lagging rural sector, the basic problems of poverty, inequality, and lack of gainful employment still hound even the IAD-covered areas. In its performance analysis of the major IAD projects, the NACIAD (1986: 58) admits that:

> Evaluation conducted after a major part of all of the physical components of IAD projects have been completed showed that achievements in terms of socio-economic impact have been limited and have tended to benefit population groups that were better situated economically and not the targeted rural poor. Likewise, the observed performance of the productive sectors failed to show an automatic chain reaction in terms of regional scale sectoral growth that can be positively attributed to such infrastructure.

In operational terms, available evaluation studies (Koppel *et al.*, 1985; IPCC, 1983) and the author's visits to some IAD sites reveal insignificant changes in the economic profile of the rural poor who constitute the majority of the Philippine population, although some sectors have derived benefits from IADs.

Generally, the IAD strategy could be credited in terms of serving as conduit of foreign assistance funds in the form of direct grants or concessionary loans for rural and agricultural development. The experience of Zamboanga del Sur and Bicol indicates that there has been an expansion of the economic base of the rural sector, since the IAD-constructed infrastructures have led to more economic activities in the area, although the benefits from such activities have not been captured by the rural poor.

In Zamboanga del Sur, even after the Phase I of ZDSDP, indicators of both social and economic development have been encouraging. The project construction of 250 kilometres of road was followed by the establishment of power lines and the increase in the mobility of the population and of visits to places both within and outside of the province. In 1976, only 8 per cent of the respondents visited Pagadian City, the provincial capital, at least once a year; however, in 1981 this figure rose to 54 per cent.

The respondents' use of electricity jumped from 5 per cent in 1976 to 24 per cent in 1981. In 1981, nearly 70 per cent of the responding households owned radios, while the number of posted letters (delivered to towns and villages by passenger jeeps) increased with the new roads constructed by the project. There was also an improvement in the level of reporting of government field officials who could already travel easily to the provincial capital. Farm productivity improved due to agricultural programmes in irrigation, extension, livestock, and crop development. Real incomes increased by between 33 per cent to 42 per cent over the five-year period. There was a decrease in mortality and a greater awareness of the need for family planning over the period concerned (ZDSDP 1985; IPC 1983). During Phase II of the ZDSDP, the emerging observation was that, the development and progress in the adjacent province of Zamboanga del Norte, with its profitable trade and commercial relations with Visayas and more stable peace and order situation, were approximated by Zamboanga del Sur because of the latter's IAD project (ZDSDP, 1985: 29).

In Bicol, the BRBDP programme areas, corresponding to the three provinces and 20 integrated development areas (IDAs) covered, showed a significant increase of 23 per cent in the average household income from all sources between 1978 and 1983. In terms of road density, there was a gradual increase from 0.39 in 1971 to 0.57 in 1982 for the whole BRBDP area coverage. While in 1978 the income source in the three provinces was basically agricultural, in 1983 the picture was somewhat changed, particularly for Albay, where 62.2 per cent of income came from business earnings, wages and salaries and 37.8 per cent from farming and fishing. In 1983 Camarines Sur was still predominantly agricultural with the income share of farming and fishing at 61.7 per cent and that of non-farm activities at 38.3 per cent. The income of Sorsogon was more or less equally shared by farming (51.6%) and non-farming (48.4%). The better economic performance of Albay may be explained by its relatively well developed road network and by the larger share of its income coming from the industry and service sector (NACIAD 1986).

3.3 *Strategy of Development for the Rural Poor*

The failure to gather baseline data on agrarian tenurial status, among others, led to inadequate IAD planning in such a way that the IRD approach hinges more on productivity than on social equity. The development structure by which the rural poor break their dependence on the rural rich has not been put in place, although IADs provide some participatory mechanisms to minimise the effects of the power of the rural elite.

As indicated earlier, one of the original IRD concerns was to institute grassroots participation in programme planning and implementation through the "bottom-up" approach. If the rural poor were to control matters that affect them through systematic grassroots participation, then the IAD strategy of development for the rural poor would logically lead to the severing of their dependence links to the rural rich. One of the key issues of IRD is precisely how to identify the rural poor as target beneficiaries (Iglesias, 1982) and eventually empower them through local resource mobilisation and utilisation. Since IAD planning depended on regional and provincial statistics based on aggregate census data (NACIAD, 1986:62), the baseline data on which plans for the rural poor were based were generally insufficient, since official census-type data do not delve into land tenure and wealth or income distribution.

Although the IAD sites in the Philippines are depressed agricultural areas with considerable incidence of share tenancy and rural insurgency, as in Bicol, the "poorest of the poor", as the IRD avowed target groups, have hardly been reached. The millions of Filipino landless farm workers, share tenants and upland dwellers remain miserably poor and desperate. Even NACIAD (1986: 58) accepts the fact that IAD projects have so far benefited the rural groups that are economically better-off. Similarly, the Los Banos-based Agricultural Policy and Strategy Team (1986: 72) questions the capacity of IAD projects to address the common problems of rural poverty and inequality by contending that:

> It is also questionable whether the IAD projects have brought about significant reductions in poverty, although they may have increased income and productivity. The bottom line, however, is that these projects do not attempt to undertake any meaningful asset redistribution and thus, in the short-term, before employment effects are significant, the benefits will be distributed according to the initial resource endowments. In brief, one can say that these projects, while location-specific, are not really "poverty programs" since they do not deliberately target the poor communities as program beneficiaries.

In his trips to two IAD projects, SIRDP in Northern Samar and ABC-LSP in Capiz, the author observed that the IRD grassroots organisations had not been established. In Capiz Land Settlement Project, the agricultural service centres (ASCs) contributed by the Department of Agriculture were the only visible IAD component serving the small upland farmers who are the dominant settlers. Being unorganised, the upland farmer-settlers lacked the capacity to bargain with the IAD project management in terms of continuity of service. During the author's visit, the upland settlers were facing tenurial uncertainty due to the failure of the government to give them homestead rights. This would have been the opportune time to organise them for the purpose of improving their effectiveness in bargaining with government entities as well as with unscrupulous landlords who attempted to ease them out of the lands that they occupied.

On the other hand, in Northern Samar, the overemphasis on infrastructure had relegated institutional development to the background. The project's institutional development officer, who was already initiating community organising activities, was discouraged by IAD management to proceed along this direction. Consequently, the attempt to encourage grassroots participation was stalled. At the same time, the agricultural development component of the project was not also proceeding very well, because there was no "push" from the small farmers and there was lack of initiative on the part of the agricultural technicians assigned to the area.

In Bicol, the strategy of empowering the poor and mobilising local resources gained some headway because of the conscious effort made by the co-operating line agencies, particularly the National Irrigation Administration, to organise the small farmers into communal irrigation associations using the community organization methodology. Moreover, the division of the whole river basin area into manageable IDAs was conducive to grassroots participation and community organising activities. Despite the deliberate efforts of the IAD personnel to organise the small farmers so they could effectively receive the agricultural development services, and in spite of the indication that household income increased over time, as already mentioned, the overall effect of the IAD programme in Bicol "was to worsen the income inequality in favour of the rich households", although NACIAD (1986: 97) reasons that the programme could not have induced the worsening of income inequality in the area since this phenomenon is not unique to the Bicol region. On the other hand, in ZDSDP area, available data gathered after Phase I indicate that the income distribution within the IAD provincial coverage "showed only a slight improvement over the same period" (ZDSDP, 1985: 17).

The Bicol data (from the Bicol Multipurpose Surveys) indicate that between 1978 and 1983 the top household income quintile had the highest income increases (between 89% and 214%), while the lowest quintile had income increases of only between 37 per cent and 53 per cent. In Zamboanga del Sur, from 1976 to 1981 the lowest farming household quartile had an increase in income of nearly 42 per cent, while the income of the highest quartile increased by around 34 per cent.

On a pilot basis, support services to agrarian reform like land consolidation and supervised low-interest credit programmes have shown that they can work well. However, they also entail high overhead costs for the government. In the Bula-Minalabac IDA in Bicol, the Land Consolidation Project led to the distribution of provisional Certificates of Land Transfer to all project farmer-beneficiaries. Sufficient support services also led to a payment rate of 90 per cent for irrigation fees, as the farm income markedly increased. IAD projects are quite effective in facilitating farmers' access to fertiliser and chemical inputs and to more widespread institutional agricultural credit, as shown by the experience of Camarines Sur.

The prospects for improved income distributions are however not promising, even in IAD-covered areas. Given the mangled land reform resulting from the emasculation of the Comprehensive Agrarian Reform Programme (CARP) by the landlord-dominated Lower House of the Philippine Congress, the Filipino rural poor are unlikely to break their dependence on the rural elite.

3.4 *Strategy of Structural Decentralisation*

The decentralisation of organisational structures of IAD projects should aim at creating changes in the local power structure so as to enhance the access of the rural poor to decision-making and to socio-economic resources (Carino, 1986, uses the term "participatory decentralisation").

In instances where IAD project operations facilitate participation, in the form of grassroots decentralisation, as in the IDAs in Bicol where beneficiaries' organisations (e.g. farmers' communal irrigation associations) are formed, the local power structure is somewhat transformed to enhance the small farmers' access to and control of socio-economic resources, such as communal irrigation systems and village-level health programmes. Viable livelihood support mechanisms such as irrigation would also enable the grassroots organisations to carry out other profitable ventures like cooperative stores, processing facilities, and improved transport (Koppel, et al., 1985). The IAD strategy of structural decentralisation should therefore focus not only in making the POs effectively decentralised but also in institutionalising grassroots receiving organisations.

Citing the finding of the USAID-GOP evaluation study conducted in 1983 (cf. Koppel et al., 1985), the NACIAD (1986: 117) points out that the major determinant of good performance and sustainable benefits is the degree of beneficiaries' involvement in decision-making from project conceptualisation to implementation. Where such involvement is seriously pursued, as in the Bula-Minalabac IDA, there is a corresponding high rate of adoption of the technological package and payment of irrigation fees, as well as good participation of farmers in irrigation maintenance activities and related investments to generate additional income. Opposite was the experience of Libmanan-Cabusao IDA which had difficulty in irrigation management due to the failure of the project to involve the beneficiaries in decision-making.

4. Some Conclusions and Recommendations

As already discussed, the NACIAD has shown some flexibility by learning from the lessons of Phase I experience. Furthermore, the lessons generated from the experience of Phase II and the current IADs in operation are also taken into account in mapping the implementation strategy for the planning or potential areas in the post-Phase II period. In the Philippine IRD experience, the spatial or geographical considerations are highlighted through the recognition of the need for area-based functional centres in the urbanising towns of the rural region which is subject of integrated development. From these centres, development impulses are transmitted to the surrounding peripheral areas. This has been described by Bronger (1980:182) as "development centre strategy" as a spatial form of decentralisation. The rural sector could be effectively reached through these development centres situated between the metropolitan headquarters and the rural peripheries.

Generally, the Philippine IAD projects are effective in stimulating growth, while their increasing number since 1973 up to the Phase II period is a clear indication of replicability. NACIAD is serious about IAD sustainability; it boldly declares (NACIAD, 1986: 75):

> The practice in second phase IAD projects and pipeline projects in involving local governments in IAD management and transferring to them knowledge and resources in IAD planning, implementation and monitoring is the major step toward building sustainable organization for integrated rural development which in turn will help build the sustainability and self-reliance of grassroots organization.

The following recommendations, based on the lessons from experience discussed above, aim at improving the performance of the current IAD schemes so as to make them more easily manageable, client-oriented and need-responsive.

The Bicol IDAs are worth emulating by other IAD projects. Operationally, a cluster of contiguous towns along the axis of the national and provincial highways could collectively constitute a sub-IAD area called IDA, which Bicol experience indicates is easily manageable. This IDA may also be described as a "development centre", which transmits development impulses to the surrounding peripheral or lagging areas.

It would be advantageous for NACIAD to continue the strategy shift from infrastructure to livelihood support, except in the case of farm-to-market roads, which are both livelihood support and rural-urban physical integrator. The potential of rural industries should further be examined since they could be the entry point for the private sector participation which is still lacking in IADs.

The IAD areas should be made into priority areas for the implementation of the comprehensive agrarian reform programme envisaged by the Aquino Administration. As previously indicated, more social equity measures should be implemented by IAD projects in order to improve income and wealth distribution and to make the rural poor independent of the traditional elite in the countryside. The stimulation of growth without social equity provisions could lead to more inequality and poverty in the long run.

The IADs should facilitate the formation of more grassroots organisations — the beneficiaries' symbol of unity, common interest, and self-reliance — because they serve as conduits for local resource mobilisation and empowerment of the rural poor. It is also through these organisations that participatory decentralisation is achieved with the beneficial result of expediting the small farmers' access to, and control of, socio-economic resources.

While the IAD special project mode should be maintained and even reinforced with funding power (as in the case of the Central Visayas Rural project) for greater authority over the co-operating agencies, systematic programming for phase-out and responsibility/resource transfer should become the core of the institutionalisation process as each IAD project is terminating. Before a new IAD project is established, thorough and objective evaluation of both completed and on-going IADs should be carried out.

REFERENCES

Agricultural Policy and Strategy Team, Agenda for Action for the Philippine Rural Sector. University of the Philippines at Los Banos and Philippine Institute for Development Studies, 1986.

Bronger, Dirk, "The Relevance of the Development Center Strategy to the Philippines", *Philippine Geographical Journal*, Vol. XXIV, No. 4 (1980).

Carino, Ledivina V. "Participatory Decentralization and Primary Health Care: A Comparative Study of Governmental and Non-Governmental Approaches", *Research Report submitted to APDCKAF*, Kuala Lumpur, 1986.

Garcia, Manuel Jr. P. "Patron Clientage: Its Implications on Agrarian Relations Improvement", Paper submitted to the Institute of Labor and Manpower Studies, Manila, October 31, 1983.

Iglesias, Gabriel U. "Managing Integrated Rural Development: Key Issues and Problems", *Philippine Journal of Public Administration*, Vol. XXVI, No. 1 (1982).

IPC, "The Socio-Economic Impact of Development Programs in Zamboanga del Sur". *Quezon City: Ateneo de Manila*, Institute of Philippine Culture, 1983.

Koppel, Bruce M. et al "An Evaluation of the Bicol River Basin Development Program". USAID-GOP, Manila, May 1985.

Limcaoco, J. Andres A. "The Integrated Area development Approach to Regional Development", *Philippine Planning Journal*, Vol. XV, No. 2 (1984).

NACIAD, "State of the Art Report on Integrated Rural Development (IRD), Philippines". Metro Manila: Program Planning and Development Department, NACIAD, 1986.

RD (Rural Development, FAO), No. 9, 1987.

ZDSDP, *Project Completion Report.* Prepared for NACIAD and ADAB, December 31, 1985.

PART II

IRD EXPERIENCES – INDIAN SPECIFICITIES

11

INTEGRATED RURAL DEVELOPMENT: Indian Specificities

Introduction

The recognition of imbalances and distortions in the economy inherited from the colonial era impelled Indian planners increasingly to use development as a major component of the Five Year Plans. Thus rural development programmes are inherent to planning in Independent India and not ephemeral beings whose lives are determined by the facts of international funding.

The emphasis on different strategies of rural development has, however, been changing over time. The shifts in emphasis emanate from some of the larger events and concerns of the society, as well from the failure of the earlier programmes to meet their objectives.

Soon after independence the community development programme was launched, cooperative institutions were promoted and agricultural development received major attention. Under the community development programme the country was divided into development blocks, each consisting of about 100 villages and provided with extension specialists in agriculture, animal husbandry, social education etc. This was supplemented with health services, family planning, small scale industry, marketing and related facilities. The block headquarters located in rural surroundings were to function as nodes through which rural development programmes could be carried out. In due course each block set up an elected advisory body.

The programme did not come up to expectations. Its failure is generally explained as follows: The villages were grouped haphazardly; neither the quality nor the quantity of services provided at block level were sufficient to meet the needs; benefits accrued to the land owning groups without touching the poorer sections of the population; and the programme as a whole was oriented towards welfare rather than development.

This was also the time when the country as a whole was facing problems of stagnant agricultural production, further compounded by rapidly growing population. Thus, a new strategy for agricultural development known as the Intensive Agricultural District Programme (IADP) was introduced, with technical cooperation from the Ford Foundation in India. Under this programme, (started in 1960), a few districts with favourable physical conditions for agriculture were selected for intensive efforts, involving provision of agricultural inputs, marketing/facilities and administrative and institutional devices deemed necessary for modernisation and commercialisation of agriculture. Over a time, the IADP was extended in a less intensive manner to about two-fifths of the Indian districts, under the name of Intensive Agricultural Area Programme (IAAP).

This new programme has been credited with the initiation of a "Green Revolution" in India. While the IADP districts in some parts of Punjab, Western Uttar Pradesh and the delta tracts in the South recorded substantial increase in productivity, it was found that in general IAAP districts performed no better than non-IAAP districts. At the same time it has been pointed out that the new seed, fertiliser technology is biased towards irrigated areas and has given rise to increased disparities in inter-personal and inter-regional income in rural areas. Yet the programme at least bailed the country out of a difficult agricultural situation.

Along with these agricultural development programmes, pilot research projects in growth centres were launched in 1969 to be operated for five years. Under these projects, block plans were prepared for about 20 blocks. A hierarchy of service centres was defined and general service centre plans were made. This project was essentially geared to increase the effectiveness of delivery of services, by identifying a set of criteria to guide locational decisions. This may also be treated as an attempt at spatial integration of investments in infrastructure and services.

The questions of rural growth (largely agricultural) and of physical access to infrastructure and services were thus addressed by these two strategies. Of the two, the former received substantial financial allocation in the development plans and as seen resulted in tangible benefits, whereas the latter remained more of a drawing board project failing to make it to the implementation stage.

The removal of wide spread poverty and unemployment which persisted subsequently became the centre of the plans. The electoral slogan '*Garibi Hatao*' (remove poverty) metamorphosed and was formalised as a major strategy for removal of poverty and unemployment with the introduction of IRDP. This was introduced on a modest scale during the Fifth Plan and later not only was extended to cover the entire rural population but also received larger plan allocations. This programme is viewed as a strategy of direct attack on poverty by providing poor rural families with income generating assets to cross the poverty line. IRDP attracted, maximum public attention, and continues to remain the major concern.

The strategy is also target-oriented, both interms of population coverage (those below poverty line, socially handicapped — Scheduled Castes and Scheduled Tribes) as well as physical coverage by setting targets of number of families to be assisted and quantum of employment— wage and self-employment — by specific period.

In addition to this, a number of programmes, directly aimed at enhancing the living conditions of rural poor had also been initiated — free house sites, subsidised housing, electric connection, health and nutrition programmes and spread of formal education.

Thus, rural development programmes in India can be profitably seen as a three pronged strategy:

(a) Economic package to promote accelerated growth in agriculture and allied activities through investments in irrigation and other inputs into agriculture as well as incentives offered to rural industrial projects. By and large this approach addressed the question of growth.

(b) The area approach — locational policies to increase rural access to infrastructural facilities — geared to tackling issues relating to spatial inequities in physical access to infrastructure.

(c) The target group approach — to directly deal with the problems of poverty and unemployment in order to reduce interpersonal or vertical inequities.

Given the prominence to IRDP and rural development in Indian plan allocations, the preoccupation of the section of academia interested in rural population has been in the recent years to review and analyse the various aspects of the programme. Similarly prior to this, the green revolution strategy, and the growth centre strategy have also undergone intense scrutiny. Such endeavours have brought to fore major issues therein.

How relevant is the programme can be gauged by an evaluation of its impact. In the process, the strength and weaknesses of the programme at various stages from formulation to implementation, the adequacy of financial and organizational support can also be noted. These aspects are analysed in two papers — by Aziz and Seetharamu — based on the experience of one of the States of India. While the performance may vary from State to State the issues involved are common.

The population in India is stratified not only on an economic scale but also along caste lines. Caste-based stratification is more strongly seen in the rural population where the social and economic handicaps are mutually interpeneterating. Two papers by P.M. Kulkarni and H. Ramachandran deal with this aspect of rural development in India. Kulkarni reviews the programme that deals with the question of rehabilitation of bonded labourers, and finds the experience is similar to that of IRDP programme. He stresses the need for additional efforts particularly at times of distress if the programmes are to yield significant results when the target is poorest of the poor such as the bonded labour.

Ramachandran's paper compares household characteristics of the scheduled caste population (lowest among the caste hierarchy — once untouchables) of various strata with comparable strata of the non-scheduled caste households. Although the four decades after Independence is too short a time to bring about substantial changes in the community which has suffered effects of centuries of accumulated maltreatment, some improvements are noted.

At the other end of the rural hierarchy, is the rural elite, while many of the programmes are not addressed to them, their role in the success of the programme is not only crucial but very complex to understand. The intricacies of their role are discussed on the basis of a case study by V.S. Parthasarathy. The paper by A.K.N. Reddy is the revised version of his Valedictory address to the International seminar. In a crisp manner he has drawn lessons from the experience of introducing technology in rural areas. The lessons are of sobering significance to the under developed countries as a whole, where new technologies are likely to play increasing role in the economic upliftment of rural poor.

Taken together these papers convey a range of rural development problems that is further widened when the magnitude of population, the social complexities and the historical burden of India are considered.

12

INTEGRATED RURAL DEVELOPMENT PROGRAMME IN KARNATAKA: An Evaluation

Abdul Aziz

Introduction

The philosophy underlying the IRDP which was launched in 1978-79 originates from the imperative that the main attack on rural poverty has to be by endowing the poor with productive assets and/or skills so that they are assured of a regular stream of income that raises them above the poverty line. Though this programme could essentially be viewed as an anti-poverty programme both at the conceptual level and in operational terms it is also meant to be an exercise in microlevel planning in so far as the planner is expected to evolve appropriate schemes for the households which seek to fully utilise the locally available resources including skills of the beneficiaries. For optimising the impact of IRDP it is expected of the planner to integrate the IRDP household plan with the block sectoral, resource and spatial plans.[1]

There have been many evaluative studies of this programme in the country which found that some beneficiaries crossed the poverty line and others did not.[2] Though not all the beneficiaries are found to have crossed the poverty line some positive signs were seen in respect of employment and income generation, asset formation and loan repayment.[3] However, reviewing the performance of IRDP as revealed by the above studies, Rath mounted a massive attack on the philosophy and the mechanics of IRDP. He argued that IRDP in practice was not an integrated programme in the sense in which the Sixth Plan document desired it to be. In his opinion IRDP did not integrate the resource based or sectoral planning with household-based planning; it was merely a household-based plan whose central attention was on identification of the rural poor and on preparing a plan for the individual beneficiaries.[4]

The position taken by Rath raises an important issue relating to the formulation and implementation of IRDP. It would, therefore, appear desirable to examine the performance of IRDP not only in terms of its objective of raising the poor households above the poverty line but also perhaps in terms of the internal logic of the programme – the logic derived from the mechanics of planning IRDP. As a follow up of this point the relevant questions to be asked are : How did the planning agency identify clusters and beneficiaries, evolve schemes of development for the households, match the households with the schemes, integrate household plans with the spatial plans, sectoral and non-sectoral plans and so on. The present paper addresses itself to these questions.

Methodology

Since the purpose of our study is to assess the impact of IRDP on the economic conditions of the beneficiary households and to relate this to the planning mechanics of IRDP this inquiry, seeks (a) to assess changes in economic conditions of the beneficiaries following the implementation of IRDP and (b) to evaluate the IRDP planning process. As part of (a) we looked at the economic conditions of the beneficiaries in the "before and after" framework with a view to bring out changes, if any, in their economic conditions following the implementation of the programme. As the entire change in the economic conditions of the beneficiaries could not however, be attributed to IRDP alone the whole exercise of assessing the impact of the programme was carried out in the 'with and without' frame. Thus, we assessed the change in conditions of those with the programme (the experimental group), and the difference observed in the *ex post* conditions of the experimental (beneficiary) group and control (non-beneficiary) group was then imputed to IRDP intervention.

The beneficiary and non-beneficiary respondents were drawn using a multi-stage sample frame. In the first stage, we selected two districts in the State – Kolar and Dharwar – representing the southern and northern Karnataka regions. From each of these districts two blocks were selected on the basis of the performance of the programme as assessed by the programme implementing agency. Of these two blocks, one was a high performing and the other a low performing block. From each of these blocks three to four village clusters where the beneficiary households were concentrated were demarcated, and the respondents for the study were drawn. Considering the time and resources at our disposal we decided to cover 75 beneficiaries and 25 non-beneficiaries from each block which gave us in all 300 beneficiaries and 100 non-beneficiaries from the four blocks under study. The final selection of the respondents was done on a random sample basis.

Since the reference period of the study was 1983-85, we selected those respondents who obtained assistance in 1983 and assessed their economic conditions at two points of time i.e., one in 1983 (before the scheme was given) and another in 1985 (after situation). The household data were collected through a structured schedule form the beneficiary and non-beneficiary households. With the help of a separate interview schedule we collected information from the district and block level functionaries on the methodology followed for planning and implementing the rural development programmes including IRDP.

Profile of IRDP and its Beneficiaries

The actual expenditure by the State on this programme during the Sixth Plan was Rs. 78.84 crores* as against Rs. 61.25 crores allocated and the actual beneficiaries numbered 7.6 lakhs** as against the target number of 5.25 lakhs. This means that the actual expenditure and beneficiaries exceeded the target by 29 per cent and 45 per cent respectively. From these figures it is difficult to arrive at the average financial assistance obtained by the beneficiaries because the expenditure figure on IRDP also includes expenses on account of administering the programme. The average assistance based on our field study pertaining to the year 1983-84 works out to Rs. 2,765. The schemewise distribution of average assistance inclusive of subsidy works out to Rs. 2,940 in the case of agriculture and allied activities, Rs. 2,764 in the case of animal husbandry schemes and Rs. 2,765 in the

* 1 crore = 10 million

** 1 lakh = 100,000

case of industry, business and service schemes.

The Union Ministry of Rural Development specified that out of the 600 beneficiaries to be covered in a given year in a block of 400 ought to be selected for schemes under the primary sector covering agriculture and allied activities, animal husbandry and related sectors, 100 under the secondary sector and the remaining 100 under the tertiary sector. Of this, at least 30 per cent of the beneficiaries ought to be members of SC and ST and that some special attention was to be given to women, ex-bonded labourers and land allotees. The composition of beneficiaries in the study region, however, does not conform to the composition specified under the ministry guidelines. While the proportion of SC and ST beneficiaries which is 44 per cent is well above the specified limit the number of women beneficiaries came to only 11 per cent of the total. The proportion of beneficiaries in the primary sector was overwhelmingly large at 87 per cent but the secondary and tertiary sectors ended up with such a small proportion as 4.7 per cent and 7.3 per cent respectively. Our discussion with the block and district authorities brought out the point that the preference of beneficiaries to animal husbandry and agriculture schemes and the lack of potential beneficiaries who could take up schemes in the secondary and tertiary sectors was the main reason for the skewed distribution of beneficiaries in favour of the primary sector.

The distribution of beneficiaries by their socio-economic category shows that among the beneficiaries selected 39.7 per cent are cultivators, 52.7 per cent are agricultural labourers, 5 per cent are those who are engaged in business and service, and artisans account for only 3 per cent. Only 3.3 per cent of the cultivator-beneficiaries have been given schemes under the ISB sector. 55.5 per cent of them are given animal husbandry schemes and 41.2 per cent are given schemes under agriculture and allied activities. About two-thirds of the artisans obtained schemes in the industries sector and rest of them were provided with animal husbandry schemes. Most of those (87%) who are in business, and service are provided with schemes under ISB sector. In the case of agricultural labourers the schemes given are somewhat more diversified. Though 63 per cent of them have obtained animal husbandry schemes, seven per cent got schemes under agriculture and allied activities and the remaining ten per cent were given ISB schemes.

Impat of IRDP

Apart from the number of beneficiary households crossing the poverty line the impact of the programme was assessed in terms of (a) changes in income and employment, (b) extent of asset formation and asset retention, and (c) extent of loan repayment among the beneficiary households.

Income Effect of the Programme

Table 12.1 shows that the average income net of paid out costs from all the scheme is about Rs.886 which flows from an average assistance of Rs. 2,765 giving a ratio of income to assistance as 0.32. Across the sectors, the net income earned by an average beneficiary is the highest in the ISB sector (Rs.1857) and this sector also gives the highest ratio of income to a assistance which is 0.74. Animal husbandry (0.28), and agriculture and allied activities (0.20) follow in that order as far as the magnitude of income generations and efficiency of assistance is concerned.

Coming to individual schemes within the ISB sector, hotel business is more remunerative with an income to assistance ratio of 1.55. This is followed by tailoring (0.92), petty shop (0.85) and weaving (0.70). The schemes given to cycle shop keepers and to the artisans such as cobblers, *dhobis* and blacksmiths are less remunerative. In the case of animal husbandry sector the milk animal scheme (0.49) is more remunerative when compared with rearing of goats, sheep and other animals. In the agriculture sector, of course, the IP set scheme tops in terms of income generation and efficiency of assistance. But the other two schemes viz., work bullocks, and bullock and carts present a hopelessly bad picture of performance. The low efficiency of work bullock scheme is understandable. It will be seen that the efficiency (productivity) of the bullocks is linked with the availability of complementary factor viz., land. In so far as the size of holdings of the beneficiaries is very small, the high value bullocks remain underutilised leading to low returns on them.

The low returns from bullock and cart scheme, which otherwise is more remunerative, should be attributed to overcrowding of these assets in a given village cluster. As the number of bullock-cart owners increased in a village cluster it would become necessary to share the available business among the larger number of beneficiaries. Obviously, this would lead to underutilisation of the bullocks and carts

Table 12.1: Net Income from Project Assistance, and Ratio of Income to Assitance by Schemes

	No of Benefi-ciaries	Average value of assistance (Rs.)	Net Income (Rs.)	Ratio of Income to Assistance
I *Agriculture and Allied Activities*	61	2939.50	600.95	0.20
1. I.P. Sets	5	5000.00	2727.40	0.54
2. Work Bullocks	37	2184.45	434.83	0.19
3. Bullocks and Carts	19	3867.63	364.84	0.09
II *Animal Husbandry*	202	2763.91	793.77	0.28
1. Milk animals	122	2487.06	1238.86	0.49
2. Other animals	80	3186.10	115.01	0.03
III *Industry, Business and Service*	37	2485.13	1856.89	0.74
1. Weaving	4	2050.13	1452.50	0.70
2. Tailoring	11	1531.81	1403.81	0.92
3. Blacksmith, Cobbler, Dhobi etc.	7	3414.28	740.14	0.21
4. Petty shop	6	2416.66	2058.66	0.85
5. Cycle shop	3	3666.66	915.33	0.24
6. Hotel Business	6	2916.66	4545.66	1.55
All Schemes	300	2765.23	885.68	0.32

causing a fall in their returns. The reason for low returns in the case of non-milk animals (goats, sheep etc.) is the high proportion of death of animals. A large number of beneficiaries who took this scheme were found to be not in possession of the animals at the time of our inquiry.

The invariable answer to the question of the status of asset possession is that animals were dead. In the case of milk animals too deaths were reported by the respondents but the proportion of animals to be dead in respect of non-milk animals is alarmingly high. The high mortality rate of animals may be a fact but there is also the possibility that the beneficiaries must have sold or killed and consumed some of these animals. Whatever may be the reason for the non-retention of the animals, it would obviously lead to low income from the scheme.

Employment Effect of the Programme

IRDP creates asset and the act of creation of assets and subsequently the process of maintenance and operation of the assets leads to employment generation. The selected IRDP schemes on an average generates 253 mandays of employment. If the full employment norm is taken to be 270 mandays in a year, then the programme would have generated in the beneficiary household a slightly less than full employment for one person. By this reckoning the ISB sector schemes are more productive in terms of employment generation (310 mandays) and the animal husbandry schemes, and schemes in agriculture and allied activities with the employment generation figures of 239 and 266 mandays respectively are comparatively less productive.

Viewing the employment potential in this manner does not make any sense because what ever employment that is generated is shared among male, female and child labour. However, so long as the rural households are facing the problem of underemployment and disguised unemployment opportunities would reduce the incidence of this problem. Therefore, the role of IRDP could be seen more in its capacity to reduce underemployment and disguised unemployment among the beneficiary households. As the above employment figures do not lend themselves to comparison across different schemes because of their heterogeneous character we standardised the female and child labour units by using the coefficients of 0.8 and 0.6 respectively employed by an earlier ISEC study[5] and present them in Table 12.2 along with the ratio of employment to assistance. It is seen that the overall ratio of employment to assistance is 0.08. That means for Rs. 100 of assistance given eight standard mandays of employment is generated. Of this, an overwhelming proportion i.e., 97.2 per cent is own and a little less than 3 per cent is hired employment. It is obvious that the employment opportunities created under IRDP are meant primarily for the family members of the household in question and this conforms to the philosophy of the programme which is self-employment-oriented.

Table 12.2: Mandays of Employment (Standardised to Male Worker) Generated and Ratio of Employment to Assistance at Beneficiary Household Level

Name of the Scheme	Total Employment	Proportion of Labour		Ratio of Employment to Assistance
		Own	Hired	
I. *Agriculture and Allied Activites*	237.1	98.7	1.3	0.08
1. IP Set	549.2	93.4	6.6	0.10
2. Work Bullocks	192.4	100.0	-	0.08
3. Bullocks and Carts	242.0	100.0	-	0.06
II. *Animal Husbandry*	*206.5*	*95.9*	*4.1*	*0.07*
1. Milk Animals	214.4	98.4	1.6	0.08
2. Other Animals	194.4	95.1	4.9	0.06
III. *Industry, Service and Business*	293.3	100.0	-	0.11
1. Weaving	297.8	100.0	-	0.14
2. Tailoring	206.2	100.0	-	0.13
3. Blacksmith, Cobbler, etc.	259.1	100.0	-	0.10
4. Petty shop	288.2	100.0	-	0.11
5. Hotel Business	368.2	100.0	-	0.12
6. Cycle Shop	313.7	100.0	-	0.08
All Schemes	*223.4*	*97.2*	*2.8*	*0.08*

The employment potential of ISB sector (with an employment to assistance ratio of 0.11) is more than that of either agriculture and allied activities sector (0.08) or animal husbandry (0.07). In the ISB sector the entire employment generated is taken by the family members. Hired employment is found in agriculture and animal husbandry sector by its proportion to total employment generated is not significant as can be seen from the Table. Schemewise, a higher than the sector average employment potential is observed in weaving (0.14), tailoring (0.13), hotel business (0.12), IP set (0.10) and milk animal

(0.08) schemes. Incidentally, these are also the schemes which have a higher ratio of income to assistance which means that the higher employment potential of these schemes is not due to the presence of disguised unemployment in them as normally is believed.

Asset Retention and Loan Repayment

The Table 12.3 shows that a large proportion (73%) of beneficiaries have retained their asset. About 8 per cent and 6 per cent of the beneficiaries reported that their assets (animals) were dead and sold separately. The remaining 13 per cent of the assets fall in to the category of a curious combination of sold/retained/dead.

Table 12.3: Asset Retention and Loan Repayment

Status of Asset	No. of Beneficiaries by per cent of Loan Repaid					
	0	1-24	25-49	50-74	75-99	100
1. Retained	84	48	42	25	1	18
2. Sold	5	1	3	4	0	2
3. Animals dead/enterprise closed	13	7	1	2	0	0
4. Some retained/and some sold	2	3	0	0	0	0
5. Some sold and some dead	32	1	0	0	0	0
6. Some retained and some sold	6	0	0	0	0	0
Total No. of cases	142	60	46	31	1	20

Coming to progress in loan repayment, 47 per cent of the beneficiaries had not made even a beginning in this regard. The remaining 53 per cent had begun to make loan repayment and some 7 per cent of the beneficiaries had, in fact, cleared the entire debt. Others had repaid loans in amounts varying from a quarter to three quarters of the debt. As expected, a larger proportion of those who retained (61%) or sold (67%) the asset had begun to repay loans. The proportion of defaulters is overwhelmingly large (79%) in the case of those who lost the asset due to death of animals or a combination of sale/ retention/death of the animal.

In regard to loan repayment, however, a point that is generally made out is that in some cases the bankers had adjusted a part or the entire amount of subsidy towards loan repayment. If the progress noted in respect of loan repayment in our study region is viewed in the light of this allegation, then there will be very little to be said in favour of loan repayment progress. We could do little by way of cross-checking on this point owing to the practical difficulties involved at the field level. Nevertheless, it is at least possible to examine whether this practice of subsidy adjustment alone could explain the phenomenon of loan repayment by the beneficiaries. As a part of this, we looked at the disaggregated picture of loan repayment at the sector and scheme levels and related it to the performance of the scheme in terms of income generation. The logic that is implied in this exercise is that if the asset generates a reasonable amount of income the beneficiaries' ability to repay loan increases which in turn facilitates loan repayment.

A cursory look at the detailed figures shows that the schemes under ISB sector and animal husbandry sector (except non-milk animal scheme in that) have shown good progress in loan repayment. In the case of agriculture and allied activities only IP set scheme falls into this category. Among those schemes where loan repayment has not begun at all or is not satisfactory the non-milk animal scheme, work bullocks scheme and the scheme of bullocks and carts stand out prominently. It will be recalled that these are the schemes which generated low project incomes. Obviously this puts a constraint on the ability of the beneficiary to repay loan. On the other hand, schemes such as milk animals, IP sets, weaving, tailoring, petty shop, cycle shop, hotel business, etc., which have shown progress in loan repayment are also schemes where income generated is of satisfactory level. Naturally, the ability of the beneficiaries to repay loans under these schemes is higher when compared with others and this point, in some measure, explains the progress of loan repayment noted in their case.

What emerges from this analysis is that the practice of subsidy adjustment alone cannot be the sole reason for progress in loan repayment; the degree of project efficiency in terms of its ability to generate a reasonable amount of income also appears to be an important factor in this. To this may be added one more fact. It was found that where the beneficiary was linked to a regular product-sale arrangement and where in turn the payment for this product was also linked to loan repayment the progress in regard to loan repayment was somewhat satisfactory. The case in point is the milk animal scheme.

Most of the beneficiaries are made members of the milk co-operatives which buy milk. When monthly payments are made for the milk sold, the co-operatives which have some arrangement with the loaner banks deduct loan repayment instalments. In this way, the milk cooperatives not only collect dues on behalf of the banks but also ensure loan repayment.

Income Mobility among Beneficiaries

Having examined the direct impact of IRDP on income, employment and asset formation at the beneficiary household level, we may now pass on to assessing the overall impact of the programme on the economic conditions of the beneficiary families. This exercise is proposed to be carried out by assessing the effectiveness of the programme in promoting income mobility among the beneficiaries. In this exercise of estimating the extent of mobility of the beneficiaries from one income bracket to the other following project intervention we have not considered it necessary to adjust the post-project income figures to the possible increase in prices as the period considered is very short. For this purpose we have devised three income brackets of which the first viz., 0-1750 could be regarded as the one where the poorest among the poor are found and the last one represent income groups (Rs. 3,500 plus) which are above the poverty line. Ideally, the families should cross the poverty line; if that is not possible, atleast they should move to the next higher income group. Such a movement of the familite is a welcome sign and would add to the credit side of the balance-sheet of IRDP performance.

This exercise of assessing income mobility among the familite is carried out in the "before and after" situation and the net effect could be obtained by subtracting from the gross effect, the effect of other programmes and natural process of development.

Keeping the above frame, the data on the overall family income of the beneficiary households derived both from project and non-project sources are presented in Table 12.4. The corresponding income figures of the non-beneficiaries are also presented. From these figures the following points emerge:

Out of the 300 families 23.7 per cent crossed the poverty line. If we removed the 20 families which were already above the poverty line (the so-called mis-identified families), the gross effect of IRDP is that it enabled 18 per cent families to cross the poverty line. Since the position regarding the number of non-beneficiary households in the non-poverty income level remains the same at 21 both before and after the project intervention in the region the effect of other projects and of the natural process of development is one had joined this group after the project intervention. This means, the gross effect of IRDP arrived at can also be taken as its net effect. Therefore, the net impact of IRDP in the study region is that it enabled 18 per cent of the beneficiaries to cross the poverty line.

Table 12.4: Income Mobility of Beneficiary and Non-Beneficiary Households
(Percentage Changes in No. of Households after Project Intervention)

Income Brackets	0-1750	1751-3499	3500 and above	Total No of Households
I *Non-Beneficiaries*	-7.1	+8.1	0.0	100
II. *Beneficiaries* of whom:	-49.2	+36.6	+255.0	300
1. Cultivators	-43.1	+12.2	+440.0	119
2. Agricultural Labourers	-51.9	+82.5	+230.	158
3. Artisans	0.0	-33.3	increase *	8
4. Business and service	-100.0	0.0	+80.0	15
Total No. of Households	221 130 before aiter	138 178 before after	41 92 before after	400

* since the base happened to be zero the small raise here gives in percentage terms an infinite increase

The crossing of poverty line by such a small number as 18 per cent of the families is not going to add much to the credit side of IRDP balance-sheet. Moreover, even this figure should be taken with a pinch of salt because it is arrived at on the basis of the poverty norm of RS. 3,500 per annum derived at 1979-80 prices. Since then, prices have risen making it necessary to revise the poverty norm, The Planning Commission has recently revised this norm to Rs. 4,800. If this norm is applied to our sample beneficiary households the number of those who crossed the new poverty line is only 27 of whom four households were above this line even before the project intervention. Among the non-beneficiaries, in addition to the nine households which had crossed the new poverty line before the project intervention. This means without project intervention one out of every 10 households had crossed the poverty line. If adjustment is made for this in the figures of those who crossed the new poverty line among the beneficiaries and for those who were already in this income group before project intervention the net number of households among beneficiaries that would have crossed the new poverty line would be a little less than 7 per cent of the families. Therefore, by the new poverty line norm the effectiveness of the programme in enabling the beneficiaries to cross the poverty line would seem to be far more disappointing.

Judged by the norm of poverty crossing, the performance of the programme appears to be less impressive. We may, however, evaluate the programme in terms of the alternative criterion referred to earlier viz., its ability to promote mobility of the families to higher income brackets. It will be seen that the number of beneficiaries in the income brackets of 0-875 and 876-1750 declined due to project intervention by 75 per cent and 39.7 per cent, respectively. There was a decline too in the case of non-beneficiary households; bit the decline observed in their case is very marginal being 14.3 per cent and 5.7 per cent, respectively in the corresponding income brackets. After the project intervention, both the beneficiary and the non-beneficiary households moved beyond the income level of Rs. 1,750 leading to a rise in the number of households in the income-brackets of 1761-2675 and 2626-3499. But while in the case of the non-beneficiaries this increase is only 4.2 per cent and 15.4 per cent the corresponding figures in respect of beneficiaries are much higher being 21.4 per cent and 65.6 per cent. Since in both the cases the change in the proportion of households in different income groups is higher among the beneficiaries when compared with the non-beneficiaries, it could be argued with some degree of confidence that project intervention did promote upward income mobility among the families.

There is then this question of who among the beneficiaries that benefited more from the programme. It will be noted that a larger proportion (33%) of households coming from business and service background crossed the poverty line. Cultivators and agricultural labourers would come second and third with about 19 per cent and 15 per cent gain, respectively. Across the different income brackets mobility is much faster in the case of agricultural labourers when compared with the other occupational categories. The rate of decline in the number of households in the first two income brackets and the rate of increase in their number in the subsequent two income brackets is higher in the case of agricultural labourers than the other occupational categories. This in a sense is a notable achievement of IRDP insofar as it has promoted a faster rate of income mobility among a class of persons who are by their very nature considered the weakest of the weaker sections.

Mobility of beneficiaries across different income brackets by schemes is presented in Table 12.5. It will be seen that the percentage decline in the number of beneficiaries after the project intervention in the lower income bracket viz., 0-1750, is found to be higher in animal husbandry and ISB sectors. The fall in the number of beneficiaries in the lower income brackets has led to the swelling of their numbers in the higher income brackets viz., 1751-3499 and 3500 and above, indicating an upward movement of the beneficiaries along the income brackets. But this movement is very sharp in animal husbandry and ISB sectors and not so sharp in the agriculture and allied activities sector. Among individual schemes mobility is faster in the milk animal scheme compared with other schemes.

Viewed from the angle of poverty line crossing, the performance of the animal husbandry sector and, within that, the performance of milk animal scheme is better when compared with the schemes in the other sectors. Even if we leave out of account those who were already above the poverty line, the performance of the schemes in terms of poverty line crossing presents the same pattern. Thus, while the number of those who crossed the poverty line (net of those who were already there) in the animal husbandry sector is 40 out of 202 beneficiaries (i.e., 20%), it is 8 out of 37 (22%) in ISB sector and only 3 out of 61 (5%) in agriculture and allied activities sector. The net number of beneficiaries crossing the poverty line is 30 per cent of the beneficiaries covered in the milk animal scheme which is the highest recorded for any individual scheme in the study region.

The low performing sector in terms of facilitating either poverty line crossing or mobility of beneficiaries along higher income bracket is the agriculture sector. The low performing schemes are work bullocks, bullock and cart, and non-milk animals.

Table 12.5: Income Mobility of Beneficiaries by Schemes
(% Change in No. of Households After Project Intervention)

Name of the scheme	0-1750		1751-3499		3500 and above		Total No.of Households
I. *Agricultural and Allied Activities*	*-24.2*		*20.0*		*100.0*		*61*
1. IP set	-66.7		0.0		increase *		5
2. Work Bullock	-22.2		17.6		50.0		37
3. Bullocks and Carts	-16.7		3.7		0.0		19
II *Animal Husbandry*	*-50.8*		*41.9*		*400.0*		*202*
1. Milk Animals	-73.2		63.9		925.0		122
2. Non-Milk Animals	-12.5		11.5		50.0		80
III. *Industry, Service Business*	*-87.5*		*28.6*		*114.3*		*37*
1. Weaving	-100.0		-100.0		0.0		4
2. Tailoring	-80.0		40.0		200.0		11
3. Blacksmithy	-100.0		-66.7		200.0		7
4. Petty shop	-66.7		200.0		0.0		6
5. Hotel Business	-100.0		-50.0		100.0		66
6. Cycle shop	-100.0		increase *		0.0		3
All Schemes	-49.2		36.6		255.0		300
Total No. of Households	179	91	101	138	20	71	300
	Before	After	Before	After	Before	After	

* Since the base happened to be zero the small increase in the number gives in percentage terms an infinite increase.

Formulation and Implementation of IRDP

As the programme has succeeded in raising only 17 per cent of the households above the poverty line it is desirable to look into the factors which constrained this programme in the achievement of its basic objective. In the previous paragraphs we have indicated the constraints which were associated with the schemes as such but here it is proposed to look at the wider issue of how effectively the programme was planned and implemented. The examination of this aspect would be done in the light of the detailed guidelines provided by the Ministry of Rural Development. Besides it is also proposed here to examine how far Rath was justified in attacking the programme on the ground that it was not an integrated programme to start with.

Plan Preparation

In the districts covered, the 25 development perspective plans were not prepared as required under the guidelines. The district credit plans have, of course, been prepared by the district lead banks. Annual action plans have also been prepared. According to the guideline the block cluster plans are to be prepared first and it is on the basis of those that the annual action plans and perspective plans for the blocks are to be formulated. However, it is rather too much to expect from the block machinery to prepare the cluster plans on the lines suggested by the Ministry guidelines. It is our impression, as is so with the PEO, that the annual action plans by and large are mere exercises indicating the annual breakup of targets, financial requirements, of the five-year IRDP plan.

Whatever may be the procedure adopted for the preparation the cluster plans the responsibility for this rests with the Block Development Officer and his assistants who form village clusters for purpose of IRDP implementation taking into account the available infrastructure facilities. Records which would have given us some idea as to how these clusters were formed are not available. But from our discussion with the concerned block level officers it is evident that each village panchayat group having 4 to 5 villages under its jurisdictions identified as a "cluster" for purpose of IRDP implementation. The Officers, after selecting such clusters, went about identifying the available infrastructure within and outside the panchayat group. This procedure is reverse of what is normally expected viz., identifying the required infrastructure and then demarcating the region which encompasses in it such infrastructure to be called a cluster. From the point of view of pure planning the approach followed by the bureaucracy may not be scientific but perhaps from the point of view of administrative convenience this may be useful in so far as each of such clusters has a panchayat and the village officer which can provide the much needed administrative infrastructure.

Beneficiary Identification

For the purpose of identifying the beneficiaries, a house to house survey is expected to be conducted by the block functionaries to ascertain and to identify the households which are below the poverty line and also to prepare family plans for them. The practice may vary, as it seems to be so in the country. But as far as our study region is concerned, it was reported that survey was conducted by the VLW and Village Accountants which was later scrutinised and approved by the *Gram Sabha*. However, to make sure that the beneficiaries were not identified without conducting a household survey we asked our respondents to indicate how they were identified for purpose of granting assistance. The distribution of households reporting as to how they were identified is presented in Table 12.6. This gives some clues as to what methods were followed in the study region for identifying the beneficiaries. It is evident that a third of the respondents interviewed reported that they were identified by the VLW and block officials and nearly 60 per cent were reported to be identified in the *gram sabha*. Some 23 of the beneficiaries reported that they were identified for the programme by bank officials and RD office. Further inquiry on the latter point brought out the following: There is a practice that though some of the beneficiaries were not initially identified by means of a household survey, later on they were recommended by the BDO and the bank managers and sponsored by the DIC. These cases are mostly the cases of ISB beneficiaries. A point that needs to be examined in this connection is, whether this channel does not provide a route for the non-poor to get into the programme. We shall shortly return to this. But meanwhile let us complete the narration of the beneficiary identification process.

After the formal survey, the households below the poverty line were listed under four per capita income groups viz., 0-175, 176-350, 351-550, 551-750. Some 120 families falling in the low income groups are selected for assistance in each of the clusters. However, in respect of ISB and minor irrigation schemes, families were selected even from the upper income groups viz., 351-550 and 551-750, because families in the lower income groups invariably would not go in for ISB and minor schemes.

The next step in beneficiary identification is the scrutiny and arrival of the list prepared by the functionaries. The method suggested in the guidelines is the scrutiny by open village assembly. Our discussions with the functionaries indicate that this was the method followed in the study region. Going back to Table 12.6 it will be seen that only about 60 per cent of the respondents admitted having attended the *Gram*

Sabha meetings where they were identified for the purpose of assistance. Grantings that the list prepared by the functionaries was also scrutinised in the same *Gram Sabha* it is evident that the remaining 40 per cent of the identified households did not pass through this process. The number of such households is more in Kolar district than in Dharwar district.

Table 12.6: Distribution of Beneficiary Households by Method of Identification

Sl. No.	Agency	No. of Households identified in				Total
		Chickballapur	Bagepally	Ranebennur	Mundargi	
1.	VLW/Others	65 (86.66)	31 (41.33)	Nil	3 (4.00)	99 (33.00)
2.	Gram Sabha	10 (13.33)	44 (58.66)	63 (84.00)	61 (81.33)	178 (59.33)
3.	Bank Officials	Nil	Nil	8 (10.66)	2 (2.66)	10 (3.33)
4.	BDO Officials	Nil	Nil	4 (5.33)	9 (12.00)	13 (4.33)
		75 (100.00)	75 (100.00)	75 (100.00)	75 (100.00)	300 (100.00)

Note: Figures in parentheses are Percentages

There is a reason for the non-conduct of *Gram Sabha* in some clusters. The purpose of holding *Gram Sabha* is to properly identify the beneficiaries by eliminating those who are above the poverty line and those who have become defaulters having not paid loans taken earlier from local co-operative societies, PLD Bank Commercial Bank. At times, the block machinery obtains defaulters' from the list of beneficiaries prepared earlier. By following this procedure the necessity of conducting *Gram Sabha* for the sake of eliminating the defaulters is skipped and the other functions of *Gram Sabha* are combined with the credit camp thereby saving valuable time. In the camp, to which *Tahsildar* and his assistants and the bankers are invited, the loan records are built and the antecedents of the beneficiary are scrutinised. The list of eligible beneficiaries is sent to the DRDS through the Block level consultative committee which in turn forwards it to the concerned bank for loan assistance. Now to say a word about the effectiveness of the beneficiary identification followed in the study region we may look at the number of beneficiaries by income groups as found on the eve of the identification process. It will be seen that out of 300 beneficiaries surveyed, only 20 had an annual income of Rs. 3,500 and above which is the non-poverty income. This means that the phenomenon of mis-identification by our figures is only 6.7 per cent which by any standards is not alarming. The lower percentage of misidentification of beneficiaries in general speaks of the effectiveness of the beneficiary identification methods followed in the study region.

It will be seen that 10 out of 20 misidentified cases were agricultural labourers, 5 were from the cultivator category and five were from beneficiaries belonging to the ISB sector. Though in absolute terms the number of misidentification in the ISB sector is small, when compared with the total number of beneficiaries the number appears to be large. Thus misidentification works out to 33 .3 per cent in ISB sector; it is, however, 4.2 per cent and 6.3 per cent respectively in the case of cultivators and agricultural labourers. Therefore, the fear that the general practice of the beneficiaries belonging to ISB sector category being sponsored by BDO, DIC and bankers outside the normal channel of beneficiary identification would lead to a high incidence of misidentification is not ill founded after all.

Family Plans

Once the beneficiaries are identified, the next important step is to evolve appropriate schemes to be given which are not only consistent with the skills and experience of the family members but also are feasible and economically viable. More than all, the schemes given should be acceptable to the beneficiaries and this can be ensured by allowing the beneficiaries to exercise their choice in the selection of the schemes or at least by giving schemes in consultation with them. The distribution of beneficiaries by manner of scheme selection in the study region is such that an overwhelming majority (92%) of the beneficiaries selected schemes on their own. Only about four per cent were given in consultation with the beneficiaries and another four per cent of the beneficiaries reported that the schemes were imposed on them.

Willingness apart, the schemes given must be consistent with the family experience and skills in the trade and also with the availability of needed inputs and product market. As part of checking on this point, it is not only necessary to look at the available infrastructure facilities but also to make a rough estimate of the market for the product. There is no evidence of any exercise having been undertaken to estimate the demand for the product. Nowhere in the region under study formal market research surveys were conducted. Intuitively, however, the concerned officers felt that there would be sufficient demand for certain products like milk and other animal products, certain household goods, consumer products and certain services. Based on such intuition schemes were identified. Having done this kind of exercise the planners then looked at the available infrastructure in the village cluster to know if this was satisfactory. Many a time, it was the availability of the infrastructure that dictated the kind of scheme to be given. Thus, cross-bred cows were given to beneficiaries of a cluster only if that cluster had milk diary society and veterinary hospital.

Acquisition of Assets

After working out the loan and subsidy amount the process of acquiring the asset begins. It will be noted that the beneficiary is normally not given cash. It is the block level purchase committee at the instance of the Block Level Consultative Committee which taking the beneficiary along visited the weekly markets and the nearby towns and purchased the asset for the beneficiary. Purchase of asset is a crucial stage because the success of the programmes depends on the quality of the asset acquired and also the number of people obtaining such assets in any given village cluster. Many a time, based on the requests of the beneficiaries without due consideration for the viability of the asset or to the skills and wishes of the beneficiaries assets are given. This may result in either the mis-match of the asset with the beneficiary or over-crowding off assets leading to lack of demand for the product or the service of such asset in the region. For example, there have been cases of a large number of agricultural labourers having been given bullocks and carts who had to share small amount of business in the region. There have also been cases where, while the skills and experience warranted granting of a particular scheme, the beneficiaries obtained a different scheme which proved to be a misfit. Further, even assuming that a particular asset acquired turned out to be very poor because of high demand for that asset. Thus, there have been cases where at any one point of time the purchase committee had to acquire tens and hundreds of animals for the beneficiaries. In such cases, the committee could hardly exercise choice and in their anxiety to complete the work of acquiring assets invariably the poor quality assets were acquired.

After the asset is acquired and handed over to the beneficiary, it is the responsibility of the Block Level Officers (BLOs) to visit the beneficiary frequently to monitor the progress with respect to the operation and maintenance of the asset for which purpose *Vikas Patrikas* are distributed among the beneficiaries on which notings are made by these officers whenever they visited them. In spite of such monitoring there have been cases of disposal of assets by the beneficiaries without the knowledge of the BLOs.

Integration of Plans

How far have district authorities integrated different plans at the block and district levels to provide for the required infrastructure for implementing IRD plans? In the study region at different stages attempts have been made by DRDS and other departments to create the required infrastructure facilities in the village clusters for effectively implementing the IRD household schemes. It is intended here to present some illustrations in support of this and also to identify other areas where integration of this type is possible and needs to be undertaken in future.

In Kolar district the major IRD schemes relate to animal husbandry as more than 75 per cent of the beneficiaries in this district come under this scheme. Naturally one would expect of the district authorities to create an infrastructure that is animal husbandry-oriented. In consonance with this, as it were, in the district there are 313 milk co-operatives which collect milk from households in different villages. The Bangalore Milk Producing Union is operating a milk route in the district which covers a route distance of 2000 km and collects 110000 litres of milk in flush season and 80000 litres during the loan season. Even in a low milk-animal priority region like Ranebennur of Dharwar district the Karnataka Milk Federation had already formed nine milk routes (of which six are now functioning); some private dairy societies have been started including the one started by IDS of Medleri, which collects milk from the households. In Haveri, a milk chilling plant has been set up under DPAP. The above account provides some evidence of how the required infrastructure particularly in the form of milk routes is made available to the IRD beneficiaries.

The marketing of milk apart, the successful operation of the milk animal schemes requires further linkages such as provision of veterinary services, fodder etc., and rearing of animals. Considering this requirement the DRDS in co-operation with the district line departments has brought about a reasonable degree of integration of the IRD plan with the sectoral and non-sectoral plans. Thus, these facilities have been created by making use of the resources that are available with the agencies handling such programmes as DPAP, NREP and SLPP. The specific instances of the enmeshing of IRD household plans with other plans are as follows:

(i) Eight vehicles are provided out of DPAP funds to operate as mobile veterinary clinics in eight taluks of Kolar district for the benefit of animals provided under IRDP. In Ranebennur and Mundargi blocks also mobile clinics have been provided out of DPAP funds. This is in addition to the rural veterinary dispensaries already set-up by the animal husbandry department.

(ii) Fodder is an important input for animal husbandry scheme. This input is provided for under a different scheme thereby integrating IRDP with sectoral plans. Thus, during 1983-84, 17 hectares of *subabul* plantation was raised in Kolar and Siddalaghatta taluks under DPAP. Similarly, during 1984-85, 94 hectares were brought under *subabul*, *hemta* grass, *Arali*, etc., in Kolar, Chickbalapur, Chintamani, Siddalaghatta and Bagepalli blocks under DPAP to provide basic fodder requirements to animals given under IRDP. The forest department has distributed *subabul* seedlings to the beneficiaries at Doni and Kadampur and raised *subabul* plantation near Garpur (all in Mundargi block). Similarly, in Aremallapura, Sunakalbidri, Honnatti, Meedlergi villages of Ranebennur block the forest department is raising *subabul* plantations.

(iii) Under SLPP, calf and sheep rearing programme was taken up in Kolar to raise standard and quality animals to be given to IRDP beneficiaries. During 1984-85, Rs.10 lakhs out of DPAP to construct a milk chilling plant at Kolar. Provision is also made for medicines and liquid nitrogen out of DPAP funds during 1983-84 and 1984-85 which will be useful for the IRDP animals.

(iv) Next to animal husbandry ISB schemes have received due

attention. These relate to schemes such as for artisans, cycle shops, petty shops, silk reeling and so on. Kolar being a sericulture area, silk reeling happens to be a very important non-agricultural activity. Rightly, therefore, DRDS has programmes for helping the silk reelers by providing the needed infrastructure facilities in co-operation with DIC and KVIC. Thus, there are three silk exchanges at Kolar, Siddalaghatta and Vijayapura which provide organised marketing facilities to the cocoon rearers and silk reelers. Silk reeling requires *Chandirkas* and IRDP provides financial assistance to bamboo workers to step up production of this product. This not only provides the needed infrastructure to cocoon rearers but also ensures market for the bamboo workers.

(v) Many of the Harijan and backward communities are engaged in mat weaving and cotton coarse cloth weaving. But these artisans not only require markets for their products but also some specific infrastructure facilities. For example, good housing facilities are needed for mat weaving and cloth weaving where a loom can be set up under congenial conditions. Realising this need, DRDS Kolar got houses built for them under, NREP. Similarly, under NREP construction of seven community work-sheds has been taken up in seven blocks in Kolar district to provide working place under one roof to the rural artisans such as weavers, blacksmiths and carpenters. Also common worksheds and workshed-cum-living accommodation have been provided under special component plan of DIC in Chintamani taluk for weavers who are assisted under IRDP by the Industries Department. In the case of these artisans carry head-loads of their product to different villages in search of buyers and that itself would result in loss of production time. With a view to help save loss of production time of such artisans attempts have been made by DRDS to establish some trading relationship between these artisans and the traders who normally live in towns.

(vi) There are also instances where DRDS and DIC are functioning as a single team to provide infrastructure facilities and thereby to integrate the household plans with the sectoral plans. Thus, in the case of SC weavers who are engaged in weaving coarse cotton cloth in Kathiriguppa village (Kolar district) DIC provided improved frame looms free of cost. The weavers were then tied up with IRDP for their working capital requirements. For marketing purpose and raw-material requirement they were linked up with the Kathiriguppa weavers Co-operative Society. However, these looms are presently idle because the weavers are reluctant to change over from their traditional pit looms to improved looms. As a corrective to this, action is being initiated under the special component plan to construct a common work-shed at a cost of Rs.1.5 lakhs and also to train them in the technique of using the new looms. Secondly, there are 66 mat weaving families (majority of whom are SCs) in Korlapatti village of Chintamani taluk. Their cases was taken up by the DIC and in 1982-83 a training programme was initiated under the special component programme for six months involving the Regional Design and Technical Development Centre, Bangalore. After the training was imparted these families were provided with improved framelooms from DIC on 60 per cent subsidy basis. Besides, they were also provided with work-shed of the value of Rs. 20000 on a 60 per cent subsidy basis. These families are also tied up with IRDP under the ISB scheme.

(vii) In Ranebennur block also such cases of inter-sectoral linkages are found. Thus, the woolen blanket weavers of Harnagiri village are provided with a common facility centre with the assistance from DIC and NREP. Loan for working capital is provided under IRDP. And they are linked to the Kurubara Unne Society of Ranebennur of marketing purposes. Young men are depute under TRYSEM to the IDS-run training center at Medleri; those trained here are later picked up for assistance under IRDP.

Gaps in the Integration Exercises

Thus, There have been cases of linkages between different agencies in the matter of provision of financial and other help to the beneficiaries and also integration component. There, in fact, has been some degree of plan integration but this was not formally done as required under the guidelines. We suggest that hereafter the planning authorities carry out the integration exercise formally and in accordance with the ministry's guidelines.

While noting that there is some degree of plan integration and that this, however, has to be formally carried out hereafter we believe that there is considerable room for extending such integration to other clusters and to other beneficiaries. In the case of beneficiaries coming under such schemes as carpentry, blacksmithy, cobblery etc., not much has been done by way of linking with either the raw-material supplying source or with the market source due to non-existence of co-operatives in their case. As a matter of fact, the problem is more severe in their case because these occupations are not remunerative. The DIC authorities, however, suggest that their conditions can be improved not merely by linking them with the input and output market sources but also by providing composite schemes. Thus, a tea shop owner, apart from being helped with working and other capital under IRDP, may also be given a milk cow to make his enterprise viable. Such instances of providing complementary benefits under IRDP may be multiplied.

Even where complementary institutional support in the form of co-operatives could be covered such as in the case of weavers and basket makers there is scope for extending such practices to other clusters. As of now such linkages in respect of these artisans are far in between and limited to a few villages. The DIC and DRDS ought to multiply these cases in the area of their jurisdiction. At least in respect of milk animal schemes such tie-ups ought to have been more numerous considering the fact that the DRDS in Kolar district has been in the field right from 1980-81. Apart from tying the households with the milk co-operatives there was need for linkages with fodder and livestock development schemes. Establishment of a fodder bank and livestock development schemes in Kolar was most essential considering the scale in which the milk animal scheme was to be operated in the district. Only recently some attempts are being made to grow *subabul* and other plants that yield fodder and to produce standard animals under the SLPP. But there have been cases of opportunities having been lost in the past owing to lack of planning and perspectives. The DPAP is one programme which would have provided enough clout to the programme of fodder development in the district had the agencies possessed the right perspective. But the funds of DPAP were diverted for other purposes which were not consistent with the objectives of the programme. To illustrate, as early as 1980-81 some Rs. 20 lakhs were spent from DPAP funds to put up an industrial estate in Kolar town (!) – an act which is not consistent at all with the objective of the programme.

Conclusions and Recommendations

The macro data at the State level and the field level information show that at each of the blocks more than the targeted 600 households per annum were assisted which caused the quantum of assistance to fall below the stipulated level. It will be seen that the reduced quantum of assistance would certainly bring down the rate of income flow. The current level of assistance contemplated (Rs. 3,000 to Rs. 5,000) was considered adequate by the authorities on the basis of the assumed capital output ratio of 1.5 as suggested by the Planning Commission. But in the light of our field data this ratio appears to be now unrealistic. As the average ratio of assistance to income found in our study is 1:0.3 which is twice the ratio assumed by the Planning Commission, it will not be unreasonable to suggest that the quantum of assistance should be at least two times of what is now provided to the poor families. This means that an assistance of the order of Rs. 6,000 to Rs. 10,000 should be given if the programme were to make any dent on poverty.

The composition of beneficiaries emerging either from the State level figures or the sample figures does not conform to the guidelines indicated by the Union Ministry of Rural Development. Primary sector schemes take away more that the stipulated two-thirds of the beneficiaries leaving less than the stipulated one-third for industry, service and business sector. The low share of ISB in IRDP allotment is not rational because, as our results indicate, the schemes under this sector are more remunerative and assistance more efficient. A larger proportion of ISB beneficiaries would have accelerated the process of poverty alleviation and diversified the village economy.

A constraint noticed in the task of bringing more number of poor families into the ISB sector is reluctance on the part of the poor to take up ISB schemes. This reluctance is possibly due to the relatively higher degree of risk and uncertainty involved in, and a set of experience and skills demanded by these schemes. The experience and skills component of the constraint can be released if more and more young men and women are first trained under TRYSEM and then linked up with IRDP. As for risk and uncertainty is concerned, this has to do mostly with the marketing of the product. If market linkages, as in the case of milk animal scheme, are established perhaps this constraint may also be released. This means that wherever possible co-operative marketing institutions should be sponsored and encouraged, and the ISB sector beneficiaries should be enrolled as members of such cooperatives.

Though the project intervention helped only 18 per cent of the beneficiaries to cross the poverty line a matter of considerable satisfaction is that a large proportion of beneficiary households particularly belonging to the landless agricultural labour class moved to higher income brackets as the schemes generated additional incomes. The additional employment opportunities generated by the project reduced under-employment among the beneficiary households.

As large as 73 per cent of the beneficiaries had retained the asset at the time of our inquiry. Considering the widespread complaint that IRDP assistance had gone into drain owing to non-acquisition and non-retention of the asset this figure of asset formation and its retention is not a mean achievement. This figure could be even higher if the block and district authorities had geared up their machinery to prevent the disposal of assets by beneficiaries. Slightly more than half (53%) of the beneficiaries had either repaid or begun to repay loans. The rate of loan repayment appears to be tied up with the retention and sale of assets in so far as a large proportion of those who retained or sold the asset had repaid or begun to repay the loan. The defaulters were found to be mostly those who had lost the asset due either to death of animals or to damage to/stealing of the asset. Loan repayment also was linked to produce-sale arrangement as in the case of the milk animal schemes where the beneficiaries were enrolled as members of the milk co-operative. It then follows that for ensuring better loan repayment loss or disposal of assets should be prevented and the beneficiaries should be tied up with co-operatives which while buying the products also deducted loan repayment instalments.

On the whole, though the programme has not prompted poverty line crossing on a substantial scale, by creating assets and increasing income and employment it has promoted income mobility among the beneficiaries and thereby initiated the process of poverty removal. But if this process were to be sustained and, in the final analysis, if it were to help those of the assisted families, which have now just moved to the higher income brackets, to cross the poverty line a second dose of assistance should be given to them.

Coming to the planning aspects of IRDP, misidentification of beneficiaries which is 6.7 per cent of the beneficiaries is less than what is reported by some studies to be the practice in other State. The low misidentification rate in Karnataka may be attributed to the practice of identifying beneficiaries through household surveys and in open *Gram*

Sabhas. Therefore, the procedure followed so far for identifying the poor may be continued. However, in respect of the beneficiaries belonging to the ISB sector where the proportion of misidentification was found to be as high as 33 per cent due to the practice followed by the planning and financing agencies to sponsor beneficiaries outside the normal channel of beneficiary identifications we suggest that beneficiary sponsorship outside the normal channel should be avoided as far as possible.

As an overwhelming majority of beneficiaries were given schemes of their own choice, the household plans, no doubt, meet the willingness criterion. To be more effective, these plans should also be consistent with the family skills and experience and with the availability of local resources and infrastructure. But there is no evidence of the planning agencies formally having evolved family plans on the consideration of these criteria. Intuition and informality appear to have loomed large in preparing the household plans. But since this approach has resulted in overcrowding of assets in certain clusters and in mismatch of schemes with the local infrastructure formal household planning exercises ought to be undertaken by the planning agencies hereafter.

Assets are acquired on behalf of the beneficiaries by the block purchase committee as per the ministry guidelines. But owing to inadequate availability particularly of animals in the local and other markets the purchase committees are reported to have bought low quality animals. Also complaints are heard from the beneficiaries about the prices of animals going up the moment wind of arrival of the purchase committee went round in the shandies. The recent decision to allow the beneficiary himself to acquire the asset may go a long way in ensuring acquisition of assets of good quality at reasonable prices. Care, however, should be taken to ensure that the beneficiary either does not over-invoice the asset or misuse the funds.

Though at the planning stage the inter-plan integration was not attempted formally, attempts were made informally by DRDS and other agencies to create the required infrastructure for effectively implementing the IRD household schemes. In their attempt at providing the infrastructure the planning authorities unconsciously established backward and forward linkages for individual schemes especially the animal husbandry and ISB sector schemes. These linkages have been established by making use of the resources that are available with the district departments and agencies handling such programmes as DPAP, NREP, SLPP and so on. However, the integration attempt has, by and large, been confined to milk animal scheme and a few of ISB schemes. The schemes in agricultural sector and some of those in ISB sector such as meant for tailors, blacksmiths, dhobis, etc., missed such linkages. Secondly, whatever linkages one finds now in the study region are not the result of a formal planning exercise; the linkages were established as a result of administrative decisions taken and implemented during the post-plan period with the help and co-operation of DIC, forest department, department of animal husbandry and so on. We, therefore, suggest that this process of informal linking of different projects should be stopped and a formal planning for achieving integration of various sectoral and non-sectoral plans should be initiated. Besides, it is also desirable that the schemes other than those in the animal husbandry and ISB sectors should be brought into this integration orbit. The question of integrating IRDP with other plan programmes brings in the question of what methodology should be evolved for securing such integration. From a review of the suggested methodologies for integrating IRDP household plans with the district and block plans a clue that emerges is this : if integration of this kind were to materialise the time perspective of the IRDP household plans should begin and end with the time perspective of other plans. It is only under such condition simultaneous planning is possible which will then create mechanics for integrating the various plans. If that is not possible, in the alternative integration could be effected if block plans are linked with the district sectoral and non-sectoral plans. For, IRDP planning is done at the block village-cluster level, and if the block and district sectoral and non-sectoral plans are already formulated the IRDP planner would then know what infrastructure would be available and what activities could be undertaken under the sectoral and non-sectoral programmes. Keeping in view the linkages that these plans would provide, the planner can then proceed to prepare the IRDP household plans. The latter will then only be an exercise in exploiting the backward and forward linkages created under sectoral and non-sectoral plans by giving appropriate schemes to the beneficiary households.

NOTES

1. Planning Commission, *Draft Sixth Five Year Plan (1978-83)*, Government of

India, New Delhi, p.21.16.

2. NABARD, *Study on Implementation of Integrated Rural Development Programme* (Mimeo), NABARD, Bombay, 1984, p.49; Programme Evaluation Organisation, Planning Commission, *Evaluation Report of Integrated Rural Development Programme*, Government of India, New Delhi, 1985, p 344.
3. Department of Applied Economics, *IRDP Evaluation and Impact Study*: Kottayam District, Cochin University, Cochin, 1984: A C Kuttykrishnan, "A Case Study of Integrated Rural Development Programme in a Kerala Village", *Indian Journal of Agricultural Economics*, Oct-Dec, 1984; and Malay Gupta "Planning for Rural Development Integrated Rural Development Programmes and its strategy : Case Study", *Indian Journal of Agricultural Economics*, July-September, 1984.
4. N. Rath, "Garibi Hatao: Can — IRDP do it?", *Economic and Political Weekly*, February 9, 1985.
5. Abdul Aziz and P H Rayappa, *Employment Potential of Selected Plan Schemes in Karnataka* (Unpublished) Institute for Social and Economic Change, Bangalore, 1978.

13

PLANNING AND MANAGEMENT OF INTEGRATED RURAL DEVELOPMENT PROJECTS: A Case Study*

A.S. Seetharamu

Introduction

The focus of this study is on the following issues: (i) the mechanisms of vertical co-ordination within, and horizontal co-ordination across different sectors of rural development; and (ii) the dynamics of participation of rural people in development projects.

The study is set in a cluster of villages (Yaliur) in the Channarayapatna block of Hassan District in Karnataka State. Yaliur is the main village of the cluster and it has seven satellite villages. There are five lower primary schools, two upper primary schools, a post office, a milk dairy society, a rural bank, electricity, *pucca* roads etc. The main village of the cluster is at a distance of 16 kilometres from the block headquarters, and is located three kilometres away from a national highway. There is only one public bus service to the main village, which arrives in the late evening, stops in the village, and leaves early in the morning. The satellite villages are within a range of three kilometres from the main village, and connected by *kutcha* roads.

Sources and Instruments of Data Collection

At the outset, a large mass of data about the development programmes operating in the district, block and cluster was collected. They pertained to the objectives and delivery system for these development programmes, including the structure and organisation of the system at

* This paper draws heavily from an earlier paper of the author in D. Berstecher (ed.) *Education and Rural Development: Issues for Planning and Research*, Paris, UNESCO, 1985.

the block level and below; the nature of interaction between the district and the block, the block and the cluster, between the various development departments at the district as well as the block level; the role-definition of the various field functionaries; the interaction of government departments with voluntary organisations and commercial establishments; the nature of intended benefits and characteristics of beneficiaries, the publicity given to development work etc.

All these data were examined so as to identity those rural development programmes that would have a particularly rich education and training component. After a detailed examination it was decided to settle upon two such programmes for the purpose of testing hypotheses regarding planning and management of education within integrated rural development project: (i) The Training and Visit System of extension education in agriculture, popularly known as the T & V system, and (ii) The Training of Youth for Self-employment, popularly known as TRYSEM.

A household information schedule was used to collect data from the heads of households of the Yaliyur cluster of villages. Another schedule was used to collect information about the T & V programme from its beneficiaries, the 'contact farmers'. The Contact Farmers formed a sub-sample of the total number of households in the Yaliyur cluster.

A third schedule was used to collect data from TRYSEM beneficiaries.

A fourth schedule solicited information from agricultural assistants relating to involvement in the T & V programme, their field and organisational problems experiences in co-ordinating training, visits and services to farmers etc.

Data from officials at the block, district and State level as well as from village leaders, members of voluntary organisations, and others were collected though less structured interviews. A few meetings of the Department of Agriculture and the Block Development Office were attended, and their proceedings duly recorded.

Sampling and Field Work

There were 422 occupied residential households in the Yaliyur cluster of villages. All of them were covered through the household-information schedule. Similarly, there were 31 contact farmers in the Yaliyur range and all of them were interviewed; all agricultural assistants in the block (28 in number) were covered as well. However, the number of TRYSEM beneficiaries for the whole block was 60, only three of whom lived in Yaliyur cluster. Hence, it was decided to include half of the 60 living outside the Yaliyur cluster but within the Channarayapatna block. Fieldwork was done from April to September 1982. Two field investigators lived in the main village of the cluster during the entire field work phase.

Study Area and Population: A Profile

A great majority of families in Yaliyur cluster are of the nuclear type. They form 87.20 per cent of the total. Families with a traditional or joint family structure are very small in number. Curiously, it is observed that there are relatively more joint families amongst those of higher-middle and high-educational status. Most respondents (heads of households) are in the age-group 41 to 50 years. All have reported that they were born in the Yaliyur cluster of villages. The role of in-migration is, in other words, very limited.

Families where the health condition of either husband or wife is critical or bad are exceptions. Out of 422 families 375 have couples eligible for family planning; 35.73 per cent of them have accepted the family planning programme. Acceptance is relatively lower in the low-educational-status families (29.56%). In three, out of four cases, it is the wife who has been sterilised and not the husband. This may be due to the general belief that sterilisation affects the working efficiency of a person.

There are 234 children below 6 years of age in the Yaliyur cluster, a majority of them in families with lower-middle (50.85%) of low educational status (29.91%). A bit more than half of them are girls. In the age-range 6 to 14, there are 540 children. Their distribution across low, lower-middle, higher-middle and high educational-status families is 29.25 per cent, 39.44 per cent, 25.18 per cent and 6.11 per cent, respectively.

The caste-status of an individual, which is based on birth and kinship, plays a crucial role in the rural development process. It is one of the key intervening variables, as far as access to development opportunities and benefits is concerned. Certain groups are considered as backward and hence eligible for government-sponsored development benefits. Apart from the backward castes, there are groups which are declared as deserving special treatment according to the constitution of India — Scheduled Castes and Scheduled Tribes (SC and ST). The percentage of SC population in Karnataka is 13.14 per cent (1971 data) (India, 14.60 percent), that of ST population is 0.79 per cent (India 6.94%).

A large proportion of respondents in the Yaliyur cluster, 79.38 per cent, have a backward caste status. There are, in addition, 6.16 per cent scheduled castes and 1.18 per cent scheduled tribes. About 13 per cent of the respondents belong to the forward castes. Of the 131 scheduled-caste/scheduled-tribe households, 24 report an annual income of less than Rs. 5,000. In 19 of them, the household head is illiterate. But illiteracy is equally common (5 out of 7) in the households reporting a yearly income of more than Rs. 5,000. Though there is a single dominant caste in the village, and though caste can be a very effective unifying social force in rural areas, it tend to be a negative factor in this particular village. Leadership is split between two leaders, both of them members of the dominant agricultural caste of the region.

Literates constitute 63.27 per cent of the Yaliyur population. There has been a phenomenal increase in the percentage of literate population in the Yaliyur cluster, from 38.76 per cent in 1971 to 63.27 per cent in 1982. Of the literates 70.41 per cent have acquired primary education, 21.87 per cent have completed secondary education, and 3.36 per cent have higher education. Among the literate and educated respondents, those who have gone out of their villages or the block for schooling are very few (only around 5 per cent). A great majority of women (87.10%) are illiterates. All the scheduled-caste women are illiterate. Likewise, 91.91 per cent of agricultural labourers among women are illiterates.

About two-thirds of all farmers cultivate their own land. They neither depend on labour from outside nor do they go out for wage-labour. However, 31.54 per cent of the respondents do not possess enough land to subsist. Hence, they not only cultivate their own land but also undertake wage-labour in agriculture. Those respondents who own land, do not themselves cultivate it but engage paid labour, while supervising and monitoring all agricultural operations, i.e. the so-called well-to-do farmers, account for around 6.35 per cent.

Those who do not possess land in Yaliyur cluster of villages are exceptions. However, over two-thirds of the landowners in the cluster are marginal and small farmers.[1] This is a very relevant factor when it comes to the design and evaluation of rural development projects in agriculture as well as under IRDP. Only marginal and small farmers are eligible for most of the IRDP and agricultural projects.

The percentages of illiteracy among marginal, small and big farmers are 49.21, 39.61 and 22.55 respectively. Whether as a cause or as an effect, the size of land-holding is positively associated with the formal schooling a farmer has received.

Wages for agricultural labour range from less than Rs. 3 to Rs. 7 and more per day. Over 91 per cent of the agricultural labourers get anywhere between Rs. 3 and Rs. 6 per day as wages.

However, the wages paid to men are much higher than for women, though in absolute terms both are very low indeed. It may be noted in passing that 136 women (32.22%) and 58 children (13.74%) from these 422 homes go for wage-labour in agriculture. About 48 per cent of the women and 65.51 per cent of the children earn less than three rupees per day.

The annual income of a household in the Yaliyur cluster ranges from a paltry figure of less than Rs. 500 to a relatively good figure of more than Rs. 15,000.[2] Twentynine families in Yaliyur cluster live in a state of acute and perpetual poverty, earning less than Rs. 1,000 a year. Five out of these 29 families have an income which is lower than Rs. 500.

The total number of families getting an annual income below Rs. 5,000 is 284 (67.29%). In other words, two out of every three families in Yaliyur cluster get an income equal to or below the figure of income set by the government for eligibility to most of the government-sponsored development programmes in rural areas. These are the families which are considered as economically backward. Consequently, the competition for benefits under the various development programmes should be quite high.

The income distribution in Yaliyur cluster is bi-modal in nature. There are two peak points, one in the range 2,001 to 3,000, and the other in the range 5,001 to 10,000. The Gini's coefficient is 0.59576.

There are two peoples' organisations in the Yaliyur cluster. One of them is the milk dairy co-operative society and the other is the village panchayat or the local self-government organisation.

There are 27 respondents in the Yaliyur cluster who are members of panchayat, the local self-government. Earlier the panchayat had been entrusted with a lot of development work. Of late, the powers of the local self-government at all levels have been drastically cut down and transferred to the bureaucracy. Now the panchayats have largely an advisory role. They also assist the bureaucracy in identification of beneficiaries. Membership in the panchayat does not carry with it as much social status as it used to. Still, the members represent the people's choice.

There is a rule for reservation of seats in the local self-government for scheduled castes and tribes. Normally they do not come forward to contest, and will instead be nominated on the committee. In Yaliyur cluster, too, there are two SC/ST members.

The village co-operative society (the dairy society) has attracted quite a few members. Membership here is not by election. Every villager who has cattle and who is willing to sell his milk to the society on the terms and conditions laid down by the Society is eligible for membership. About 42 per cent of the respondents are members of the village co-operative society. These members usually get loans from the bank to buy more cattle. They repay the loan on a daily basic by selling milk to the society.

In sum, people of the Yaliyur cluster of villages constitute a community whose developmental needs and aspirations are quite high. They are a relatively literate lot, mostly engaged in farming, on the look-out for opportunities for self-development. They live in nuclear families and are given to a life of hard labour on their own farm or in agricultural labour for others. Meanwhile, there have been visible signs of a complementary development effort 'from above'. A rural bank was established in 1981 to serve the people, and to assist the government in implementation of development programmes. The dairy co-operative society, too, was formed in 1981, and the IRDP programmes were promoted. The Training and Visit System of Extension Education in Agriculture was launched in 1980 in the cluster. Taken together, these details provide the context of rural development in Yaliyur village cluster which the following sections will analyse in greater depth.

The Training and Visit System of Agricultural Extension

This programme, popularly known as the T & V system, is sponsored and assisted by the World Bank in several countries of the world. Karnataka State in India adopted the T and V system in 1979. Writing about it, Robert S. McNamara, the former President of the World Bank, observed that:

> '. . . (the objective of this programme) . . . is to improve and expand agricultural extension through an intensive system of training and visits, and, thus, to reach a large member of farmers quickly with advice covering the entire production cycles. The cost of such service is relatively small. The results are highly visible, and bolster the farmers' self-confidence and pride in their work. The scheme can also help assure that other investments in agriculture achieve their potential' (Benor and Harrison, 1977).

Farmers who are relatively young, dynamic, and receptive to innovations forms the target group of the T & V system. They are called 'Contact Farmers'. Representing (at least in theory) different cross-sections and interest groups of rural society in terms of land-holding, income, caste, age, etc., they are to be the linking-pins between the organisational framework for rural development especially the T & V System, and the rural population. They are in other words the change-agents in rural areas.

We present on the following pages the results of detailed interviews with the Contact Farmers (CF), Assistant Director of Agriculture (ADA), and Agricultural Assistants (AA) in the study area. This area was chosen so as to comprise two adjacent ranges, Yaliyur and Baladare. Each of these has a different story to tell as far as the T and V system is concerned. In Yaliyur, most of the 31 CF figuring on the ADA's official list were not at all aware of the programme nor of the role assigned to them; the T & V system had apparently been implemented in a very half-hearted way. In the neighbouring range of Baladare, on the other hand, excellent work was being done according to the ADA. Hence, it was tempting to examine what factors accounted for the programme's success in one context, and for its failure in an apparently similar one. The results of this analysis are presented separately for the CF of Yaliyur and Baladare, as well as for the area as a whole.

The Profile of Contact Farmers

We analyse here the profile of the 66 Contact Farmers (CFs) in Baladare and Yaliyur with two main questions in mains firstly, what distinguishes the active and functioning group of CFs in Baladare from the inactive group in Yaliyur who are hardly aware of their being Contact Farmers? Secondly, what distinguishes CFs in general from the household heads interviewed in Yaliyur village cluster?

With a majority of CF in Baladare are young and belong to all cross-sections of the village society, a majority of CF in Yaliyur are rather old and belong to either the dominant or the forward caste. Some 77 per cent of CFs live in nuclear families. Traditional family structures thus seem to be more common among them than in the general household sample (87.2 per cent of nuclear type).

Though most CFs in Baladare have primary education (20 out of 35), there is also an illiterate (1), and quite a few with secondary education (10), higher, technical and professional education (1 each).

In contrast, the CFs in Yaliyur range have, on the whole, a somewhat lower level of education. While 22 out of 31 are primary-educated, there are five secondary level-educated and four illiterate CFs. In comparison with the overall household survey, CFs are a distinctly a better educated group.

Also, the families of CFs have higher levels of school education than the average household (Table 13.1).

Table 13.1: Comparison of Educational Status (Percentages)

Educational Status of Families	Contact Farmers	Yaliyur Households
Low	10.6	32.0
Lower-middle	40.9	37.9
Higher-middle	39.4	24.9
High	9.1	5.5

Note: The difference is particularly apparent in the low as well as in the higher-middle educational-status categories.

While 29 out of 35 CF in Baladare cultivate their own land, the figure for Yaliyur is 24 out of 31. There are five CF in Baladare as well as Yaliyur whose main occupation is agricultural labour though they have small pieces of land. There is also, in both Baladare and Yaliyur ranges, the typical landlord CF, who owns land and gets it cultivated.

Twenty-eight out of 35 CF in Baladare and 29 out of 31 CF in Yaliyur have more than ten years of experience in farm work.

All CFs in Baladare and Yaliyur have at least one acre of land. There are a few who have more than 20 acres. The distribution is, however, skewed in favour of larger-sized holdings in Baladare.

It is important, in this connection, to find out how many CFs are marginal, small and big farmers. Marginal and small farmers are not only trained in scientific methods of cultivation under the T and V system, but are also eligible for subsidies, loans and many other developmental opportunities. Nineteen out of 31 CFs in Yaliyur and six out of 36 in Baladare belong to the marginal and small-farmer category. There are, in other words, substantially more big farmers amongst the CFs in Baladare — the range where, it will be recalled, the T and V programme is functioning much more effectively than in Yaliyur. Compared with the overall proportion of marginal and small farmers in our larger household sample, which is 67.79 per cent, CFs are, on the whole, are characterised by bigger land-holdings.

Next to Ragi and Paddy, practically all CFs in Baladare and Yaliyur grow coconut. Yet the T & V system as managed by the Department of Agriculture excludes coconut — because it falls under the jurisdiction of the Department of Horticulture.

There are only a few CFs in Baladare range whose income falls below Rs. 5,000 rupees per annum. Their proportion is higher in the Yaliyur range. But in comparison with the overall household sample, where no less then 67.29 per cent had an annual income below Rs. 5,000 per year, Contact Farmers are economically much better-off.

Further more, incontrast to Yaliur Range (3 out of 31) there are quite a few CF (13 out of 35) in Baladare whose income exceeds 15,000 rupees per annum.

Finally, the CFs are invariably members of one or the other village organisations such as the village panchayat, the Coir Corporation Society, the Dairy Society, the Farmers Co-operative Society, the Youth Club, etc.

Compared with the overall household sample, where only 6.4 per cent were member of panchayat, and 42.4 per cent had joined the Dairy Society, CFs are clearly more prone to participating in development organisations at the grass-rots level.

Selection of Contact Farmers : Theory and Reality

The CF is the centre of all nonformal educational activity in the process of rural and particularly agricultural development. It is to him that the elaborate, time-consuming and complex T and V System is geared. It is through him that the entire village community is to catch up with new knowledge, scientific skills, and modern attitudes with respect to agricultural practices. Hence, the selection, role-definition, and performance of the CF is crucial to the rural development process.

It is in this light that the guidelines for selection of Contact Farmers have to be looked into. This is all the more important as the village society is a heterogeneous one in terms of land-holding, income, educational level, etc. One in terms of caste and occupation is there some homogeneity. With these cocnsiderations, the Government of India has laid down certain guidelines[3] for selection of Contact Farmers. They stress, *inter alia*, three important principles of selection: firstly, that the village people themselves should participate in the selection of CF; secondly, that the CF should be experienced and practising farmers; and thirdly, that they should include a fair representation of both small, medium, and big farmers.

Principle of Peoples' Participation

The first principle of selection of CF is that the 'selection of CF may be left to the farmers themselves'.[3] This highly democratic directive has been flouted. In the case of Yaliyur, the CF have been selected by the ADA's office and their list has been kept without even informing, let alone regularly meeting, a great majority of them. In contrast, at Baladare, all the CF are aware of their function. But in 29 out of 35 cases it is the Agricultural Assistant who simply informed them that they were to be CFs. The AAO added five more to the list, and the village leader got another one included. None of them has thus been genuinely elected.

Principle of Practical Experience

All Contact Farmers except one are practising farmers. All the them have landed interests. Ragi and coconut cultivation are popular among almost all the CFs. However, as we pointed out the T and V system planned and managed by the Department of Agriculture covers only Ragi and paddy. Coconut, practised by virtually all farmers, is left out. There is no co-ordination of functions at the grass-roots level between the field staff of the Departments of Agriculture and Horticulture. The general feeling is that it is 'not required'.

Principle of Representative

It is proposed that due representation should be given to small and medium farmers when selectioning CFs. The CFs are supposed to influence the farmers around them by applying and transferring the knowledge and skills transmitted to them by the AA. Hence the Contact Farmers should be from all cross-sections with respect to land-holding.

However, the distribution of CFs in Baladare is skewed in favour of large-sized holders. Twenty-nine out of 35 CFs in Baladare own more than five acres of land. Big farmers in Yaliyur (more then 5 acres) are only 12 out of 31.

The principle of representativity has been better observed in the Yaliyur range where T and V is not managed well, whereas it has been flouted in the Baladare range where the programme is better managed. Thus, paradoxically, the T and V system is planned well where it is not properly implemented, and it is implemented and managed better where it is not properly planned.

For the agricultural field staff, there are many advantages in concentrating on big farmers. They are better educated and earn a relatively better income. They are more receptive to what the AA may propose. They can take risks by following new agricultural practices. Considerations of costs of inputs and services do not weigh as much with them as they may do in the case of marginal and small farmers. They will have more business or other transactions at the town or block headquarters. They will thus carry a 'good' impression of the work of the AA to his superior officers and others who matter. They may have links with administrative and politically powerful persons. In short, they are the people who 'matter' in rural areas.

What will be the overall effect on rural development of this concentration on big farmers? The big farmers will be able to increase their productivity and income by applying the lessons of new agricultural technology. In fact, it is quite possible that overall good production due to big farmers may increase more quickly. At the same time, the marginal and small farmers, whether they are contact or follow farmers, tend to withdraw from or ignore the T and V system. They will begin to think that it is meant only far the big farmers who have the means of investment to match the T and V suggestions. In this way, the objectives of the T and V system will ultimately be defeated. Further, the gap between the haves and the have-nots, the landed gentry and the poor marginal and small farmers, will increase. The objective of equity will thus remain a distant dream.

Other Principles

The selection of the CF with respect to other principles such as that of social status, receptivity to new ideas, representation of diverse agrotechnical conditions, enthusiastic entrepreneurship etc., have all been by the large observed in both ranges. The CFs are members of village organisation and belong to all ages, two out of three CFs in Baladare being young or middle aged. It is only in Yaliyur that a majority of CF listed in the ADA's office tend to be older and, in a few cases, even very old.

Responsiveness to New Agricultural Practices

There are many aspects of farming which go to makeup the package of new agricultural practices: soil-testing and selection of crops on the basis of its results; use of new seeds and chemicals for treatment of seeds; spacing of cultivable land; systematic preparation of seed-beds and transplantation in case of a few crops; use of fertilizers and manures in correct proportion; adoption of preventive measures to check crop diseases; use of appropriate pesticides in correct proportion in case of affectation of crops; use of weedicides; use of modern agricultural implements; improved practices in regard to storage of grains, etc. The farmers' responsiveness to all these dimensions of modernised agriculture is essential for the success of the Green Revolution. The farmers' response in turn depends upon two things: (i) farmers' socio-economic characteristics, their motivation, abilities, etc., and (ii) the management and monitoring of the T and V programme at the grass-roots level, and its co-ordination with other developmental opportunities in the form of subsidies and loans for inputs and services. It is these latter aspects that are being looked into now.

CF Response to Soil Testing

None of the CFs in Yaliyur had his soil tested, whereas in Baladare 15 out of 35 CFs have done so. Among these 15 CF, 13 have an annual income of over Rs. 5,000. In most cases it was the Agricultural Assistant who had the soil tested for the CFs. Twelve out of the 15 subsequently planned their cropping pattern on this basis.

The Tiller's Weapon

The most common, inexpensive and popular weapon in the hands of the Indian farmer is the plough made of wood. There have been several improvements of this traditional plough. For a few years now the plough made of steel has been recommended, marketed and popularised through the Department of Agriculture. It is sold at subsidised rates for marginal and small farmers and agricultural labourers.

Yet, only two CF in Baladare and one CFs in Yaliyur use exclusively the modernised steel plough. Another 23 CFs in Baladare and 14 in Yaliyur use it along with the traditional plough. There are still ten CFs in Baladare out of 35 and 11 in Yaliyur out of 31 who depend exclusively on the traditional plough.

The educational level of the CF has nothing to do with the use of the traditional plough. But several CFs who use the traditional plough in Yaliyur belong to low-income groups. Furthermore, it is mostly the CF who belong to the SC and ST category in terms of caste-status who use the traditional plough.

All the 25 CFs in Baladare who use the modern plough have been motivated by the AA. In Yaliyur the CFs are motivated from several sources, the Agricultural Assistant being only one of them.

Finally, it is interesting to observe that though 40 CFs use the modern plough for cultivation, only two of them have obtained a subsidy to purchase it.

Seeds of Progress

The quantity of food produced also depends upon the quality of seeds, and the way they are used. Twenty-eight out of 35 CFs in Baladare prepare the seed-bed for paddy and coconut cultivation as per the guidelines of the Department of Agriculture. There are still six CFs who do it in their traditional way. In contrast, at Yaliyur range 22 out of 31 CFs prepare the seed-bed in a traditional way.

However, a majority of CFs in both ranges have recognised the value of high-yielding varieties (HYV) of seeds. Thirty out of 35 CFs in Baladare and 20 out of 31 CF in Yaliyur use HYV.

It should be recalled in passing that quite a few farmers in Yaliyur range had used improved seeds a few years earlier and got a better than normal yield. They tried to retain a small portion of this yield for purposes of seeding in the following crop season, but could not do so owing to their low economic status. They needed food-grains to sustain their living, to exist. So they used up the seeds preserved for the purpose and had to revert to the locally available, cheaper seeds that they could borrow from relatively better-placed farmers. These pitiable contingencies of human existence in rural areas call for support from the government to the poorest, however knowledgeable, farmers. This can take the form of a seed library (call it by whatever name) from where they can borrow seeds on a no-profit no-loss basis. Mere education and transmission of knowledge do not serve the purpose.

Most of the CFs who use the improved seeds in both Baladare and Yaliyur have primary or even secondary education. Similarly, a majority of them belong to the higher-income groups.

Thirty-three CFs in Baladare out of 35 reported that it was the AA of the range who afore the first time suggested the use of improved seeds. The CFs of Yaliyur mentioned several sources: only three credited the AA for the suggestion, while six CFs have learnt it by observing other farmers, None of the CFs mentioned the radio as a source of motivation.

Why don't all CFs resort to improved seeds? Only two CFs in Baladare and eight in Yaliyur have ventured a reply to this question. While the CFs in Baladare reported that the improved seeds are expensive, four CFs in Yaliyur feel that the management and care of the farm with improved seeds is too expensive. The other four CF in Yaliyur feel that a mixture of both locally available and improved seeds is best fo higher yields.

Chemical Treatment of Seeds

The seeds need to be treated with chemicals as a preventive measure before seeding. Nineteen CFs in Baladare and 20 in Yaliyur have no problem of treating seeds with chemicals. They use ready-made seeds packed in certified bags. Nine more CFs in Baladare treat the seeds with chemicals on their own. However, there are six CFs in Baladare and five in Yaliyur who reported that they definitely do not treat seeds with chemicals.

The nine CFs in Baladare who treat seeds with chemicals on their own are primary – and secondary-educated. All of them get an income over Rs. 5,000 per annum, and five of them are in the above Rs. 15,000 range. The AA of the range advised all these nine CFs on the treatment of seeds.

Transplantation of Crops

Transplantation is a popular step in paddy cultivation. It is a method of transferring a tender plant into previously cleaned areas in the same plot. Spacing of plants, weeding and cleaning of transferred plants are all attended to at this stage. Systematised knowledge concerning the transplantation of plants leads to optimisation of production. Practically all Contact Farmers reported that they transplant their crops – 32 in Baladare and 26 in Yaliyur. By contrast, all CFs in Yaliyur do it in their traditional way, as handed down for generations, whereas 19 CF out of 35 in Baladare are guided by the AA's advice on scientific methods of transplantation.

Consumption of Manures and Fertilizers

All Contact Farmers in Baladare as well as Yaliyur use both manures and fertilisers on their farms. The manure is available locally either in the form of cow-dung or other animal and vegetable waste, sold in measures of a cartload.

The synthetic or chemical fertilisers are used by all CFs except three in Yaliyur. Two of the latter are illiterates while one is secondary-educated. But all three get an income of over Rs. 5,000 per annum. The CFs who use synthetic fertilizers belong to all educational categories including illiterates and all income-groups including the lowest range. However, there is a concentration of the CFs who use fertilisers in the category of primary education and in the income-groups Rs. 5,001 to Rs. 10,000 and Rs. 15,001 and above.

In 34 out of 35 cases in Baladare it is the AA of the range who persuaded the CF to use synthetic fertilisers. In Yaliyur the number of CFs crediting the AA for this is hardly two.

Pest Control in Agriculture

It is common knowledge that crops are affected by pests. There are two ways in which pest affectation is controlled. One of them is to take preventive measures and the other is to resort to plant-protection measures.

Only six CFs in Baladare have reported that their crops are not affected by pests. Out of these six, four had taken preventive measures.

Those who do not undertake plant-protection measures when their crops are affected are rather exceptions. There are two such CFs in Yaliyur and one in Baladare.

It would have been interesting to test the knowledge and skills of CFs regarding the quantity and timing of the use of pesticides, weedicides and insecticides. But this was beyond the competence of the present study. However, in a study by Pannikar, exploring reasons for sub-optimal performance of 317 cultivator households in two census villages of Palghat and Kuttanad areas of Kerala State, it is reported that:

> '. . . Input (fertilisers) use was closely as per the guidelines of the Directorate of Extension Education, Kerala Agricultural University. Adoption of HYV was widespread, but yields were low. Reasons for sub-optimal performance were explored. It is felt that the HYV (as against traditional varieties) attract a variety of pests and diseases at the reproductive stages (as against vegetative stage for traditional varieties), leading to indiscriminate application of insecticides, pesticides and weedicides. This results in serious health hazards for plants, wipes out natural enemies of pests such as frogs, insects, fish and to some extent even spiders' (Panikkar, 1981).

This observation is significant from the point of view of proper education of farmers in the use of agricultural inputs and management of the farm.

Storing Food-grains

Given the poverty levels of farmers in India they do not come across long-term storage problems of food-grains as they do not produce enough. However, every farmer faces the problem of storing food-grains. This is essential to prevent infection from fungi and protect the seeds against insects. Quite an amount of research-based, tried and tested knowledge is available about storage practices. It forms part of the T and V programme also. But it is observed that only three CFs (in Baladare as well as Yaliyur) follow the guidelines of the AA in storing their food-grains. All the rest do it in their traditional way.

Relationships between Agricultural Assistants, Contact Farmers and Follow Farmers

The management of the T and V programme at the grass-roots level depends upon several factors: the vigour and sincerity with which the AA takes the job to his head and heart; the concern of higher officers in the hierarchy regarding the observance of training and visit schedules; the mechanisms of reinforcement, both positive and negative, of the work of the field functionaries, etc., and ultimately the response of the contact and follow farmers. In this sense, the relationships and interaction between Agricultural Assistance, Contact Farmers, and Follow Farmers were examined by this study.

In terms of contact between the AA and the CF, the T and V programme appears to have performed well in the Baladare range. Its performance is dismal in the Yaliyur range. Thirty-four out of 35 CF in Baladare have reported that they know their AA well, and they could give his name. The 35 man can recognise the AA but cannot recall his name. In contrast, only five CFs in Yaliyur know the AA by name.

The AA is scheduled to meet one group of CFs once a week for training, and one in the following week for visits. All the 35 CFs in Baladare have reported that the AA meets them at least once a fortnight, though none of them has reported any weekly meetings.

The picture is altogether different in the Yaliyur range. While only three CFs have reported about occasional meetings with the AA, not a single group meeting has been conducted so far.

Almost all the CFs in Baladare experience field problems in the planning an management of their crops. In 33 out of 35 cases such problems have been referred for the AA. But the member of CFs who have referred their field problems at Yaliur to the AA is hardly four.

All the CFs who have raised questions on farm management with the AA report that the AA knows the answers to all field problems that they have raised so far. Fifteen Contact Farmers in Baladare went on to say that, in case the AA does not know the answer, he carries the problem to his superiors and brings back the solution in the subsequent meeting. But the CFs in Yaliyur appear to be highly dissatisfied with the performance of the AA of their range. Nineteen out of 31 reported that their AA does not care about their field problems. In fact, when asked what suggestions they would offer to improve the work of the AA in their range, ten CF in Yaliyur range recommended that 'action should be taken against the AA' for non-performance.

The Contact Farmers who are the immediate target of the whole T and V system are supposed to spread the T and V messages in their environment by precept as well as practice. In this way it is hoped that all the farmers in the area, and especially 25 to 40 so called 'Follow Farmers' for every CF, will take to the T and V technology. Hence, the T and V will spread through a process of chair reaction. These are the noble objective of the T and V system. But the actual field situation is not so rosy.

Twenty-five out of 35 CFs in Baladare have reported that they have interactions with follow farmers. There are only two such CFs in Yaliyur. These interactions are limited and are far from regular. In most cases the advice is given only when follow farmers take the initiative. Many FFs, on the other had, who consult the CFs about agricultural practices do follow the advice of the CFs. In 17 out of 25 cases in Baladare the FFs have acted upon the advice of the CFs. In fact, 12 CFs have reportedly supervised the farming operations of the FF to whom they had offered advice.

The Department of Agriculture organises a variety of agricultural extension programmes other than the T and V field days, field demonstrations, field excursions, specialised agricultural training, are illustrations of such programmes. Twenty-six out of 35 Contact Farmers in Baladare are aware to these educational programmes. Most of the CFs characterised the educational programmes in which they participated as useful or partly useful. None felt that the programmes were useless. Though it is hard to believe, the CFs in Yaliyur reported that none of them is aware of any of these programmes.

Concluding Impressions – T and V System

The general feeling as regards the planning an management of the T and V system in rural areas is one of the dissonances. Whilst in the context of the Yaliyur range the T and V programme is planned well managed badly, in the context of Baladare range it is planned badly but managed well. The T and V programme, as being implemented now at Baladare, will not serve the objective of either growth or equity. Though it is planned well in Yaliyur, it exists largely on paper and generalizations on an almost non-implemented programme would be futile.

Certain striking contrasts appear between the AA of Baladare and that of Yaliyur, as one looks at the management of the T and V programme. The AA of Baladare is young. He appears to be enthusiastic in popularising the T and V. He has excellent relations with the farmers his range, as could be observed while moving with him in rural areas. He has taken the T and V work to his heart, displays concern about farmers' problems and commitment to his work. Though relatively new to the job, he enjoys the confidence and open appreciation of the his superior officers including the ADA as well as the village leaders.

The AA of Yaliyur is getting old. He is nearing 50 years of age, and he has about 28 years of extension education work experience in rural areas. He has been in the same position for all these 28 years, though the designation of his post has been changed time and again. He has only a few years left before retirement, and displays open apathy towards rural development programmes including the T and V. He hardly visits the villages of his range, has limited contacts with farmers though he knows all of them and all of them know him. Perhaps, these observations reflect upon the service conditions, promotion policies and prospects of the field level functionaries in extension education programmes in particular, and rural development programmes in general. They are the immediate agents of the delivery system for rural development. There is a need to re-examine the status of this human-resource factor in development.

The Programme of Training Youth for Self-Employment

The programme of 'Training Youth for Self-Employment', popularly known as TRYSEM, is one among several schemes included in IRDP — the Integrated Rural Development Programme already referred to earlier in this study. The IRDP was launched all over the State by the Government of Karnataka during 1979. Its target-group are the poorest of the poor families in rural areas.

IRDP programmes are planned at the block level, based on the identification of the poorest families. For this, a household survey is carried out in a group of villages called a cluster. A cut-off point of household income distinguishes the potential beneficiary-families from the rest.

The IRDP programmes are implemented through the Block Development Officer, who co-ordinates his work with the banking institutions, training agencies, voluntary organisations, marketing centres, etc.

'Training of Youth for Self-Employment' is essentially a non-agricultural programme. In addition, it is one of the few programmes which have a rich education and training component. It involves a nonformal education stage as well as financial support in the form of loans for purchase of equipment, subsidy in the form of stipend during the training, and later on, assistance in marketing the products.

Preference is given to scheduled castes, scheduled tribes and women. There is no insistence on a qualifying level of formal education. Nor is there usually any certification of the training obtained. The curriculum on the various training programmes is planned in such a way as to suit local conditions. Paramount is the objective to assist the trained youth in setting up self-employment, and to discourage them from taking up paid employment; it is considered that the latter would defeat the objective of the programme and render the training futile.

A variety of specific training schemes are proposed under TRYSEM: training in rearing cross-bred cattle; fisheries; horticulture; seed farming; sericulture; repair of electrically-operated pumpsets; production of bakery products; artificial insemination; poultry-raising; radio assembly and repair; wool production; mat-making; embroidery; preservation of fruits and other consumable goods; blacksmithy; masonry; carpentry; bee-keeping and tailoring.

The BDO will select the training centres in consultation with the District Rural Development Society (DRDS).

The trainee is not supposed to spend anything on his training, as the DRDS is supposed to meet all training expenses. The trainee has to launch his employment after a feasibility study and in consultation with the BDO, the District Industries Centre, the teachers of the training school, and officers of the DRDS, the local banking organisation, the marketing officers, etc.

The present study has tried to examine the implementation of TRYSEM programmes in Channarayapatna block. Half of the beneficiaries under the TRYSEM during the years 1979-80 and 1980-81 from the sample of the study. For this purpose, the 62 beneficiaries were listed in alphabetical order of names and every alternatie person was chosen for the study. Only 30 of them could finally be contacted, as one had left his village.

The Programme and its Clients

TRYSEM, it should be pointed out, is a programme addressed to unemployed youth in rural areas. There may be several definitions of 'Youth' in terms of age; if the period between 18 to 25 years is taken as 'youth', then 22 out of the 30 respondents fit into the programme. There are two respondents who are below 18 years; this fact is all-decisive, as it makes them ineligible for bank loans. There are, on the other hand, six respondents who are older than 26 years. In Channarayapatna block, therefore, the clientele of TRYSEM meets only in part the official definition of 'youth'.

It is equally interesting to observe that a majority of TRYSEM beneficiaries are women. There are 24 respondent women among 30 respondents. Ten respondents are married, two of them are widows, and the rest are unmarried.

All respondents are educated, with a minimum of seven years of primary education. Eight respondents have even passed the final secondary-school examination. Two are trained in nursery education, and others are working as teachers for adult education centres during the evenings. The TRYSEM clients are thus much better educated than the average womenfull in the area. It will be recalled that illiteracy is rampant among the 411 sample wives interviewed by this study.

The 30 respondents are distributed in seven areas of the block. Many areas in the block have been left out in selecting TRYSEM beneficiaries. There are certain constraints, such as lack of infrastructure facilities, or a community zeal, which stand in the way of a balanced selection.

The Industrial Extension Officer (IEO) is the chief source of awareness about the TRYSEM programme for a majority of the respondents; he has been mentioned in 22 out of 30 cases. The IEO is attached to the Block Development Office (BDO), though his parent department is the Department of Industries and Commerce.

Another eight respondents mentioned in addition the Women Welfare Officer of *'Mukhya Sevika'* and other sources. One of these eight has come to know through reading printed pamphlets circulated by the BDO, and another two have read about it on the notice-board of the block office.

A majority of respondents have been motivated for the TRYSEM programme by economic considerations. Fifteen out of 28 have reported that they joined TRYSEM so as 'to earn money'. Another six respondents said that they wanted to spend their time in a meaningful way. Three respondents said that the training offered under TRYSEM matched with their traditional family occupation and so they got interested. There are two respondents who wanted to get a certificate under TRYSEM programme and use it later to get a job.

Twenty-two out of 28 respondents have been trained in tailoring by three voluntary women's organisations. The duration of training was six months for all respondents. Two trainees discontinued the tailoring course. One of them did so as she got married.

Three respondents from the block headquarters have been trained at the Agricultural Equipment Training Centre. Channarayapatna, in a sandwich course on smithy, carpentry and welding. Three other respondents have been trained in carpentry at the Artisan Training Institute in Holenarasipur, a nearby block. All these six respondents are males. The duration of training for them, too, was six months.

The TRYSEM scheme includes stipends for the trainees, paid on a monthly basis. It is observed that varying amounts have been paid to the trainees as stipend. While 11 respondents have received Rs. 50 per month during the six-month period of training, 17 respondents have received 100 rupees as stipend. Almost all the non-trailoring TRYSEM beneficiaries have received Rs. 100 per month. It is not entirely clear as to why the amount varies from Rs. 50 to Rs.Pw100. One explanation is that in the case of those who received Rs. 50 only, the other Rs. 50 were retained as a recurring deposit towards purchase of the sewing or tailoring machine after the training.

Most of the respondents did not need to spend from their pocket either on, board and lodging, or on transport, as their places of residence were near the training centres.

But for five respondents the training centre is far away from their homes. Especially the three respondents who were trained in carpentry at the Artisan Training Centre at Holenarasipur, a neighbouring block headquarters, found it hard to manage their training with the stipend given. They had to spend Rs. 30 to Rs. 40 over and above the Rs. 100 they received as stipend every month.

Programme Relevance and Follow-up

A majority of TRYSEM beneficiaries (15 out of 28) reported that the training they had received was useful to them. Ten respondents found it 'not very much' useful, while three respondents reported that it was useful 'to some extent'. It needs to be pointed out that not all who have received training (28 respondents) have also received loans and subsidy (14 respondents). Of those 14, who did have follow-up support, 11 stitch clothes of the villagers to earn money, while one of them stitches clothes of family members — her family is well-to-do and she does not need to earn money. The scheduled caste beneficiary is not using the machine. There is no demand for her work. Another respondent has given up stitching as it is not profitable. Four of those who received neither loan nor subsidy, also use their training by stitching at the women's welfare centre or at friends' places. Another three non-beneficiaries have their own tailoring machine. Training has been useful to them. For the three carpentry-trained beneficiaries, too, the training is useful as they do piece-work in the village. One carpentry-trained respondent has secured a job.

Follow-up Assistance

The purpose of training under TRYSEM is to give the beneficiaries a capacity for self-employment. However, financial support for the purchase of equipment, machinery or other essential items was given to only 14 respondents. For this purpose, the IEO arranged a loan from the bank and a subsidy from the government, given through the BDO under the IRDP programme. One of these 14 respondents, being a scheduled caste lady, got the equipment free of cost. For the 14 respondents who have got follow-up assistance, a time-gap between training and employment has been observed. Five respondents had to wait for nearly a year after completing their training, while another nine respondents had to wait for nearly a year and a half. Needless to say, better planning and management should be able to secure financial assistance immediately after the period of training.

Fourteen respondents have thus not received any financial assistance for self-employment after their training. It is not that all these 14 respondents had aspired for financial assistance but failed to get it. This is the case of only nine out of the 14: the local bank had refused to grant financial assistance to two out of these nine respondents as they were minors, being below 18 years of age and thus not eligible for the assistance. Another four out of the nine respondents could not get the loan, as they failed to pay a deposit towards the purchase of the equipment. Perhaps these four were the poorest of the poor. One of them was found to be a widow. In the case of two more respondents the loan had been sanctioned, but not yet released. The bank was waiting for the subsidy from the government.

Of the remaining five respondents who had not applied for

follow-up assistance, one quit the course after four months. The other four did not want a loan or subsidy, as they already had the equipment or purchased it on their own; one respondent (trained in welding, carpentry and smithy) got a paid job as a welder in the District headquarters.

It must also be noted that the amount of loan and subsidy is not the same for all beneficiaries. While one belonging to a scheduled caste, got the tailoring machine for free, the others have got loans ranging from 640 to 800 rupees. The subsidy also varied form 140 to 290 rupees.

The rate of interest on bank loans for TRYSEM is fixed at one per cent. There is no fixed period for loan repayment for any beneficiary. They have been advised to repay in monthly instalments depending upon their income. There are these who have been repaying as low an instalment as Rs. 20 per month, while other have paid as much as Rs. 80 per month. Only one beneficiary has repaid the full amount.

The TRYSEM Market

Only 15 TRYSEM beneficiaries are in a practical sense self-employed. Those who are trained in tailoring stitch clothes, and those who are trained in carpentry take up piece-work of making windows, doors, tables, chairs, etc. They do this work in the village itself. As we saw, one trainee who was trained in welding got a job.

Women trained in tailoring, in a few cases, find it difficult to get orders for stitching as there are already professional tailors at work in their villages. But it is the case of the scheduled caste respondent which is most pathetic and cruel. Though she got trained in tailoring, has completed the eighth standard of schooling, and has got a tailoring machine free of cost, she has not been able to get along with this job. There is, she says, no demand for her skill, and hence she is not using her machine. She did not like to spell out the reasons. In all likelihood, the caste Hindus do not want to give their clothes to her for stitching. Moreover, even the other scheduled caste families may prefer to got to caste Hindu tailors.

Economic Condition of TRYSEM Beneficiaries

How far has the TRYSEM improved the economic condition of the respondents? Those respondents who were just trained, and the others who were provided financial follow-up assistance, as well, must be considered separately for this analysis.

Nine of those who were just trained reported that the training did not improve their economic condition while another three reported that there has been a slight improvement. Likewise five respondents among the 14 who had been given financial assistance for purchase of equipment their economic condition. It is only in the case of eight respondents that the project has effected 'slight improvement'. This will be the case of most tailoring women who apparently earn an additional Rs. 30 per month. There is, finally, one beneficiary who has reported that the TRYSEM programme has definitely improved her economic condition. She is a tailor who manages to earn some Rs. 60 to Rs. 70 per month.

General Impressions of Respondents

The respondents had been asked to give their general impressions or anything else they wanted to say about the TRYSEM programme. Six respondents had nothing to say. Eleven respondents complained that the IEO who so enthusiastically involved them in the project did not follow it up after the training was over. Either he did not take sufficient interest in getting them financial assistance from banks, or failed to get them a certificate for the training they had received. Three other respondents further criticised the IEO for not auctioning the clothing they had stitched during training and carrying it away 'God knows where'. Two respondents have complaints against the bank for raising 'unnecessary' objections in sanctioning assistance. Five respondents have complaints against the educational content of the programme: four of them, trained in tailoring, designed that new patterns and styles should have been taught instead of concentrating too much on the parts of the machine and on theoretical aspects. One who was trained in welding, smithy, and carpentry in a period of six months desired that he should have been taught only one trade during that time.

Planning and Management of the TRYSEM Programme

The planning and management of the TRYSEM programme must be assessed from the perspective of the 'success' of the whole project. Has the TRYSEM programme been successful? One may have to define 'success' at the outset: should 'success' be interpreted in terms of coverage of beneficiaries, successful completion of training, the variety of training programmes offered, provision of financial assistance to youth for self-employment, the opening-up of markets for the skills in which the persons are trained? Or should it be gauged by its overall effects in raising the levels of income and quality of life of the persons covered?

A minimum of seventh-standard education has been required in selecting beneficiaries for the TRYSEM training. because of the formal education of the beneficiaries, sources of programme awareness other than personal contacts have come to light. The beneficiaries have come to know about the programme not only through verbal messages from the IEO and the Women Welfare Officer (WWO), but also through printed pamphlets, advertisements in local newspapers, notice-board displays at the BDO's office, etc.

Beneficiaries have been invariably selected by the IEO or the WWO of the BDO's office. A better planning in selection could have avoided some problems at a later stage. For instance, two persons were below 18 years of age were selected and then refer financial assistance from the bank on the grounds they were minors. In fact, quite a few beneficiaries the TRYSEM programme cannot strictly be called 'youth'.

A great majority of TRYSEM beneficiaries are women. There is nothing wrong with that from the point of view of raising the status of rural women. But it was not planned that way. It has happened like that because of insufficient demand for a variety of trades under TRYSEM. When the IEO could not get sufficient response for other trades he requested the women welfare officer to locate persons to reach the target fixed for the block. This suited the *Mukhya Sevika* as she is expected to promote women's welfare. So she publicised it with the IEO at places where there was already some community enthusiasm for women's welfare in the form of active women's organisations. In this way they found several women willing to undergo training under TRYSEM.

This type of planning based on social demand and target fulfilment is likely to lead to several types of imbalances. One of them will be the imbalance in skill development. That is, only a few skills such as tailoring will be covered and in a few years there will be a large supply of tailors not matched by demand. Even now, those trained under TRYSEM and assisted to purchase equipment find it difficult to get a market as there are professional tailors in their area, tailors for whom it is a caste occupation. Another imbalance refers to locational and distributional aspects of the TRYSEM programme. Only a few areas where there is already a given level of development or development consciousness will get patronised, while those areas which are relatively under-developed will be ignored.

A few final observations on the management of the TRYSEM programme: the training aspect of the programme has been managed relatively well. There were few dropouts, as most of the trainees lived near the training centres. A majority of trainees reported that the training was useful to them. However, the financial follow-up support for self-employment could have been managed in a better way. Nearly 50 per cent of trainees could not get any financial support. Those who did had to wait for a long time. There was a minimum time-gap of eight months. Had the papers for financial assistance been initiated well in advance for the completion of the training, it would have been possible to minimise the time-gap. Finally, the marketing of the products from TRYSEM has been almost completely ignored. Consideration of all these aspects would go a long way in making the TRYSEM programme more successful and relevant for the non-agricultural dimension of rural development.

Summary of the Main Findings

At two points the present study has dealt with problems of verticals and horizontal integration in the delivery system for rural development. first, it presented an institutional analysis focusing on the taluk or block; in the Indian setting, the block is supposed to be the principal linking-pin for different programmes of the rural development. In addition, the study subsequently employed interviews with field-level functionaries and clients of two selected development projects to identify problems of integration in the practical operation of these projects.

What conclusions can be drawn from this two-prong analysis of the delivery system for rural development? The institutional analysis, though geographically limited to Channarayapatna block in Hassan district, does suggest certain generalisable conclusions: the block provides the point of intersection for various vertically-structured institutions, distinguished by their functional specialisation. Each of these observes a vertical chain of command, and maintains its particular institutional culture. The high degree of differentiation which these multiple delivery channels represent does not seem to be matched by a commensurate degree of integration. There are several reasons why the Block Development Agency, and at a higher level the District Rural Development Society, do not provide the effective 'linking-pins' for which they were conceived. The first is that an agency as crucial as the Department of Agriculture remains outside the BDO's co-ordinating power; but even for agencies within the BDO's purview, the BDO cannot exercise direct control over their block-level staff. His administrative rank is too low; moreover, his staff resources are too depleted to allow for effective co-ordination and supervision.

NOTES

1. Marginal holding means less than one hectare of cultivable land and small-holding means a holding in the range of one to two hectares. Land beyond this limit is considered as a big farm. Cultivable land means dry land, the conversion rate being 1 hectare of wet land to 2 hectares of dry land. The classification of land as dry or wet depends upon the type of crop grown along with the source and availability or irrigation.
2. The income data analysed in the present study are not directly reported by the respondents, but computed by the researchers, based on information about their produce during the previous year and any additional income from wage-labour, cattle, dairying, poultry, sheep-tending, household industry, etc.
3. Directive issued by the Director of Agriculture, Karnataka State, on 11-6-1979, and addressed, amongst others, to the Deputy Director of Agriculture in Hassan District.

14

A SCHEME FOR THE ALLEVIATION OF EXTREME POVERTY: An Evaluation

P.M. Kulkarni

I. Introduction

With the adoption of direct intervention as the principal strategy aimed at poverty alleviation in India, the emphasis has shifted, towards providing assistance directly to those identified as 'poor'. This has given rise to what are called target group or beneficiary-oriented programmes. These programmes can be broadly classified into those for self-employment and those for the creation of wage employment. The Integrated Rural Development Programme (IRDP) is the main instrument for providing productive assets for self-employment to the rural poor. Though initially proposed as a programme for the integrated development of rural areas, it was identified and recognised as essentially an anti-poverty programme. Furthermore, at the stage of implementation, it was treated as a programme for providing productive assets to poor rural households. Since most of the rural poor were agricultural labourers and marginal farmers, the demand was for land. But because of the inability to acquire and distribute cultivable land to the landless, the next best alternative, that was also acceptable to the rural poor, was to provide cattle and sheep. Naturally, a majority of the poor received milch cattle, draught cattle, sheep or goats. The purchase of the assets was financed by banks, to which the recipients had to make repayments, and only a part was given as a subsidy, which was the net benefit to the beneficiaries. The beneficiaries were then expected to utilise these assets for income generation, pay off the loans, and 'rise above the poverty line'.

The functioning and impact of this programme have been examined in a number of studies that have collected data from the administrators as well as from the beneficiaries. In a review that has received widespread attention and that has generated considerable debate, Rath (1985) has forcefully and convincingly argued that : (i) in terms of poverty alleviation, the programme has achieved very little — only about 20 per cent of poor beneficiaries were able to cross the poverty line, and if an adjustment is made for loan repayment instalments, this percentage would fall below 10 ; (ii) this failure is, as is often believed, not administrative, 'in the sense that more careful administration, can convert the bulk of failures into success' (p. 244); and (iii) the poorest of the poor, the landless agricultural labourers, have fared the worst (for a comment on this paper, see Dantwala, 1985). Rath has further pointed out that 'the poorest who are at the bottom rung of the economic ladder do not get proportionately larger loan and subsidy compared to those above them'. The programme has made a provision for differential subsidy, but the difference is too small to be of significance (the capital subsidy increases from one-fourth of the price of the asset in the case of small farmers, to one-third of the price in the case of marginal farmers and agricultural labourers).

However, in another scheme designed for a group that can be considered to belong to the poorest section of the society, the basic approach is the same as that of the IRDP, but the amount of subsidy is much larger. In fact, the entire cost of the asset is paid by the government with the result that there is no bank loan and thus no burden of repayment. This scheme, called the 'Bonded Labour Rehabilitation Programme', was introduced with the aim of providing assistance to those labourers who were released after the bonded labour system was abolished in India. It has been in operation since 1978, and thus has been functioning contemporaneously with the IRDP. The administration of the scheme is done by the same agency that is responsible for the implementation of the IRDP and the same guidelines are followed. An examination of the functioning of the bonded labour rehabilitation programme, thus, provides an opportunity to see how a programme very similar to the IRDP, with the added benefit that there is no burden of loan on the recipients of the assets, has worked for the extreme poor — the formerly bonded labourers. The results can then be compared to the findings of studies on the IRDP.

In this paper, some findings from an evaluation study of the bonded labour rehabilitation programme in Karnataka are presented. These are, later, compared to the functioning of the IRDP in the same State as observed in evaluation studies that were carried out at about the same time. The comparison is meaningful because the administrative practices and efficiency and the socio-political setting remain unchanged. The background of the bonded labour rehabilitation programme is given in the next section. This is followed by a description of the functioning of the programme and its impact. A comparison with the findings of the IRDP studies is given in section IV, followed by discussion.

II. The Bonded Labour Rehabilitation Programme In Karnataka: Background

The practice of poor labourers working as bonded servants to landowner-cultivators was widely prevalent in rural India. Lacking land or other assets that could be pledged or mortgaged, poor landless families would often pledge the labour of someone in the family in order to secure a loan. Such a person would then work as a 'bonded labourer' committed to provide service exclusively to the lender and not free to participate in the labour market. The work would be done either purely towards interest until the principal was repaid or for a specified period towards repayment of the loan. Such arrangements often continued for long periods or were renewed annually. The terms were generally unfavourable to the borrowing family which was in a weak bargaining position whereas the lender had the benefit of assured labour.

The Government of India abolished the bonded labour system in 1975. The State Governments were asked to identify those working as bonded labourers and make arrangements to release them. In pursuance of this, 1,20,561 bonded labourers were released in India by 1981, over half of whom (62,689) were in Karnataka. The abolition of the bonded labour system and the consequent release of the labourers was only the first step in the amelioration of those who were hitherto bonded. Most of them did not have adequate income generating assets and it was feared that many would relapse into bondage (though illegal). Therefore, in 1978, the Government of India introduced a programme for the rehabilitation of freed bonded labourers. The main feature of this scheme is to provide assistance to the freed labourers in the form of certain income generating assets such as draught cattle, milch cattle, sheep, goats and materials and tools for skill/craftbased enterprises.

The cost of assistance per freed labourer had a ceiling of Rs.4,000 initially which was enhanced to Rs.6,250 in 1986. The administration of the programme is entrusted to a department of the State government. In Karnataka, the Department of Rural Development and Panchayati Raj is responsible for the implementation of the programme.

An evaluation of the bonded labour rehabilitation programme in Karnataka was attempted in 1987. Information on the nature of bondage, the process of procuring an asset, facilitates available to utilise it, retention of the asset, income generated due to it, as well as current income and living conditions was obtained from a sample of freed labourers covered by the scheme. The study was conducted in four districts of the State in which a very large number of bonded labourers were identified and given assistance and a total of 411 released labourers who had received some assistance were interviewed. Information about various aspects of the scheme was obtained through informal discussions with village leaders, social workers, and government officials.

The Bonded Labour System in Karnataka

In Karnataka, the system of bonded labour is commonly called the '*jeetha*' system (for some information, see Srinivas, 1955). The practice of taking loans and working in lieu of interest until the loan was repaid was not widely prevalent at least in the recent past. Only about 13 per cent of those contacted in this survey had worked in this manner, the rest had worked on annual contracts. Generally, a poor family, with some male members (rarely did women work on bondage) capable of working full time, would enter into an agreement with a landlord to provide the labour of such a person for one year and receive a certain amount of money. Thus, the money received by the household of the labourer could more correctly be described as an 'advance wage' rather than as a 'loan'. The labourers were expected to provide service exclusively to the lender. They were not free to participate in the labour market and it was not easy to terminate the contracts before the end of the year. The landlords provided food (2-3 meals a day) and clothing (2-3 sets a year). The labourers were expected to do any work assigned by the landlords. Naturally, this was mostly related to agricultural operations and animal husbandry. There were no fixed hours of work and since many stayed in the houses of the landlords their services could be used even at odd hours.

It was observed that the bonded labourers came generally from the weakest sections of the society. Of those contracted in this study, 78 per cent belonged to the scheduled castes or tribes and most of the others also belonged to communities that may be considered as backward. Over 87 per cent were illiterate and even among those with some schooling, not many had reached middle school level. Most lived in mud and thatched houses which had only one or two rooms. About half (45%) belonged to landless households, and those who owned lands had small holdings with rarely any irrigation facility. Only about 19 per cent owned some cattle. This description of the social and economic condition of the bonded labourers may appear superfluous, since who else but the very poor would work as such? But it is useful to note that those assisted in this programme were indeed very poor and as a group may be considered to have been among the most disadvantaged.

III. **Implementation and Impact of the Rehabilitation Programme**

Provision of Assets under the Scheme

The block development offices are entrusted with the task of suggesting suitable types of asset to be given as an outright grant rather than on credit as in the IRDP. The selection of schemes is based on preferences of the released labourers and opinions of the government officers about the suitability of these preferences to local conditions, and to skills and abilities of the potential beneficiaries. Among those contacted in the study, there was no overwhelming preference for any single scheme — about 18 per cent each preferred a pair of bullocks and sheep/goat units and about 11 per cent each preferred a cross-bred cow and buffaloes. A majority received the preferred type of asset. But many of those who wanted a pair of bullocks were denied it because they did not own any land, and many who wanted a sheep/goat unit were denied it because of the feeling that an asset of this type may be frittered away and would not be of use in the long run. There was not much preference for schemes base on skill, craft or business, generally termed as ISB (Industry Service, Business) schemes. Thus, ultimately, the animal husbandry schemes dominated. Among the sample beneficiaries the largest proportion had received buffaloes (28%), followed by a sheep/goat unit (25%), a pair of bullocks (15%), a cross-bred cow (11%), combination of milk and work cattle (8 per cent), combination of cattle and sheep (8%), and an ISB scheme (5%).

The procedure for the procurement and distribution of assets was the same as in the case of other similar schemes. Generally, assets were purchased by the block office and rarely was cash given to the released labourers. On the part of the beneficiaries, some paper work was required and they had to incur some expenditure in this connection for trips to the block office, documents, and expenses of middlemen. Some incidental expenditure — on transport of animals, photographs, etc. — and the insurance premium were charged against the sanctioned amount for individual beneficiaries. The quality of assets was generally good. Most milk cattle were either in lactation of expected to calves within a short time, and the bullocks generally in the age range 3-7 years. However, many recipients felt that the animals were overvalued. The incidence of ineligible persons receiving the assets was negligible, nor does the evidence indicate a substantial incidence of fictitious beneficiaries. The implementation of the rehabilitation scheme, overall, can be considered to have been done in a satisfactory manner.

Table 14.1: Rates of Retention of Various Types of Asset

Type of Asset	Per cent retaining the asset up to the survey date *	Per cent retaining the asset at the end of 1 Year after procurement	2 Year after procurement	3 Years after procurement	No. in the sampler given this type of asset
Bullocks	79	97	92	83	61
Cross-bred cows	68	94	87	58	47
Buffaloes	62	93	83	68	115
Bullocks + Buffalo	100	100	100	100	33
Sheep/goat unit	47	49	46	38	104
Bullocks + sheep	91	93	93	84	32
ISB	32	36	28	--	19
All	65	81	75	63	411

* Percentage distribution is not given since there are too few observations.

Retention of Assets

The first step in studying the impact of rehabilitation is to see to what extent the recipients have retained the assets (or are continuing with the enterprise). For this purpose those who have lost the original asset but have replaced it can also be treated as having retained the asset since they would also be 'in business'. Overall, 65 per cent of those who were given assistance were found to have retained the asset (or its replacement) up to the survey date. Retention rates for different durations since procurement are given in Table 14.1. The retention rates of bullocks (a pair of bullocks or a pair with another cattle or sheep) are very high, of milk cattle moderate, and of sheep/goats and ISB assets very low. There is heavy attrition in the first year itself in case of sheep/goat units and ISB assets whereas for other types of assets, attrition in the first year is negligible.

Retention of assets depends on a number of factors — related to the asset (quality, risk of death or of being unproductive, amount and flow of income, etc.), related to the owner (experience in handling the asset, availability of own raw material or fodder, facilitates such as shed, ability to purchase necessary materials, and ability to avoid disposal of the asset for normal consumption), and related to institutional support (for marketing, credit, veterinary services, etc). It was found that the quality of assets was generally good, but the risk of death was very high in the case of sheep/goats. Most of the released labourers had experience in handling cattle, but it was on behalf of the owners, and hence they may not have been knowledgeable about certain special problems. Less than 20 per cent of the recipients of cattle had owned such animals in the past and hardly any had owned graded animals. Since almost all the recipients were very poor, the ability to purchase necessary material was low, and the need to dispose off assets for consumption purposes urgent. Further, institutional support for credit and marketing was available mainly to members of co-operative societies and only 20 per cent of owners of milk cattle had become such members. In the light of this, the retention rates observed appear quite satisfactory. In fact, many officers involved in the implementation of the programme as well as many village leaders had not expected a high degree of retention of assets.

The levels of retention for two schemes- sheep/goat units and ISB — are, however, very low. In addition to the high losses on the account of death of sheep/goats, there have been heavy losses due to sales. The difficulty with these animals, unlike milk cattle, is that there is no continuous flow of income. The owner cannot be patient too long and is therefore inclined to sell one or two animal(s) at a time. To lesser degree, this problem is faced by the owners of buffaloes since buffaloes have long dry periods during which no income is generated. Lack of training in handling assets, and the fact that often cash was given instead of materials, are responsible for the low success rate of ISB scheme recipients.

Income Generated Due to Assets

Information on income and expenditure was obtained for the year 1986-87 from those who have retained the assets. The average net income due to an asset is Rs.874. Higher income is derived from cross-bred cows and bullocks-buffalo combination is moderate and due to sheep/goat units very low.

Those who have retained ISB assets were able to earn good incomes due to these, but the number of such persons is small of course, even among the owners of a particular asset, there are large variations in income and some have in fact lost small amounts (Table 14.2). On the other hand, many owners of milk cattle earned over Rs. 2000 during the year due to the asset. The mean incomes are generally lower than those observed in studies on beneficiaries of bank finance and thus indicate lower rate of return. However, as mentioned above, the conditions were not vary favourable to a better utilisation of assets and therefore this finding is not surprising. The low income generated from sheep/goat units is in correspondence with the low retention rate for these.

However, in the case of bullocks, in spite of low incomes, the retention rate is higher. This could be attributed to high opportunity cost. But equally important is the fact that in an agrarian setting, the ownership of a pair of bullocks confers some respectability on the household which by itself is very valuable.

Impact of Rehabilitation

To study the impact of rehabilitation on incomes, the 'before and after' approach could not be used because of non-availability of incomes prior to rehabilitation. However, it can be safely assumed that almost all the bonded labourers were very poor in the past, a not too

Table 14.2: Net Income due to Various Types of Asset

Net Income due to the asset during 1986-87	Types of asset							
	Bullo-cks	Cross-Bred Cows	Buffaloes	Bullocks + Buffaloes	Sheep/ Goats	Bullocks + Sheep	ISB	All
				Percentage Distribution				
Negative	18.8	25.0	39.4	6.1	6.1	13.8	*	20.1
Rs. 0-199	14.6	12.5	7.0	6.1	53.1	20.7	*	19.0
Rs. 200-499	10.4	6.3	7.0	15.2	10.2	10.3	*	9.3
Rs. 500-999	12.5	25.4	18.2	18.4	6.9	*	18.7	
Rs. 1000-1999	27.1	15.6	8.5	24.2	12.2	37.9	*	18.7
Rs. 2000 or more	8.3	28.1	12.7	30.3	0.0	10.3	*	14.2
Total	100.0	100.0	100.0	100.0	100.0	100.0	*	100.0
Mean (Rs.)	784	1657	568	1554	273	835	(2457)	874
No. who have retained the asset	48	32	71	33	49	29	6	268

Note: These incomes refer to only those who have retained the asset or its replacement.
( ) Based on less than 20 observations.

Table 14.3: Levels of Household and Per capita Incomes by Asset Retention

Percentage Distribution of Total Household Income in 1986-87			Percentage Distribution of Per Capita Income in 1986-87		
Household Income	Those who retained	Those who did not retain	Per Capita Income	Those who retained	Those who did not retain
Less than Rs.3000	33.6	42.7	Less than Rs.3000	32.5	37.8
Rs.3000-4999	34.3	37.8	Rs.600-999	36.2	43.4
Rs.5000-6399	12.7	10.5	Rs.1000-1299	11.2	9.8
Rs.6400-7999	7.8	4.2	Rs.1300-1599	10.1	4.2
Rs.8000 or more	11.6	4.9	Rs.1600 or more	10.1	4.9
Total	100.0	100.0	Total	100.0	100.0
Mean (Rs.)	4505	3872	Mean (Rs.)	877	800
Per cent with Household income of Rs.6400 or more	19.4	9.1	Per cent with Per capita Income		
			Rs. 948 or more	35.1	25.9
			Rs.1322 or more	19.4	9.1

Notes: (i) Rs.6,400 per annum is the cut off point for poverty line being used currently.

(ii) For rural Karnataka, per capita income of Rs.1,322 in 1986-87 corresponds to Rs.240 in 1960-61, the cut off point for poverty line, and per capita income of Rs.948 in 1986-87 corresponds to Dandekar-Rath poverty line for rural Karnataka (Rs.172 in 1960-61 prices).

unrealistic assumption since otherwise they would not have been bonded. Therefore, those whose current incomes are above or even a little below the poverty line can be considered to have raised their income levels. Two alternate poverty lines are used here — Rs. 6,400 per household per annum as proposed by the Planning Commission and Rs. 948 per capita per annum which corresponds to the Dandekar Rath line for Rural Karnataka (adjusted to 1986-87 price index). It can be seen from Table 14.3. that among those who have retained assets, 19 per cent have crossed one line and 35 per cent have crossed the other line. However, it would not be correct to attribute all of this to the rehabilitation programme, since even some of those who did not retain the assets and thus were unable to make use of the programme have incomes above the poverty lines. But the levels of incomes for the latter group are lower than the levels for those who have retained the assets. The difference of about Rs.600 (Rs.4,505 — Rs.3,872) in mean household income and of about 10 points in per cent above the poverty line may be attributed to the impact of the ownership of assets. Other indicators such as per cent income earned from sources other than wage labour, and per cent owning at least a watch, a radio or a bicycle also show that the ownership of asset has made an impact (Table 14.4).

Table 14.4: Some Indicators of Income/Present Condition by Retention of Assets

Indicator	Status of Asset		
	Retained	Not Retained	All
Mean Household income in 1986-87 (Rs)	4505	3872	4285
Mean per capita income in 1986-87 (Rs)	877	800	851
Percent households with :			
Household income over 6400 Rs.	19**	9	16
Per capita income over 948 Rs.	35*	26	32
Percent of income earned from sources other than wage labour	33**	20	29
Percent of households owning atleast a watch/radio/bicycle	24	17	22
No.of households in the sample	268	143	411

*, ** The means/percentages for those who have retained the assets are significantly higher than for those who have not, at 5%(*), or 1%(**) level of significance.

Tabulations by districts (not shown here) which eliminate the effect of regional factors, also show that those who have retained the assets are better off than those who have not in terms of some of the indicators considered. These differences persist even when controlling for certain background variables such as land ownership and caste.

In addition to these comparisons, the income levels of some of those who are yet to be given an asset (called non-beneficiaries) when compared with the levels of those who have received the assets also show that those who have retained the assets are better off than the non-beneficiaries.

Present Living Conditions

The improvements in income levels would be of no value if the living conditions — quality of life — remain unchanged. The available evidence shows that there has been some improvements in this regard since rehabilitation. Though most of the labourers continue to live in small mud and thatched huts, many have better roofs and more rooms than in the past. There has been only a marginal improvement in land in government programmes. On the other hand, many more own livestock now than in the past. Though about half of the released labourers continue to be in debts, especially because of expenditure on account of marriage, the reliance on landlords is low. Only about 8 per cent of the households had someone working as bonded labourer at the time of survey. There has been an increase in the tendency to send children to school. Finally, in response to a direct question on the present condition as compared to that during bondage, over 75 per cent replied that there has been an improvement. However, instead of an increase in income, the main reason for this feeling is that they are free of bondage, free to work at own initiative and time. Overall, it can be stated that there has been some improvement in the living conditions of released labourers. Though most continue to be poor and leading a life far from comfortable, the small changes are significant and more that improvements in income, freedom from bondage has given them a feeling of a better life.

IV. Comparison with Findings from IRDP studies in Karnataka

How does the bonded labour rehabilitation programme fare as compared to the IRDP, both in terms of implementation and in terms of impact? Data from three studies on the IRDP that were undertaken in Karnataka during 1985-86 are available for this comparison. The department of Rural Development, Government of India, carried out a concurrent evaluation of the programme in collaboration with a number of research institutions and universities. The results of this evaluation are available (Kurien, 1987) for the country as a whole, as well as for the States and of these, the findings for Karnataka are used here. The Institute for Social and Economic Change participated in the concurrent evaluation, and some of the data for Karnataka, in the collection of which the Institute was involved, have been presented by Rao and Erappa (1987). Though these form a subset of the data used by Kurian for Karnataka, the analysis has been done independently, certain aspects have been examined in details and therefore are used here in addition to the results of Kurian. The third study is an evaluation of the IRDP in Karnataka that was done in 1986 quite independently of the concurrent evaluation mentioned above. The results are given by Aziz (1987).

First, the implementation, the important aspects are : selection of beneficiaries, identification of suitable schemes, procurement of assets and support in the utilisation. In the IRDP, there is some evidence of non-poor households also getting the benefit. But because of difficulties in assessing the levels of income, the estimates of misclassification would not be very accurate. In the bonded labour rehabilitation programme in Karnataka, the task of identification was done earlier, soon after the abolition of the bonded labour system, a time when there was no scheme of providing assistance. This, probably, is the reason why there are not many instances of ineligible persons getting the benefit. The proportion belonging to the socially most disadvantaged sections of the population, the scheduled castes and tribes, is higher among the bonded labour beneficiaries. But this is because most of bonded labourers belonged to these groups. In both the IRDP and the bonded labour rehabilitation programme, the selection of schemes for individual beneficiaries was done by taking into account the preferences of the individuals and the assessments of the government officers about the suitability of these. The share of the ISB scheme is much lower in the bonded labour rehabilitation programme as compared to the IRDP. But this may be attributed to the fact that only a minuscule proportion of the bonded labourers came from artisan households and hence the demand for craft-based schemes was very low. The procurement of assets in both the IRDP and the bonded labour rehabilitation programme was done by the purchase committees at the block levels. There was no difference in the procedure adopted except that there was no involvement of bank officials in the latter. The feeling among many beneficiaries that the assets were overvalued is common to both the programmes. Another common factor is the absence of any serious attempt to provide training in handling (or managing) the assets. The beneficiaries in the bonded labour programme have a small advantage because they get the asset as a grant and not as a loan. But many of the IRDP beneficiaries also do not make repayments regularly and hence, in practice, the advantage amount to little. Thus, there do not appear to be any material differences in the implementation of the two programmes.

All the IRDP studies have given data on per cent who were continuing with the scheme (those who have retained the original asset or its replacement are treated as continuing with the scheme) at the end of two years. These are given in Table 14.5. It can be seen that 70 per cent or more continued with the scheme for at least two years. This is true in the case of the bonded labourers as well as indicates that the tendency to carry on with the business was large even for a group as disadvantaged as the bonded labourers. Data are also available on the net income from the asset, that is income after deducting all costs except the value of family labour. Information on total household income is also available in some of the studies. Some caution is required in using these data for comparison. The estimation of income is always difficult and different studies have adopted different procedures for this purpose. It is difficult to say which one is more accurate and therefore the available data should be used only to see the order of magnitude. The mean net income from the asset in one year varies from Rs.886 to Rs.1,411 in the three IRDP studies. The bonded labourers could get only Rs.682 on an average from the asset. There is large variation in the incomes earned by different individuals and in both the IRDP and the bonded labour samples, a good proportion have earned over Rs.2000. This indicates that, even though the average for the bonded labourers appears to be lower, there is scope for earning substantial incomes from this scheme as in the IRDP. One of the studies on IRDP has attempted to measure the net impact of the programme in terms of per cent of households rising above the poverty line. Aziz, by comparing the improvement in the income level of beneficiaries with the improvement in the case of non-beneficiaries in the same are, has estimated this to be about 18 per cent. From the bonded labour study, about 10 per cent can be said to have crossed the line because of the programme. The other two IRDP studies did not have a non-beneficiary group as control and therefore it is difficult to assess the net impact from their results. Measured in terms of annual household income, the net impact of the IRDP is estimated to be Rs.801 (based on some unpublished data in the study by Aziz) and Rs.632 of the bonded labour rehabilitation programme. Thus, it can be seen that the bonded labour programme has not fared as well as the IRDP. However, except for the poverty line indicator, the difference is not much. In terms of continuation both the IRDP and the bonded labour programme can be considered to have performed very well, and in terms of income generation and crossing the poverty line, quite poorly.

Table 14.5: Indicators of Impact of IRDP/Bonded Labour Rehabilitation Programme in Karnataka

Programme/Study	Per cent continuing with scheme for atleast two years	Net income from the asset in one year (Rs.)	Net percent households rising above the poverty line[1]	Net increase in annual household Income[2]
IRDP				
Kurian (Karnataka)	77[3]	993[4] -	-	-
Rao, Erappa	72	1411	-	-
Aziz	87	886	18	801
Bonded labour	75	682	10	632

Notes: 1. Computed as :(Percent of beneficiaries crossing the poverty line) - (Per cent of non-beneficiaries crossing the line), in the study of Aziz and as (Per cent above the poverty line among those who retained the asset) - (Percent above the poverty line among those who did not) in the bonded labour study.

2. The net increase is the difference between in mean annual household incomes computed in a manner similar to that in notes 2.
3. This is the per cent who have the entire asset intact.
4. Approximate value, computed from the given distribution.

Source: Kurian (1987), Rao, Erappa (1987), Aziz (1987) and unpublished data from the studies.

As mentioned above, it would not be appropriate to use the income data for making cross-study comparisons. However, it is possible to compare the extreme poor and the not so poor in each study. Such internal comparisons would not be severely affected by the differences in the procedures of income estimation. Aziz has given data separately for 'bottom', 'middle', and 'upper' groups. The upper group is very small and does not aid any comparison. However, the 'bottom' and 'middle' groups can be considered to represent high and medium degrees of poverty respectively. Similarly, the agricultural labourers and land owners, in both the IRDP study can be considered to represent high and medium degrees of poverty. Per cent continuing with the scheme and net income from it are given for these groups within each of these three studies in Table 14.6. The extreme poor have lesser propensity continue with the scheme but the difference between them and the not so poor is very small, only about nine points. The picture is not clear about the income generated by an asset. Overall, it can be said that though the extreme poor have lower tendency to retain an asset as compared to the others, over 60 per cent do manage to continue with the enterprise for over two years. Clearly, even the extreme poor are interested in keeping the assets provided and making utilisation of these. They are only a little less successful than those who have better endowments and this difference is probably attributable to the compulsions of poverty rather than to lack of interest in enterprise. The fact that even the formerly bonded labourers, most of whom had never owned any cattle earlier and had not been involved in even a small enterprise, tried to hold on to the available productive assets indicates that the poor have an ardent desire to engage in some enterprise of their own. The popular belief that many poor would simply sell off the given assets does not get support from the available data. Moreover, though the poorest among the poor do not fare as well as the others, they do not fare much worse either.

V. Discussion

The findings of the study on the bonded labour rehabilitation programme and the IRDP studies indicate, mainly, that most of the beneficiaries do keep the assets and stay in business for over two years, the incomes generated by the assets are small on an average, and the poorest fare only a little worse as compared to the others. The principal aim of the programme is obviously to enable the poor to have better incomes and in this dimension the results are unimpressive. The assets have not generated as much incomes as expected — the capital output

Table 14.6: Continuation with Schemes and Income earned by Degree of Poverty

Programme/Study	Percent continuing with the scheme for atleast two years		Net income from the asset in one year (Rs)	
	High	Medium	High	Medium
	Degree of povery			
IRDP Rao, Erappa	64	75	1367	1400
IRDP Aziz	83	92	863	767
Bonded labour rehabilitation	69	78	426	804

Note: The Classification by degree of poverty varies in the studies : for details, see text.

Source: Same as in Table 14.5.

ratios are well off the expected 1.5:1. There are, no doubt, variations in this, and some, including those who were extremely poor, have been able to earn substantial amounts from the assets. On the other hand, many have earned very little and they constitute a relatively greater proportion of the beneficiaries. Of course, all enterprises face some risks and earnings from these would vary. But when a substantial proportion do not earn well there is a need for looking at the causes. Since most of the beneficiaries had received and had also preferred cattle, it would be worthwhile to see why they have not been able to earn adequate incomes. Most of the beneficiaries had experience in handling cattle. But this was done generally for the landlords and at that time the labourers did not have any financial responsibility. The management of assets requires certain skills which may not possess. There were little efforts towards imparting any education on these lines. Besides, there may not me a continuous flow of income from certain assets. The worst case is that of sheep or goats which do not produce regular income. Milk cattle have dry periods and these can be quite long for buffaloes. There may not be much demand for the work of bullocks either for farm operations or for transport in certain seasons. During such periods, the maintenance, and more specifically the feeding, of these animals must be done from certain other sources. The inability to do so turns the cattle to scavenging which leads to gradual deterioration in their condition, and affects their productivity. The poor are very vulnerable in this regard. It would be advisable to save part of the income earned during the productive periods for use during the unproductive periods. But for the very poor it is difficult to save almost anything. The income from other sources, generally wage labour, is so low that all the income earned during the productive cycle of the asset is also required for routine consumption and savings would be possible only by reducing the household consumption below the minimum requirement. Whatever the reason, the inability to support the animals during certain periods leads to gradual deterioration in their condition and affects their productivity in future.

There is some scope for improvement in the income even within the present programme structure. A more aggressive policy of education in asset management and protective monitoring of assets during the early phase would be helpful. A wider spread of dairy co-operatives could provide better credit and marketing facilities. Linking the ISB schemes with specific training programmes would also be valuable. But these steps would be inadequate to provide protection during unproductive cycles and periods of distress.

One would expect that if an asset is not generating adequate income there would be tendency to dispose it off. The high levels of retention are, therefore surprising. What leads people to keep the animals at home and try to carry on with the business when these yield so little? Possibly there is some hope that sooner or later the assets would become more productive. Besides, there is not much to lose by keeping an asset as long as one does not have to make any further investment in it. The availability of family labour takes care of routine requirement. But this goes against the commonly held belief that the assets given under the anti-poverty programme are disposed off quickly. There is often a reference to the 'circulating cow'. The available evidence indicates that the very poor are seriously interested in using the assets given and earning some incomes out of it. For many this may have been the first such opportunity. That many are not quite successful in an efficient utilisation is a different matter. But the attempt is sincere and therefore, if the incomes can be greater, the impact would also be more favourable. Undoubtedly, there would be some who may try to dispose off the assets and some who may be just unlucky. But, overall, it appears that there is a strong desire to won assets that would help in earning incomes.

The smallness of the income generated by such programmes does not necessarily lead to a call for an abandonment of the programmes. Even some strong critics of the IRDP do not deny that it has a role to play. But certain alternative approaches have been considered. The main proposal on these lines is that of generation of employment. Certainly massive employment generation programmes could help rural poor households to earn greater incomes by taking full advantage of the available labour and this would not have the hazards associated with enterprises like the IRDP schemes. But then there is no harm in an employment programme acting as a complement to a programme of transfer of assets. Ownership of assets like land and cattle is of intrinsic value in a agrarian society. And the maintenance of the kind of assets given in anti-poverty programmes can be, and often is, combined with outside employment. Therefore, if a household that has received such assets can also earn income from wage employment at fair rates and if such employment is available during the lean period of the production cycle of the assets, it would be possible to spend some money on the assets and prevent their deterioration. The compulsions to sell assets at the time of distress would also be less and the prospects of making prolonged and efficient utilisation of assets would be brighter. In order to achieve this, the development programmes need to go further and provide better support at the individual level including specific assistance at times of distress. A beneficiary oriented programme should strive to treat each beneficiary household individually and, within the general framework of anti-poverty programmes, provide the specific relief that is relevant at a point in time.

REFERENCES

Aziz, Abdul, 1978. 'Integrated Rural Development Programme in Karnataka: An Evaluation',(mimeo). Institute for Social and Economic Change, Bangalore.

Dandekar, V.M. and N. Rath, 1971, *Poverty in India*, Indian School of Political Economy, Poona.

Dantwala, M.L. 1985, 'Garibi Hatao' : Strategy Options", *Economic and Political Weekly*, Vol.XX, No 11, pp.475-76.

Kurian,N.J., 1987, 'IRDP : How Relevant Is It ?', *Economic and Political Weekly*, Vol. XXII, No. 52, pp. a161-176.

Marla, Sarma, 1981, *Bonded Labour in India*, Bibla Impex, New Delhi.

Rao V.M. and S Erappa, 1987, 'IRDP and Rural Diversification : A Study in Karnataka' *Economic and Political Weekly*, Vol. XXII, No. 52, pp. a151-160.

Rath and Neelakantha, 1985, "Garibi Hatao: Can IRDP Do It?" *Economic and Political Weekly*, Vol. XX, No. 6, pp. 238-246.

Srinivas M.N., 1985 'The Social System of a Mysore Village', in *Village India*, Mckim

Marriot (ed.). The University of Chicago Press, Chicago.

Thorner Daniel and Alice Thorner, 1957 'Types of Employer-Labourer Relationships in Indian Agriculture', *Indian Journal of Agricultural Economics*, Vol. XXII, No. 2, pp. 84-96.

15

RURAL DEVELOPMENT PROCESS AND THE SCHEDULED CASTE POPULATION

H. Ramachandran

An economy characterised by poverty and glaring inequality, invokes programmes that are essentially addressed to various strata - particularly that segment of the population that occupies the lowest layer. The rural scheduled caste population suffer both social disabilities and economic deprivations. As such a number of rural development efforts of the State are addressed to the scheduled caste population. However, the social and economic exploitation of this segment of Indian society has a much longer history spanning centuries than the attempt to promote equality through special privileges provided for in the Constitution of India and through development programmes. As a result the disparities between scheduled castes and non-scheduled caste population persist as have been noted in a number of studies. We, therefore, refrain here from further elucidations of this disparity and move on to some questions pertaining to rural development process *vis-a-vis* the scheduled caste population, that have not attracted much attention.

More recently, the impact of development programmes has become a subject of enquiry. Much of these studies using the methodology of controlled group experiments and programme evaluation tend to analyse the impact of specific programmes. However, such attempts serve oniy a limited objective – to evaluate the success/failure of the implementation of the programmes and to introduce corrective measures where found necessary. The question that needs further attention is whether beyond the impacts seen by controlled group studies and project evaluation exercises are there perceivable larger changes in the population.

The development of scheduled caste population has been attempted through reform movements, education, and reduction in their economic poverty through direct state intervention. Available studies on scheduled caste population tend to compare them and the rest of the population on a number of attributes. Almost all such studies consider the two groups as distinct, homogeneous groups, neither of them differentiated by economic classes. This framework of analysis stems from the fact that the bulk of the rural scheduled castes are landless labourers. Nevertheless, since a considerable proportion are outside these poorer occupations it becomes necessary to compare various classes in each of the two major social groups. Socially, the fact that scheduled castes are not homogeneous but are arranged in an hierarchical manner consisting of various sub-castes has been recognised. The emergence of a middle class which occupies and performs elite role among them has also been indicated. From these indications one may venture to look at the rural scheduled caste households not as a homogenous group but differentiated by economic classes. This framework allows one to compare the attributes of scheduled castes and non-scheduled castes population to corresponding classes.

If the development programmes – particularly those that are geared to improve the living conditions of the lower strata – are successful, then it would get reflected in the weakening relationship between economic strength/status on the one hand and the ability to use the programmes on the other. Thus, a part of this study labours on the nature of relationship between economic status/strength of various socio-economic groups and their propensity to take advantage of development processes. A part of this discussion also revolves around the question of the relationship between social disabilities and economic deprivations. Have we reached a stage when we could think of selective discrimination among the socially handicapped population?

In order to facilitate a reflection on these questions, we resort to an empirical analysis of rural household data. The analysis that follows is based on household data generated from 245 randomly selected sample villages in Tumkur district of Karnataka.[1] A description of the study area is given elsewhere.[2]

All the households in the 245 sample villages numbering 29785, at the time of the survey were covered by the fieldwork conducted during

April-June 1977.[3] About 21 per cent of the sample households were scheduled castes and in terms of their population, their share was 19 per cent. The criteria adopted to aggregate the rural households into homogeneous groups or strata must reflect the stratified nature of the society. Given the rural population that is heavily dependent on agricultural sector, we have opted to classify the households according to the size of the agricultural holding owned by the households if the major source of income of the household is agriculture.[4] Households whose major source of income is other than agriculture is grouped according to the main occupation of the head of the household. The distribution of households according to these groups are given in Table 15.1 for ready reference.

Table 15.1: Distribution of Sample Households by Broad Occupation Groups

Occupation Groups	SC No.of house-holds	Per Cent to Total	Non-SC No. of house-holds	Per cent to Total	Total	Percen-tage
1	2	3	4	5	6	7
Agricultural labourers	2016	37.19	2324	11.45	4340	16.88
Artisans	219	4.04	980	4.83	1199	4.66
Marginal Farmers	1337	24.66	3531	17.40	4868	18.93
Small Farmers	1153	21.27	5740	28.29	6893	26.81
Medium Farmers	455	8.39	5437	26.79	5892	22.91
Large Farmers	8	0.15	273	1.35	281	1.09
Business/Trade	35	0.65	579	2.85	614	2.39
Professionals and Salaried	125	2.30	1154	5.69	1279	4.97
Others	73	1.35	274	1.35	347	1.35
Total	5421	100.00	20292	100.00	25713	100.00

The pre ponderence of scheduled caste in traditional rural occupations (about 87%) is clearly seen. However, since the scheduled caste population is a part of the same socio-economic system, the pattern of their occupational distribution is similar to that of non-scheduled caste population. If we compare, for example, columns 3 and 5 of Table 15.1, we find a high degree of similarity.

With this background of the data base, we return to the relationship between economic status as reflected by the above socio-economic categories and household characteristics reflected by some illustrative indicators.

Many government programmes are directed at improving access to farm related assets through credit facilities on preferential rates of interest and highly subsidised inputs that go into agricultural production. Some of these have been directed at rural target groups of marginal and small farmers. As a case in point, we compare ownership of two production related assets – irrigation wells representing traditional assets and pumpsets representing modern assets.

Table 15.2: Per cent Households Owning Irrigation Wells and Pumpsets

Occupational Class	Percent scheduled caste households owning assets to scheduled caste households owning land in each occupational class		Percent non-scheduled caste households owning assets to non-scheduled caste households owning land in each occupational class	
	Irrigation wells	Pump-sets	Irrigation wells	Pump-sets
1	2	3	4	5
Agricultural labourers	0.9	0.1	2.6	1.0
Artisans	0.5	0.5	3.2	0.6
Marginal farmers	3.7	1.4	12.4	3.7
Small farmers	7.6	1.6	19.1	9.3
Medium farmers				
Large farmers	17.7	6.3	41.4	25.4
Business/Trade	0.0	0.0	4.2	1.7
Professional/Salaried	3.2	0.8	7.4	4.9
Others	1.4	1.4	6.6	3.7
All Households	4.5	1.3	20.3	11.2
Coefficient of variation	4.7	5.9	2.7	3.1

In absolute terms the disparity between the two social groups are sharp when we study the proportion of households owning these assets. Whereas, only about 5 per cent of the scheduled caste households owning land has irrigation wells, among the non-scheduled caste households it is over 20 per cent. Corresponding values for pumpsets are about one and 11 per cent. However, among the farming classes the differences among the two social groups are much less marked (Table 15.2). As the size of the land-holding increases, the disparity in the ownership of irrigation wells decreases. It is also to be noted that the proportion of households owning the assets in each occupational class is more unequally distributed in the scheduled caste households.

The ownership of two assets discussed above, which are associated with irrigation are detrimental to the use of modern agricultural practices like use of high yielding variety (HYV) and fertiliser. The general level of use of these agricultural practices is very low in both social groups (Table 15.3). While the differences between the social groups are marked, there is a strong relationship in each of the two groups between size classes of holdings and use of modern agricultural practices. This is true both of scheduled caste and non-scheduled caste households.

Table 15.3: Per cent Households using Modern Agricultural Practices

Occupation Groups	Percent Households Using HYV SC	HYV Non-SC	Fertilisers SC	Fertilisers Non-SC
Agricultural Labourers	0.4	0.6	3.3	3.4
Artisans	0.5	0.6	5.1	6.0
Marginal Farmers	2.0	6.9	12.2	30.0
Small farmers	2.9	8.5	17.1	44.0
Medium and Large farmers	6.7	18.5	28.9	60.8
Trade/Commerce	5.7	1.9	8.6	5.4
Professional/ Salaried	1.6	4.5	13.6	13.9
Others	0.0	1.8	1.4	4.0
All households	1.9	9.7	10.9	36.4

Institutionalised formal sources of finance like co-operative banks, Land Development Banks and Commercial Banks have programmes specifically to aid weaker sections and scheduled castes in rural areas, who have for long been exploited by private money-lenders. One might see then some impact of such programmes by studying the differences in access of different groups to these sources of agricultural finance.

Despite concerted efforts and public programmes to extend institutional credits to rural sector, a large proportion of households indicate private money-lenders as a source of agricultural finance (Table 15.4). However, among scheduled caste households, 40 to 70 per cent have indicated access to formal sources of loan and among non-scheduled castes the corresponding figure ranges from 45 to 77 per cent. It therefore, appears that access to the formal sources of loan does not differ substantially between the major social groups.

Table 15.4: Sources of Loans for Agriculture

Social Groups	No. of Households who receive loans from				
	Co-operative Banks	Land Development Banks	Commercial Banks	Money Lenders and Others	Total
Scheduled Caste	507	181	161	373	1222
Non-scheduled Caste	3884	1972	846	1998	8700
All Households	4391	2183	1007	2371	9952

In the context of total households in different occupation groups, the percentage of borrowers from formal institutions is rather low (Table 15.5). Despite this, the class differences in access to them are clearly seen. Among each class of farmers, the use of these institutions increases with land holdings, irrespective of the caste dimension. Among the weaker sections, the scheduled caste households appear to have a slight advantage in access to these institutions. The differential access between the two groups is rather small in the case of cooperative banks.

Although the living conditions are directly related to income, the relationship is disturbed by special programmes that intervene directly to improve the standards of living of poorer sections. The impact of these programmes are brought out by a set of indicators. While the dominant house types in rural areas are *kutcha* houses, among the scheduled caste households, the *pucca* houses constitute six per cent and in the case of non-scheduled caste houses, it is about 14 per cent (Table 15.6). However, unlike productive inputs such as agricultural land and other inputs into agriculture, the differences between scheduled caste and other households are more marked in higher status occupational classes. One may also noticed the incidence of much larger proportion of *pucca* houses among the households in non-traditional rural occupations in both social groups.

Table 15.5: Source of Loan for Agriculture by Occupational Classes

Occupation Group	Percent household borrowings from					
	Commercial Banks		PLD Banks		Co-Operatives	
	SC	Non-SC	SC	Non-SC	SC	Non-SC
Agricultural Labourers	3.7	2.3	1.0	0.9	1.3	0.5
Artisans	1.9	4.0	0.0	0.8	5.1	5.8
Marginal Farmers	10.5	12.8	2.8	2.4	3.2	1.8
Small Farmers	13.8	18.0	4.8	6.9	2.3	2.9
Medium/Large farmers	16.0	25.5	16.0	17.4	2.8	6.3
Business/Trade	5.7	4.8	0.0	1.6	11.4	9.3
Professional/ Salaried	7.2	7.5	3.2	4.2	2.4	3.5
Others	1.4	3.7	0.0	1.5	2.7	1.5
All Households	8.6	15.6	3.5	7.5	2.4	3.7

Although the proportion of electrified households is very low, there is a large gap between the two social groups. While there is a strong relationship between households with electric connection and occupational class in both the groups the disparities are sharp almost in every occupational class. Both among the scheduled caste and non-scheduled caste section, it is business/trade and professional/salaried classes which record largest proportion of households with electricity. In the case of non-scheduled caste households these two classes are followed closely by medium/large cultivators.

Table 15.6: Housing

Occupational Class	Percent Households having *pucca* houses, and electricity to households in each occupational group			
	Pucca Houses		Electricity	
	SC	Non-SC	SC	Non-SC
Agricultural Labourers	5.0	7.0	1.1	5.4
Artisans	15.7	9.3	7.4	14.0
Marginal Farmers	5.1	8.2	1.8	8.1
Small farmers	5.5	7.1	1.1.	14.1
Medium/Large farmers	5.0	19.2	2.2	31.2
Business/Trade	8.6	9.8	14.3	34.4
Professional/Salaried	18.4	26.0	20.8	52.6
Rent receivers/pensioners/ Animal Husbandry Allied Activities/Others	4.1	13.6	2.7	24.5
All households	5.9	13.5	2.7	20.2

The government in order to help weaker sections and the scheduled castes in the area of rural housing, introduced schemes for distribution of free dwelling sites and assistance in the form of Janata housing. Since these were specifically directed at the rural poor one might expect some impact, more in the case of free site distribution than in the case of Janata housing that called for some amount of financial inputs from the prospective beneficiaries. About 20 per cent of scheduled caste households had the benefit of acquiring free house sites and six per cent possessed Janata houses. The corresponding values for the non-scheduled caste households being less than three and one percent respectively (Table 15.7).

Within the scheduled caste households, the largest beneficiaries of the sites have been small and marginal farmers, both groups recording over 25 per cent of households with free sites. However, among the non-scheduled castes households the weaker sections represented by agricultural labourers, artisans and marginal farmers were the largest beneficiaries. It is significant to note that among the scheduled caste, a substantive proportion of households that do not belong to economically weaker sections for example professional/salaried, medium and large farmers, business/trade groups have benefited. One can also see that the variation across different occupational groups is rather small in the case of scheduled castes as compared to non-scheduled castes. Whereas such programmes are basically oriented towards weaker sections, the distribution of beneficiaries do not indicate clearly the class bias of the programme.

Table 15.7: Distribution of Households with Free Sites and Janata Houses

Occupational Class	Per cent SC and Non-SC Households having free Sites and Janata Houses			
	Free Sites		Janata Houses	
	SC	Non-SC	SC	Non-SC
Agricultural labourers	20.4	7.4	7.0	2.4
Artisans	16.2	5.9	4.2	2.3
Marginal farmers	25.2	3.1	5.2	0.4
Small farmers	27.7	1.3	5.0	0.2
Medium and Large farmers	16.0	1.8	0.4	0.2
Business/Trade	8.6	5.4	8.6	3.4
Professional/Salaried	14.4	2.3	4.8	0.7
Others	23.3	6.7	8.2	1.8
All Households	19.8	2.6	6.6	0.7

Having had a look at some illustrative indicators dealing with productive sector and household living conditions, we use a simple calculus in order to show firstly that the relationship between economic status and access to government programmes is negative in general and attempt to arrange rural households in hierarchic groups in order to underline the need for selective discrimination even among scheduled caste households.

Towards this end we rank the sixteen groups of rural population based on their performance on selected indicators. These indicators could fruitfully be grouped into five categories viz. assets, agricultural infrastructure and practices, education and exposure, living conditions and gains from state programmes (Table 15.8).

We have simply ranked the sixteen groups of rural households along these 23 indicators in order to place the rural groups on a hierarchic scale of five broad dimensions. Notwithstanding the shortcomings of this calculus we believe that a general comparison of various groups across the five dimensions of household attributes could be useful.

Table 15.8: Indicators of Hierarchy of Rural Groups

I *Assets*:	(a)	Per cent Households with Agricultural lands.
	(b)	Per cent Households with wet/garden land.
	(c)	Per Household wet land in acres.
	(d)	Per cent Households with irrigation wells.
	(e)	Per cent Households with pumpsets.
II *Agricultural Infrastructure and Practices*		
	(a)	Per cent Households using HYV.
	(b)	Per cent Households using fertiliser.
	(c)	Per cent Households borrowing from co-operative credit societies.
	(d)	Per cent Households with membership in co-operative societies.
III *Education and Exposure*		
	(a)	Male literacy rates.
	(b)	Female literacy rates.
	(c)	Per cent school enrolment of male children.
	(d)	Per cent school enrolment of female children.
IV *Living Conditions*		
	(a)	Per cent Households with *Pucca* houses.
	(b)	Per cent Households with electric connection.
	(c)	Per cent Households consuming regularly (i) Pulses (ii) Milk (iii) Butter-milk (iv) Vegetables (v) Fruits.
V *Gains from State Programmes*		
	(a)	Per cent Households with free sites.
	(b)	Per cent Households with Janata houses.

The degree of relationship between the ranking of the 16 groups of five dimensions is recorded in Table 15.9. There is a high degree of correspondence between the ranking of various groups on assets and agricultural practices/infrastructures. Similarly, the ranking on living conditions and education/exposure is also similar.

Ranking of the groups based on assets does influence the performance of the groups on other indicators. But what is significant is the low degree of relationship between socio-economic status and the level of education/exposure of the group. The degree of relationship between asset status and living conditions is also low. The consistently observable negative coefficients on the fifth dimension – gains from state programmes – speak of the compensating effect of the state interventions. The weak relationship between status and educational level is an indication of the ongoing rural change.

Table 15.9: Correlations between Ranking of Rural Groups on Households Attributes

Attributes		Rank Correlations				
		1	2	3	4	5
Assets	1	1	0.90	.44	.47	-.66
Agricultural Infrastructure/Practices	2		1	.32	.34	-.52
Education/ Exposure	3			1	.96	-.73
Living Conditions	4				1	-.77
Gains from State Programmes	5					1

If we combine all the dimensions together the ranking of rural groups is as follows:

(1) Non-scheduled caste medium/large farmers.
(2) Non-scheduled caste professional/salaried.
(3) Non-scheduled caste small farmers.
(4) Scheduled caste professional/salaried.
(5) Non-scheduled caste trade/commerce.
(6) Non-scheduled caste miscellaneous occupations.
(7) Non-scheduled caste marginal farmers.
(8) Scheduled caste medium/large farmers.
(9) Scheduled caste small farmers.
(10) Scheduled caste Trade/Commerce.
(11) Non-scheduled caste artisans.
(12) Scheduled caste marginal farmers.
(13) Non-scheduled caste agricultural labourers.
(14) Scheduled caste artisans.
(15) Scheduled caste agricultural labourers.

(16) Scheduled caste miscellaneous occupations.

While a detailed study of changes that have taken place in the simple households between the survey conducted in 1977 and now is currently on, the empirical results presented above is firstly to stress the necessity to consider alternative methodologies to monitor development as well as the need to change development strategy arising there from.

NOTES

1. A research study on Integrated Rural Development was initiated by Prof. V.K.R.V. Rao towards the end of 1976 at the ISEC, based on Tumkur district of Karnataka. A number of studies have been completed under this project earlier. This paper uses data generated by the Tumkur project.
2. See Ramachandran H. (1982), *Behaviour in Space-Rural Marketing in an Underdeveloped Economy*, Concept, New Delhi.
3. After checking the consistency of data and non-responses some households were left out of the analysis. This study pertains to 25713 rural households.
4. Marginal farmers (< 2 acres), small farmers (2-5 acres) medium farmers (5-25 acres) and Large farmers (25 + acres).

16

RURAL ELITES AND DEVELOPMENT: A Case Study

V.S. Parthasarathy

Introduction

The main thrust of this paper is to examine how, men in positions of power or have access to power or other resources, operate at the micro level to aid developments. How do they interact with the local populace and to what extent they are instrumental in implementing the governmental programmes for the benefit of the rural masses? Do they exploit the situation for their own ends? The introduction of rural development programmes in an integrated manner covering different aspects of village social life is a feature of the post-independence era in India.

The panchayats functioned in the village, it was different from the one which was introduced in 1959. They were traditional panchayats, which were functioning under a group of village elders who belonged to dominant castes. These panchayats were interested in the perpetuation of the then existing social system and to maintain harmony in the villages. With their limited exposure to the external world and with less pressure of population, they were concerned only with the internal affairs and not with the world outside. (For a description of Karnataka village at the time when Independence came, see Srinivas, 1976). As far as the villages were concerned, the rural elites belonging to the dominant castes knew what was good to the villagers, and with their patron-client ties and total economic dependence on the dominant castes, the general mass of villagers were in a helpless condition. This was associated with lack of education, lack of employment opportunities outside one's village and poor communications.

With Independence, the political system underwent a major change, and all citizens irrespective of their differing social status acquired equality in the eyes of law and the state. With democracy all citizens whether rural or urban, high or low, rich or poor, were involved in the governing process. This resulted in people becoming aware of their rights and duties as also the knowledge that they had the right to the resources of the nation. Such a desire was also encouraged by the introduction of planning as a process of the over-all economic development of the nation and also as an instrument of change. This was evidenced the introduction of the Community Development Programmes for the development of rural areas. Later on certain other programmes like IADP were also introduced and experimented. "The organisation pattern used in all the programmes ignored the need for institutions" at micro-level, through proper decentralisation of power. The programmes were administered in a top-down manner where participation of beneficiaries in the development activities was not considered. The target was the rural poor, a very unorganised segment requiring concerted attempts to organise them" (Ray, 1985: 87). An attempt was made to remedy the situation by introducing democratic institutions at the village level and with decentralisation of power.

In order to effectively implement various development programmes and to get a continuous feedback, the state has involved the elected representatives in the process of planning. While the State and Central legislatures deliberate on planning at the macro-level, agencies such as Taluk Development Boards, the Panchayati Raj institutions and their members are brought into the picture with the Block Development Office as the executive unit. This has led to the close involvement of the elected representatives in the implementation process. In addition, many other institutions like co-operative societies and banks have also been involved in this process.

The State government indicates a broad *modus operandi* to these institutions about development programmes. The actual details as to how it should be operated and to whom they should be given has been left to the local officials and the elected representatives. In this process, the elected representatives and the officials have become a means for access to governmental programmes. This in turn has helped the officials and the elected representative to become patrons of the rural masses, whom they can exploit later to their future advantage. This has also led to close co-operation between officials and the elected representatives.

The elected representatives at different levels have access to resources differentially and there seems to be close co-ordination between the members of the same political party operating at different levels. The point, I wish to make here is that our political representatives have become so powerful that at the grassroots level nothing moves without their knowledge and intervention. Therefore, at the level of ordinary peasants, it is difficult to have access to benefits without the protection and patronage of the elected representatives. On the other hand the elected representatives need the support of the peasants to remain in power.

It is the policy of the government now to hand out benefits to individuals and households through the Panchayats. The Panchayats have become key agents in development. In such a situation, the Panchayat members, especially, the Chairman will become a powerful man with plenty of access to resources, which pushes the poor peasants to a position of dependence. To receive any benefit, one should be favoured by the members of the Panchayat and its Chairman. These panchayats are again linked to Taluk Development Boards which are above panchayats. These Taluk Development Boards, which are the resources distribution centre through the Block Development Office, not only co-ordinates and supervises the work of the panchayats but also have close linkages. The members of the Taluk Development Board derive their positions from the rural masses and represent them at the higher level than the Panchayat. It is here, that one can observe closely the inter-action between the rural elites and the rural masses. This is the main reason for selecting a Panchayat for observation and study.

The Elites

In the context of rural society it is very difficult to define elites. Traditionally, in the rural society, the elites and the leaders were the same. However, where old values and attitudes have undergone change and leaders have started emerging from the lower and less privileged classes there is need to make a distinction. But, inspite of this I shall use the two interchangeably in my discussion.

"Elite in the most general sense, denotes a group of persons who in any society hold positions of eminence. More specifically, it denotes a group of persons who are eminent in a particular field-especially the governing minority and the circles from which the governing minority is recruited" (Gould and Kolb, 1964:234) and the leader is "(1) a person who assumes a dominant role of others in a given social situation by originating the action; (2) a person who is regularly dominant over others, and directs the behaviour of subordinates" (Zadrogny 1959:186). With these broad definitions for the present, let us examine how best we can identify the elites in rural society. An understanding of the definitions reveals that social status plays a very important role in identifying the elites while leadership hinges on one's achievement. In this study, the people who are under observation held positions of power or continue to hold power although the power they wielded may not be comparable with that wielded by men in the larger society. In addition, a majority of them belong to social groups of high status, viz., dominant castes. In this paper, I have used the positional approach to identify the elites. In this approach the elites are identified on the basis of their occupying positions of power or influence. However, this is complicated by the fact that several kind of elites exist in the same society viz., traditional elites, hereditary elites, political elites, intellectual elites and the emerging elites as a by-product of economic development.

In a traditional society, the elite groups were restricted to the higher castes and the elite status moved from one generation to the next generation in these groups. In the post-British period this position began to undergo change although the basic social structure remained intact. This can be seen in the powerful Backward Classes Movement of South India (see Srinivas, 1969: 69-74). However, in the Post-Independent India, with the abolition of untouchability, adoption of adult franchise and secularism, opportunities were thrown open to all castes, classes and categories. Many privileges and opportunities which were the monopoly of certain classes of people became accessible to one and all. More importantly access to education and positions in government led to major changes occurring in the composition of the elites. Added to this, the introduction of democratic and representative institutions and reservation to scheduled castes and tribes and women, have all facilitated to the emergence of new elites.

In the political sphere, wealth and caste dominance determine who gets elected. At the village level, it is the members of the dominant caste, who control the Panchayat which means the political elites and the traditional elites merge together. This is true at the level of the state also. Although, the other castes, especially the scheduled castes and tribes have representation in the Panchayat, they either play an insignificant role or second fiddle to the dominant castes, unless such a representative is very atriculate, has the support of his community and also that of the political bosses at the State level. Such a situation will continue for years to come as long as the dominant caste has the political and economic power. The other castes for their very existence and being entangled in patron client relationships, cannot break the hold of the dominant cases. In such a situation, even though, the members of the lower castes acquire political representation in the micro-level institutions, they have to depend on the members of the upper castes for their own survival and needs. The linkages that have been established by the dominant castes with the bureaucracy and the political institutions are firm and many.

Any understanding of the role of rural elites in development requires an understanding of the politics in the villages. This is all the more necessary as most of the villages in the state are faction ridden and it is accepted that factions do have a role to play in the social life of the villagers. When Community Development programmes were introduced in India, its failure was attributed to the rampant factionalism in the villages though subsequently some scholars opined that factions can also play a positive role if properly utilised. But with the introduction of democratic institutions in 1959 and with the decentralisation of power and the constitution of group panchayats and election, the factions underwent a lot of change in the character of their functioning.

The Unit of Study

The unit of study for our present purpose is a group of panchayat consisting of several villages. A Panchayat, for administrative and development purposes, functions as a single whole. For the purpose of study,* Kuppe Panchayat in Madbal Hobli, Magadi taluk, Bangalore District, was selected. The preference for Magadi was for the reason that I had conducted field-study of a village about 10-12 km (as the crow flies) from Kuppe a few years ago (Epstein *et al.*, 1983) and further a Ph.D thesis had been completed on a constituent village of the Panchayat (Karanth, 1984).

Magadi taluk is situated in the dry area and is dependent on rainfall

* Pseudonyms have been used for the names of individuals and for some villages.

for agriculture. Neither the big rivers flow through it nor does it have any major irrigation facility. Wherever wet land cultivation is done, it is done through lift irrigation, or with water taken from tanks. Industrially also, this area has not progressed well. However, in recent years, with the introduction of sericulture and with the declaration of Magadi taluk as a 'seed' area, some change has been observed in the economic life of the people.

With the lack of natural resources the mainstay of the people in the taluk is agriculture. Excepting for a minor forest around Durga Hill, and scrub jungle here and there, forest wealth in the taluk is very poor. Proximity to irrigated Mandya district and the metropolitan Bangalore city, provides avenues of employment to the agricultural labourers in the taluk and also provides market for the local agricultural produce, especially vegetables. A weekly market (shandy) is held in Magadi town on every Friday and it attracts quite a number of villagers from all parts of Magadi taluk. In addition, Magadi town acts as a shopping centre for the villagers around.

Being administrative centre for the taluk, Magadi town is frequented by villagers for some work or the other. Whether for getting a loan or for providing a higher education for the children, Magadi is the nearest place for them. Though ordinary villagers visit Magadi frequently, a majority of rural elites and leaders visit Magadi regularly on their own errands or on behalf of others. It is a meeting place for these people to transact business, to exchange information and to work out the strategies in their area. In addition, for some of the very active elites, Bangalore city is like a neighbouring village. With their active involvement in local politics and with their close linkages to taluk level and state level politics, they have to be physically mobile. In fact, during my field-work, it was easier for me to contact these elites in Magadi town rather that in their own villages.

Kuppe Panchayat with its headquarters in Doddi, a hamlet of Kuppe, is situated south-east of Magadi town, at about 8-9 kilometres. This may be because Doddi is of larger size than Kuppe and it is situated on the main communication line. In addition, at the time the Group Panchayats were estabilished the Lingyats of Dodi dominated the scene and they were able to get the headquarters established in their hamlet. The communication to toher villages in this panchayat ahd not developed at that time and the ideal location of the hamlet helped in establishing the headquarters. It may be noted that the location of Doddi is such that all other villages and hamlets are situated around

Doddi. It is easily accessible not only to Magadi town but also to Bangalore city, Ramanagara, Channapatna, etc. A metalled road from Magadi to Ramanagara passes through Doddi and yet another road connects Doddi to Bangalore city.

The Kuppe Panchayat consists of nine revenue villages and covers an area of 3360 acres and 27 *guntas*, with a cultivable area of 2175 acres and 36 *guntas*. The remaining 1184 acres and 31 *guntas* are covered by forests, fallow land and settlement area. It has an undulated landscape with a minor state forest surrounding Durga hills. The bulk of the land is devoted to dry land agriculture interspersed with mango and jack gardens here and there and one comes across pieces of land irrigated through wells or tank.

Agriculture and sericulture are the main occupation of the people. Animal husbandry and firewood gathering and selling, constitute subsidiary sources of income (Karanth, 1984). It is a familiar sight in this part of the country to see villagers carrying headloads of fuel to the market in Magadi and sometimes, if the quantity is considerable, to the Bangalore market. The firewood collection and selling is done mostly by the Lambhanis who have settled in these villages in separate settlements called *'tandya'*.

The main crops in this Panchayat area are ragi, mulberry, pulses and groundnut and to a limited extent paddy and horsegram. While ragi provides staple food, commercial crops like mulberry, pulses and groundnut provide ready cash. The growing of mulberry and rearing of silk-worms has become, in the past 15 years, the mainstray of the economy of the villagers. While the bulk of the land is devoted to growing staple food and to cash crops like pulses and groundnut, it has become common to devote a small patch of land to the growth of mulberry. This allotment of land depends on the capacity of the farmers to rear cocoons and the availability of domestic labour resources. When adequate water supply is available, mulberry can be harvested 5-6 times in a year, providing occupation to the farmer throughout the year. But on the land dependent on rains, 3 to 4 crops can be grown. Therefore, more and more farmers are going in for well-irrigation through energised pumpsets. This land improvement is not confined to large farmers. With the availability of easy credit facilities provided by the government, it has become possible for farmers to improve their economic conditions through the practice of sericulture. When crops like ragi, pulses and groundnut only were being grown there was only seasonal demand for agricultural labour and now with the introduction of sericulture, the demand for labour has grown and many villagers tell me that the wage rates have also increased.

The Kuppe Panchayat has a population of 4322 distributed in 766 households. The households and population are distributed unevenly in the villages and hamlets, with Rajpura, N palya, Doddi and Putha being of considerable size. Rajpura is the largest and this point has led to many conflicts with Doddi which had become the centre of power.

The villages and hamlets of this panchayat are easily accessible from Doddi. Rajpura which is the biggest of the villages in this panchayat is about 3 km to the west of Doddi and is connected to it through a foot-path. It is usual for villagers from Rajpura to walk by this path and catch the buses for either Magadi town or Bangalore city or Ramanagara and beyond. There are two *kutcha* roads connecting Rajpura and the Ramnagara-Magadi main road, of which one is 5 km and another is about 3.5 km. All other villages and hamlets in this panchayat are accessible from Doddi. Thus, Doddi is situated at a place of easy accessibility to all the villages and hamlets of the panchayat and also to other towns and villages. Doddi with its hotels, bus facilities, schools and some offices, has become a meeting place for villagers of the panchayat as well as villagers of neighbouring villages.

A perusal of Table 16.1 indicates the dominance of Okkaligas in some villages and of Lingayats in some others. And there are some villages and hamlets where they are absent. The Lingayats and Okkaligas play an active part in the social and economic life, with the other castes playing a secondary role and this point becomes significant when we discuss the role of elites and politics in this Panchayat. This is also significant in another sense that villages with common castes in residence have greater contact and a tendency to act in cooperation because of kinship and other links. The power struggle in this panchayat is between Okkaligas and Lingayats, with the other castes tilting the power balance or by taking a passive role. This role again is strengthened by the fact of patron-client relationships that exist between dominant and other castes.

The following details give an idea of the different facilities available in different villages and hamlets of the Panchayat :

1. Kuppe: 1 Urdu Primary School — Electricity — No Borewell — No Hotel.

Table 16.1: Caste Composition of the Villages and Hamlets in Kuppe Panchayat In percentages (approximate)

Kuppe	100	Muslims
Doddi (Hamlet)	70	Lingayats
	10	Okkaligas and other castes
M Doddi (Hamlet)	20	Harijans
	50	Bovis
	50	Okkaligas, and other minor castes
K O Mata	100	Lingayats
Tandya	100	Lambanis
Rampalya	50	Bedas
	50	Idigas
N Palya	50	Bedas
	50	Lingayats, smiths, Harijans, etc.
Putha	50	Okkaligas
	25	Bovis
	5	Other castes
	20	Harijans
Durga	25	Satani
	40	Lingayats
	35	Others
Rajpura	60	Okkaligas
	16	Other castes — Washerman, Barber, Lambani, etc.

2. M Doddi: 1 Kannada Primary School — Electricity — 1 Borewell — No Hotel

3. Doddi: 1 Nursery School (TDB) — 1 Govt Primary School and Middle School — 1 High School (aided) managed by a Lingayat Mutt — 1 Govt Health Centre — 1 Veterinary Govt Hospital, 1 Vyavasaya Seva Sahakara Sangha Niyamitha Society — There used to be a milk cooperative society which has become defunct now — Electricity — piped water supply — sericulture market — Grainage — Post Office — Hotels, Shops, etc — well connected by public transport — VLW Quarters — electric lineman's quarters — HQ of Kuppe Panchayat — village Accountant's Office — frequently visited by officials — flour mill.

4. N Palya: 1 Primary School — electricity — 1 borewell.

5. Rampalya: Electricity — no school — one borewell proposed.

6. Rajpura: 1 Nursery school — 1 Govt primary and Middle School — Electricity — 1 Chaki Centre — 2

Borewells, one of which is meant for supplying piped water. The piped water supply has been sanctioned and the work is yet to start — hotels, shops etc. — flour mill.

7. K O Mata: No school — electricity — 1 borewell.

8. Tandya: 1 Nursery School — electricity — 1 borewell.

9. Durga: Pilgrim centre — connected by public transport — 1 primary school — electricity — piped water supply maintained by the temple — 1 borewell — hotels and shops — number of choultries.

10. Putha: 1 primary school — electricity — 1 borewell — chaki centre.

According to the village accountant, the income of this panchayat was Rs.7,584.27 during the year 1983-84. The University of Agricultural Sciences, Bangalore, had adopted Putha village for agricultural development. While at Doddi there was concentration of common facilities, the other constituent villages, mainly Rajpura and Putha were featured by their absence. This is, as I understand, due to lack of active leadership in these villages, at the time these facilities were given and due to their inconvenient locations. When the new generation of leaders started occupying positions of power, there was awareness in them of the situation and attempts were made to fill the lacunae. In recent years, Rajpura and Putha villages have been given Chaki centres (silk-worm rearing) which is absent in Doddi and this is due to the fact that a large percentage of people in the former villages depend on sericulture for the bulk of their income.

The elites and leaders in other villages are aware of the fact that they cannot get certain facilities in their villages as they have already been provided in Doddi. But for any new or additional facilities that are to be granted to the villages, there will be acute competition and political influence from the villages. The fact that good communication network is one of the means of development is well noted by the villagers and there is clamour for getting the road well improved so that buses could ply into their villages thereby bringing economic prosperity.

Although there is clamour for these facilities, the general conditions of the village roads and drainage etc., remain poor. This fact also applies to Doddi. Excepting for the main road where the buses ply, all other roads are in very poor condition. About drainage, less said the better. If this was the condition when the panchayat was functioning, one cannot expect anything better in its absence. The reason the elites attribute to this situation is the paucity of funds in the panchayat and its total dependence on the Taluk Development Board for additional funds.

As far as facilities and benefits for individual households are concerned, in the last few years, a large number of schemes have been evolved by the government and under these schemes, lot of loans and subsidies, technical advice and inputs are available to the villagers.

Caste and Politics

There are 13 elected seats in the Kuppe Panchayat and four seats are reserved for scheduled castes and tribes. The following gives the details of constituencies :

1. Rajpura and Kuppe: 1 Constituency — 4 seats (3 General and 1 reserved)
2. Doddi: 1 Constituency — 4 seats (3 General and 1 reserved)
3. Putha and Durga: 1 Constituency — 2 seats (1 General and 1 reserved)
4. K O Mata, N Palya: 1 Constituency — 3 seats (2 General and 1 & Tandya reserved)

The following list gives the details of members with their village and political party affiliations for the years 1978-83 :

Congress I	1. Patel R N (Chairman)	Okkaliga	Rajpura
	2. SG	"	"
	3. R (woman)	"	"
	4. S	SC	"
	5. B	Okkaliga	Putha
	6. K	Lambani(ST)	"
	7. K N	"	K.O.Mata
Janatha	8. Patel N	Lingayat	"
	9. G (V chairman)	Bedda	"
	10. Doddi R	Lingayat	Doddi
	11. A (woman)	"	"
	12. Sri	"	"
	13. D	Odda (SC)	"

A perusal of the above list indicates that Congress I was holding the panchayat in its control with a simple majority. There was equal representation to Okkaligas and Lingayats with 4 seats each. The Panchayat previous to 1978-83 Panchayat was dominated by Janata party members with the power controlled by Doddi members. At the time when Group Panchayats were introduced, the bulk of the villages in this area were supporting the Indian National Congress and a very small minority were with the opposition group. At that time, the great divide of the Congress had not taken place and it was the dominant political party. The first elected members, with the bulk of them belonging to older generations and the democratic way of functioning being new, there was some sort of unity among the rural elites in the Panchayat. This situation was exploited by the more articulate elites to corner benefits for their own villages or hamlets, which was not objected to by the others.

With the gradual appearance of the new, younger and educated elites in the Panchayat, the scenario began to change. However, the same conditions continued to prevail till 1969 when the Congress divided into two. It was then that the realignment started taking place which ultimately led to division in the Panchayat on the political party basis. This opportunity gave occasion to the younger members for giving vant to their feelings regarding the development of Doddi at the cost of the other villages and hamlets in the area.

With the realignment of political forces in the taluk as a consequence of state and national level politics, and with the Congress I in power in the state, it was possible for the Congress I to wrest power from the Janata Group in the Panchayat. Several strategies were used to achieve this and this will be elaborated later.

It is interesting that while Doddi, K.O. Mata and parts of N Palya and M Doddi are with the Janata, the remaining villages and hamlets are dominated by Congress I . The Congress I areas are featured by the dominance of Okkaligas and the other areas, in particular, Doddi and K.O. Mata, by Lingayats. The smaller caste groups like Lambanis, and the artisan castes align themselves according to the situational contexts. However, the Harijans, a majority of them, seem to have permanent loyalties to the Congress I. This is because, the Scheduled Caste in general have the impression that Indira Gandhi, the leader of the Congress I , is devoted to the cause of the Scheduled Castes and the down trodden, and they did benefit from certain programmes initiated by her during her regime.

The case of the Muslims in Kuppe is different. It is a single caste (religion) village viz., Muslims. They have not benefited either in the Janata regime or Congress I regime. Therefore, their alignment to any particular group or party varies from election to election. Prior to 1978, their village was part of Doddi constituency, which returned Lingayats to the Panchayat and during the election in 1978, it became part of Rajpura constituency which returned Congress I candidates to the Panchayat.

The Role of Elites in Development: The Mechanism

Prior to 1959, excepting for uninhabited villages, all the other villages with their hamlets in Kuppe Panchayat had village Panchayats in their villages. Their function was to look after the civic functions in the villages. It was only in 1959, with the Group Panchayats Act, that a number of group Panchayats came into existence.

With the formation of the group panchayat i.e. a common panchayat with its headquarters in one of the villages, and the members of the Panchayat being elected on the basis of adult franchise, whoever controlled the panchayat had access to resources. Although earlier, for the village panchayats, elections were held, the members usually came from the dominant castes and among them the stronger factional groups, and stakes were very small and the factional groups could continue to flourish. In the larger panchayats, the constituencies for election were delineated on the basis of population size and on many occasions, one or more villages together formed the constituency, sometimes cutting across castes. This necessitated the factional groups to move beyond the village for their operations. Once the factional groups moved beyond the village, the factional rivalries within the village could not become a rallying point for villagers from outside the villages. As a result, for the factional groups, the alignment with the political parties proved a fertile ground for their operation.

It can be seen that in Kuppe Panchayat different villages have different political party domination. While Rajpura and Putha have Congress I dominance, Doddi and K.O.Mata have Janata dominance. This is the current picture. However, if we go back to the time when group panchayats were formed, the Indian National Congress was the main political party in all the villages. That means to say, that the more powerful faction in each village had thrown in its lot with Congress I. While the opposing factions, generally weaker had thrown in their lot with the minor political parties.

During the first group panchayat election, the members representing Indian National Congress came to power in the Panchayat. That was the time when Doddi R, a Lingayat emerged as a leader from Doddi. The other members from the other villages in the group panchayat being in the same political party supported him strongly. Doddi R is an intelligent and articulate leader who had an interest in developing the villages. With most of other members being elderly and traditional in outlook, it was possible for him to have their confidence, and with his dynamism he could establish rapport with new bureaucracy. Although, here and there one comes across the comment that Doddi R was corrupt, no one, even his enemies, denied the fact that he was an enterprising person who had a basic interest in the development of the villages. In this efforts, he was also ably supported by H G C, now a Janatha MLA, an Okkaliga, who was the President of the Taluk Development Board. As said earlier, the leader of Rajpura village, a respected leader of the Okkaligas, strongly supported Doddi R in his activities. To quote R N, a son of the Rajpura leader, who was a member of the Taluk Development Board, and rival of Doddi R now and who represented the Congress I interests in the Panchayat, "At the time Doddi got all the facilities and benefits, my father was a member of the Panchayat and Doddi, being situated on the main road, according to the policy of the government, got all the facilities like the Post Office, High School, etc. My father was able to secure to Rajpura village, a middle school and electricity . At that time, when my father was the Vice-Chairman of the Panchayat, he was not in a position to demand anything for the village as there was only a footpath connecting it to other villages. Later, when H G C was the President of the Taluk Development Board, my father through HGC's good offices, got the footpath converted into a road under the Rural Communication Scheme." On the other side, the villagers are jealous towards Doddi, but at the same time, they acknowledge the fact that Doddi had several advantages : (1) It was selected as the headquarters of the group panchayat; (2) its favourable location; (3) the emergence of Doddi R as a capable leader and (4) the co-operation of the other villages in the initial stages of the establishment of the group panchayat.

The absence of caste cleavages and the unity of purpose in the panchayat facilitated Doddi R to make sincere efforts to get development benefits to the village. About 15 years ago, a high school was established in Doddi. The Lingayat elites of Doddi and K O Mata under the leadership of Doddi R, persuaded the Degal Mutt (Lingayat) of Kanakapura to start a school there which they did and also collected funds from the neighbouring villages for the construction of the school building. This was a facility which was very much needed and the villagers responded enthusiastically. In achieving these objectives, Doddi R had the able support of another Lingayat rural elite, Patel N of K. O. Mata. It must be remembered that K O Mata is a small Lingayat village about half-a-kilometre from Doddi and it stood to gain from the development of the latter.

Sometime during the fifties, the government had drawn an electric line to Doddi which was a boon to the villagers. However, not many could use this facility at that time and as a result, the government was incurring loss. The government, it seems, even wanted to disconnect the line. To prevent such a thing from happening, Doddi R personally met the officials and pressurised them into not disconnecting the lines. He stated then that he assured the officials that he would see to it that electricity was used to activate pumpsets etc., so that the line became profitable. And Doddi R did succeeded in his efforts. During the same period the villages Rajpura and N Palya also got electricity. It is alleged that when electricity came to Putha village, politics was brought in there, by Rajpura Congress I leader, R.N. Justifying the concentration of development facilities in Doddi, Patel N of K O Mata stated that "We did not make any attempt to distribute the infrastructural facilities to all the villages, because we wanted all these facilities in a central place". It also said that Doddi R was responsible for providing drinking water supply and sericulture grainage centre and veterinary hospital in Doddi.

When a government health centre was established in Doddi, there were problems. H G C became President and Member of the Taluk Development Board with the help of Doddi R, Patel N and others. In spite of Solur Siddappa, (an important taluk level leader), pressurising Doddi R against HGC, Doddi R stood by him for the sake of party loyalty. With all this, when Doddi R wanted a resolution to be passed by the Taluk Development Board, HGC, it appears, did not oblige, although HGC had the majority in the Board. This was because, HGC said that he wanted a health centre in his village. Doddi R was also a member of the Taluk Development Board and it was then that the break between HGC and Doddi R came. Doddi R undaunted by his failure in the Taluk Development Board, approached important officials and the concerned minister and succeeded in getting a health centre to Doddi.

All these could be done in the village, because of the support he received from the other members. But then this could not continue for long. With the break in the monolithic Congress with Indira Gandhi heading a faction, and the other, by Nijalingappa, Doddi R opted to remain with the Congress O headed by Nijalingappa. Even this did not make much difference. With the death of Rajpura Okkaliga leader of Panchayat, his place was filled by his son R.N. R N had had his education in Bangalore, and soon after his father's death he came back to the village and filled the gap left by his father. His father was an acknowledged leader of the village and R N, automatically succeeded to it. For sometime the relation between R N and Doddi R appeared normal though a cleavage was developing. It only needed an incident. This came in the form of election to the Magadi Marketing Society. The Directors were to be elected by the representatives of the village co-operative societies and R N had been assured of nomination to the society by Doddi R. But later under Solur Siddappa's pressure, Doddi R went back on his words and sent a Lingayat member to the Magadi Society instead of RN. This led to the final rift between Doddi R and R.N.

The break between these two leaders resulted in a realignment of political forces in the Kuppe Panchayat. R N who was in Congress I from the beginning continued to do so and Doddi R became a member of the Janata party in which the Congress O had merged. This had an impact on the factional groups in the villages in Kuppe Panchayat. For example, in Rajpura, there is a faction opposed to R N. Once the rift occurred between R N and Doddi R this factional group in Rajpura became staunch supporters of Doddi R and the Janata party. This happened in the Putha village also. This was reflected in the Panchayat elections held in 1972 when the power was wrested from the Janata party by the Congress I group. The villagers believe that whoever has political power can deliver the goods. It is on this belief that R N and his supporters operated in capturing the Panchayat in 1978. Till then the caste feelings in the Panchayat were dormant and then it came to the fore in the elections.

Where there are factions in the village, then the faction which is associated with the ruling political party can achieve a great deal, while the others cannot. To quote an example: A Chaki centre had been sanctioned to the village Rajpura by the Government of Karnataka and the ruling faction had pointed out a piece of land owned by the Government for the construction of a building for the centre. When the land was to be registered, the opposing faction made a claim with the Assistant Director of Sericulture that this land belonged to a private party. Then on the basis of this complaint, the above official suggested that the village should allot another piece of land for the building. This was done because the opposing faction did not want the ruling faction to get the credit for establishing a Chaki centre. The ruling faction, which had political influence with the M L A of the taluk, made contact with the Joint Director of Sericulture and through him succeeded in getting the original piece of land approved for the building.

Doddi R was not only an active figure in the Kuppe Panchayat, he was also active in the taluk level politics. But during this period, R N of Rajpura also moved to the taluk level. R N on the advice of the taluk M L A and along with M L A's brother H G N, contested for the Taluk Development Board from their respective hoblis and both of them were elected. Unfortunately, for Doddi R, who also contested for the Taluk Development Board from Magadi (*kasaba*) hobli did not get elected. However, this was compensated by his election to the Primary Land Development Bank, Magadi, against R N of Rajpura. He subsequently became President of the Primary Land Development Bank. This is a prestigious position at the taluk level, and one which places enormous financial resources in the hands of the President, which he can use to confer favours and increase his influence and prestige. During my field-work, I had occasion to observe the way Doddi R functioned as President of the PLDB. He used to be available to the villagers throughout the week from 10 am to 5 pm at the bank in Magadi.

In the case of R N of Rajpura, his election to the Taluk Development Board, coupled with his kinsman H G N (brother of sitting M L A) becoming Chairman of the T D Board and added to it, with the dominance of the Congress I in the Board, enhanced his influence, prestige and power. This gave linkages to the taluk level and state level politicians which as astute politician could make use of. The conflict between Doddi R and R N extended to the taluk level also, which resulted in each developing his own following.

This conflict had an impact in other areas also. There is a cooperative society in Doddi to cater the the needs of the villagers in this area. The Directors of the Society are elected by the member villagers. The budding elites will have their initial experience in the elections held for directorship. R N of Rajpura also succeeded in putting his persons on the society which enabled him to control this institution and the resultant patronage.

It must be pointed out here that the active members belonging to the dominant castes have a strong economic base, fair knowledge of the wider politics, and a certain amount of education. For them, politics is a full time activity, and they are members of large households and with someone to look after their family agriculture, they can afford to spend their entire time to their selected calling. They are very mobile and quite often it is very difficult to meet them in their villages, a problem which I faced during my field-work. They are also progressive farmers who use modern methods of agriculture. Another perceptible character is their enormous hunger for information. They read newspapers regularly and listen to radio news. The first thing they would ask me whenever I visited them was whether I had brought any newspaper. They would discuss with anyone the finer points of politics and did not hesitate to discuss the latest trends in politics.

An observable feature in this Panchayat is that when a facility is successfully provided to a village, there will be a number of individuals who will claim credit for bringing the needed facility. They elaborately describe how, inspite of impediments they had succeeded in securing it to the village. If there was any delay in securing it, or a total failure to get it, it was ascribed to the non-cooperation of the opposing rural elites. While this is the version put forwarded by the elites, the common villager, has his own view point. He usually attributes some personal motive to the elite who brings a facility to the village. In other words, it was not the desire to do good, but to further a self-interest that was responsible for bringing a facility to the village.

It is also relevant to mention here the case of the construction of Madbal–Rajpura road which had been sanctioned by the Taluk Development Board. This work was pending at the time of fieldwork because of the hostility between two groups in the village. This road if completed, facilitated access to the hobli headquarters, and since this distance was shorter than that between Rajpura village and Doddi, the children could easily go to schools in Madbal village. A road had been laid between Madbal and Ajjahalli during the time of C R Rangegowda, who was an M L A for one term. Had this road materialised under the original plan, it would have by-passed Rajpura village. Pressure was brought on the government through HGC, MLA, for making the road pass through Rajpura village. The Executive

Engineer, PWD, after inspection recommended that the road pass through Rajpura village which was accepted by the government. The construction of the road involved private lands and some pieces especially belonging to Janatha party. The initiative for the road construction was taken by R N (Congress I). At the time when the government started acquisition proceedings, the affected Janatha party members went to the court on a petition and succeeded in stalling the work.

Sometimes the enlightened rural elites took initiative in getting certain benefits which otherwise would have gone to some other village. The case in point is the Putha village. The University of Agricultural Sciences, Bangalore, periodically adopts villages for development. A few years before the field-work was done, the UAS had selected a neighbouring village, Pura, for this adoption. It is said that because of the backwardness of the Pura villagers, they neither made use of the opportunity nor cooperated with the officials. Therefore, the UAS officials thought of adopting some other village instead of Pura village. When N of Putha heard of this, he consulted some of his villagers on the need for getting their village adopted for development, and he, through the BDO, whom he had known well, approached the UAS officials and got his village adopted. The benefits from this adoption are: (1) help in adopting new techniques of agriculture, (2) Guidance and supply of improved seeds; (3) training facilities for select farmers; (4) frequent demonstrations in the use of new techniques and (5) visits by select farmers to experimental farms.

Another arena where the rural elites are very active is the Co-operative Society. This society is situated in Doddi with the name *Raitha Seva Sahakara Sangha* which was in existence since 1949. It was called then as Multipurpose Co-operative Society. It was working well till 1957 when it closed down. The then Secretary and the President of the Society had misappropriated the money. At the instance of the Cooperative Department, the society was revived in 1966 and it was functioning at the time of the fieldwork although there was a case of misappropriation against the Secretary in the year 1983. The society, had an elected Board of Directors and the Secretary, however, is a salaried person.

The membership of the Board of Directors conferred certain prestige and gave access to the resources of the society. Therefore, there was struggle among the rural elites for control of the society which gave them a patronage of large number of villagers. This society was also an arena for opposing groups to extend their control and power.

The society was very important in the lives of the villagers. This was from the point of view of credit that was available to them. Secondly, agricultural inputs and all rationed articles including kerosene were distributed through the society. The Directors of the society were in a position to confer favours through loans to their followers. If the President and Secretary joined hands, then they could also have a dip into the money of the society. The co-operative society which was there to serve the interests of the society instead served the interests of the Board of Directors who were none other than the leading elites in the area and who also held positions in other democratic institutions.

In the Doddi society, till five years ago, power was held by Doddi R and his group. But after the rift between R N and Doddi R, both belonging to different political parties, not only was the Panchayat was captured by R N (Congress I) group, but also the society. R N and his followers gleefully told me that they contrived to elect a Lingayat of Doddi as President of the Society. This President happened to be an agnatic relative of Doddi R and was also opposed to him.

There are many development programmes which are meant for individual or households rather than for the village as a whole. Such programmes are a god-sent to the rural elites as they give the opportunities to enhance their prestige and power by acting as go-between between the government and the concerned individual or household. In theory everyone has direct access to the government through its bureaucracy. However, in practice it is different. Especially, for the villagers, particularly for the village poor, bureaucracy is unapproachable and they can have access to the benefits only through the intervention and recommendation of their leaders or patrons, who are the rural elites, possessing power and prestige. This is a crucial fact.

The Government had decided to acquire 3 acres and 13 *guntas* of land situated on the periphery of the Rajpura village settlement for distribution as "Janatha" sites. This piece of land belonged to one D under the Tenacy Act and he belonged to R N (Congress I) group. R N tried all means to prevent the acquisition of land as it belonged to his client. R N had influenced all the officials in this connection and it seems that the then BDO had falsely recorded that the said land had been acquired and sites distributed. It took, it seems, three years to get the matter settled. The opposition group succeeded in getting this land acquired and distributed. It was commented by the Janatha party group that in the distribution of sites, the major beneficiaries were people belonging to R N group. To save one person R N was willing to sacrifice several others. Only the watchfulness of the opposition group prevented such a thing happening. Where the factional rivalries are intense there the opposition groups acting as a policeman, try to prevent such a misdeed happening.

In another case, a smith, who is an astrologer in N Palya village wanted to take a loan for buying a pumpset. He had 0-15 *guntas* of land on which he grew betel leaves and arecanut and the pumpset was needed for this field. At the suggestion of Doddi R he approached the authorities for a loan and they rejected his application on the ground that he did not have a minimum land of one acre. Doddi R then suggested that he should ask for a loan for goldsmithy work. This amount would have been too small for a pumpset, therefore, he did not try. Again Doddi R suggested that he should try for a loan under the IRDP scheme for livestock. When he approached the officer through Doddi R, the officer told him, "your main purpose is to get a pumpset. If a loan is sanctioned for livestock, you will not buy them and instead, use the money for buying a pumpset". On this ground the loan was refused. Though in this case, the smith failed to get the loan, in spite of Doddi R's support, it is interesting to note how alternative channels are tried to secure the benefit.

The areas in which the common villager requires help and assistance from the rural elites are old age pension, loans for agriculture, pumpsets, and other inputs, in securing sites, loans for house construction, regularisation of encroached lands, backward class and scheduled caste certificates, etc. There are innumerable number of state and central schemes in operation and it is rarely a common villager knows about them. The rural elites, who are in regular contacts with officials and politicians are in the know of it. The real elites make use of these schemes to help their followers and also enhance their prestige.

Another area in which the rural elites are in great demand is in the area of employment. The villagers believe that there is nothing like having a salaried employment and once their children attain a certain level of education they strive to get them salaried jobs. For a person of middle level education, the most preferred job is that of a Constable in the Police Department, for which post they are willing to pay bribe also. The other one is the Village Accountant's job. Of course the cases of highly educated are different. I know of several cases where attempts were being made to secure the constable's job/post through the help of the local elites.

The elites state that they take up villagers' cases in order to help them, but the statement should not be accepted at its face value. The amount of time they spend for public cause and the money they spend in travel are expected to be compensated. It is said that in the last several years Doddi R after he became an active figure in the Panchayat and taluk, his economic status had gone up. He had a reasonable amount of land and owned a flour mill in the village. It is also alleged by his opposition group that he got a commission on every pumpset bought in the area. It must be remembered that he was the President of the Primary Land Development Bank, Magadi which gave loans to the villagers for land improvement, pumpsets, wells, etc. In contrast R N of Rajpura village, was hereditarily economically well-off and did not seem to have made money. His money appeared to come from sericulture and innovative agriculture. In fact, he made quite an amount of money through raising improved cotton seeds. He also keeps pigs. Now he also runs a flour mill in Rajpura village. A flour mill started functioning in the village five years ago by Angadi R of the Congress I group. Since starting of a mill in this village would affect the flour mill run by Doddi R, he used his influence to delay the grant of licence. However, R N using his influence through the Panchayat Extension officer, succeeded in obtaining the licence for Angadi R. Angadi R kept the flour mill for two years and then sold it to R N.

In a system where economic interests predominate, the rural elites try to exploit the situation and they are aided in by the close linkages which they have established with the bureaucracy.

Excepting in Kuppe village, where Muslims are the only community, the Scheduled Castes and the Lambanis are spread in the other villages are hamlets. The Muslims, however, are concentrated in a single settlement, with 44 households and they seem to take minimal interest in the affairs of the Panchayat, Kuppe was at one time, a reasonably medium sized village, but quite a number of Muslims over a period of time out-migrated. The beneficiaries of this migration were the dominant castes of the neighbouring villages, especially, Lingayats of Doddi, who bought off their lands. It is well known that Muslims as a community is not very much rooted to soil and they look to commerce and trade for their living. In Kuppe village, even households having some land, have trade as their occupation. Their movement is generally towards towns like Magadi and cities like Bangalore. In addition, almost every household in the village has taken to *bidi* manufacture. With their isolated situation and with their interests out side the Panchayat, neither the Muslims take interest in the affairs of the village nor others take any interest in them. It is not surprising that not a single leader has emerged as a spokesman for their community. This is reflected in the condition of their village. The village is featured by the absence of drainage, good roads and borewell. There is an Urdu primary school and is housed in a dilapidated building.

If this is the situation of Muslims, the conditions of scheduled castes and Lambanis are somewhat different. They do not live in isolated conditions and they are spread over in the villages and hamlets of the Panchayat. Although their settlement are separated from the main settlement in the village or hamlet, they have access to the facilities provided for the village as a whole. With their economic dependence on the dominant castes and their subseservient relationship, they have been able to have access to the development programmes through the rural elites. The rural elites belonging to dominant castes behave as though they are the real beneficiaries for the scheduled castes and Lambanis. As a result, no rural elites in the real sense have emerged amongst them.

Elites and Development Programmes: An overview

Primarily the active elites belong to upper caste and upper class categories and have a vested interest in getting involved in the development processes. While on the one hand their activities help the rural people, more importantly, the elites benefit economically as well as politically. Given the present social structure and the kind of democratic institutions that have been introduced in the villages, the government also cannot implement the development programmes without involving the rural elites (they act as a link between the taluk and the Panchayat). Thus the rural elites become an essential element of the development process.

The development of the village depends to a greater extent on how decision are made at the Panchayat level. "This will have to be analysed in terms of the characteristics and type of people at the helm of affairs, risk taking, utility of certain innovative activities and the process of group consensus for some of the development activities"

(Mehta, 1972:142). We have. in the previous sections discussed the way the rural elites operate in channellising development programmes to the benefit of their villages. In the process of implementing development programmes conflicting situations arise, and such situations themselves will help rural elites to have access to the government programmes. But for the conflict between the dominant caste elites of Rajpura and Doddi village elites, certain developments could not have taken place in the villages. As it was seen as long as there was cooperation and friendliness between the elites of constituent villages of the Panchayat, there was a unilateral development of a hamlet. Once the conflict arose, the different elites parted their ways, and the development pattern changed. The other villages in the Panchayat also started getting attention.

The democratic institutions at the micro-level have become indispensable. This is evidenced by the fact that when the term of the Panchayats came to an end in 1983, the government instead of at least temporarily asking these panchayats to continue, handed over the Panchayats to the administrators who were all officials. This resulted in the rural elites holding power positions in the villages becoming powerless and more importantly the interests of the villages greatly suffered. All the panchayat activities come to a standstill. With the administrators looking after a number of panchayats at the same time, they had no time or interest in looking after the panchayat developmental activities.

During this period, however, the rural elites continued to be active in their role as intermediaries between the taluk level administrators and the village folk; but they were helpless as far as the Panchayat activities were concerned. For example, during this period, a good number of street bulbs had fused out, but there was no one to take an interest in their replacement. When I asked the villagers as to why they had not approached the administrators, they pleaded their ignorance of the existence of administrators and the only people they knew were the local elites, who were indifferent as they had no power.

In recent years there have been argument about the role of the dominant castes in rural areas and some scholars consider that their roles and power are exaggerated. However, this study reveals that the dominant castes were always a strong element in the rural areas, and that with the introduction of democratic institutions and development programmes for rural areas, they are becoming stronger. It can easily be argued that the dominant castes, with their economic and political power represent upper class interests, and consequently, there is no conflict between the caste and class interests. In fact their interest coincide.

"Prominent politicians at the taluk level, especially those who belong to the ruling party, act as valves regulating the flow of funds from State Government to the poor and the underprivileged. They can block or divert the flow in directions entirely different from the ones intended.

Political rivalry at the taluk level shapes the politicians' attitude towards the poor. They gradually realise that the best way to ensure political support is to do "social work". Those who aspire to political power have to build a political base by intervening in the administration to divert government funds and assistance in favour of their clients."

The above statement refers to the study of Chakravarti village which is about few miles from Kuppe panchayat. Our study substantiates the above conclusions. Thus, we are in a situation where upper class interests are butteresed by the state's development interests in the poor and weaker sections. The rural elites need the assistance of the poor to perpetuate their class interest while the poor themselves have an interest in these elites to have access to benefits.

Acknowledgements

I am grateful to Prof. M.N. Srinivas for his valuable comments on the earlier version of this paper.

REFERENCES

Bottomore, T.B., 1971. *Elites and Society*. London : Penguin Books.

Epstein, T.S., M.N. Panini, M.N. Srinivas and V.S. Parthasarathy. 1983. *Basic needs viewed from above and from below: The case of Karnataka State, India*, Paris: OECD.

Gould, Julius and Williams L Kolb (Eds), 1964. *A Dictionary of the Social Sciences*. London: Tavistock Pubs.

Karanth, G.K., 1984. *Change and Continuity in Agrarian relations : A Case study of Karnataka village*. New Delhi: Unpublished Ph D thesis submitted to the Jawaharlal Nehru University.

Mehta, S.R., 1972. *Emerging Pattern of Rural Leadership*. New Delhi : Wiley Eastern Private Limited.

Panini, M.N., n.d, *The Political Economy of Poverty-Eradication in Karnataka*.

Unpublished.

Ray, C.N., 1985. Rural Development Programme in India. *Man and Development*, VII (1):74-105.

Srinivas, M.N., 1969. *Social Change in Modern India*. Berkeley and Los Angeles : University of California Press.

Srinivas, M.N., 1976. *The Remembered Village*. Delhi. Oxford University Press.

Zadrogny, John T., 1959. *Dictionary of Social Science* Washington : Public Affairs Press.

17

TECHNOLOGIES FOR RURAL DEVELOPMENT: Lessons from Astra's Experience*

A.K.N. Reddy

A Personal Introduction

After almost two decades in the field of electrochemistry I felt that, like most of the work in in advanced institutions of education, science and technology, my own work was largely irrelevant to India's poor, the majority of whom live in villages. I also felt that I should re-orientate my efforts towards technologies for rural development. Such a viewpoint found sympathy from many other colleagues at the Indian Institute of Science. This shared vision led in 1974 to the formulation and implementation of the ASTRA programme through which it was hoped that the Application of Science and Technology to Rural Areas would be a weapon (or "*asthra*" in Sanskrit) in the interests of the poor.

However, the attempt at working in rural areas quickly revealed my serious shortcomings. I was born and raised in a city and therefore knew virtually nothing about life in villages; I had received a western type of education and therefore found it difficult to understand traditional attitudes and approaches; and I was a member of the elite, coming from the family of a professional, and therefore found it very dif-

---

* This paper is based on a Keynote Address first delivered at the Rural & Community Services Centre, The Tata Iron & Steel Co., Ltd., Jamshedpur, on 4th March 1987, and then developed for the Valedictory Address to the Workshop on "Rural Development" organised by the Asian Institute of Technology, Bangkok, and the Institute of Social and Economic Change, Bangalore, on 9th July, 1988, at the Institute of Social and Economic Change.

ficult to see the world through the eyes of the poor.

All this meant that I had to undergo a great deal of unlearning (in addition to learning) to be able to function in rural areas. Thus far, my learning experience has spanned 14 years of which the first nine were as the Convenor of ASTRA, and the remaining were focused on its community biogas plant project at Pura village, Kunigal Taluk, Tumkur District, Karnataka.

Many lessons have emerged from this experience. Since these lessons may be of some use to others wishing to make similar efforts, they are set down below.

LESSON 1: Rural people may be poor and illiterate, but they are not irrational, and we must understand this rationality.

In fact, the poorer they are, the more does their survival depend upon their rationality, i.e., upon a proper evaluation of costs and benefits. And, in their attitude to returns and risks, they invariably take the "worst case scenario" more seriously than the "best case scenario", because the former can lead to total ruin whereas the latter only means marginal improvement. In other words, they are highly risk-averse. For example, their choice of traditional seed varieties in preference to high-yielding varieties (HYV) is often dictated by the fact that the latter can give lower yields than the former if the inputs are not in the optimum range. As the nursery rhyme goes: "when she was good, she was very very good, but when she was bad, she was horrid".

We must therefore proceed under the assumption that, given the options within the range of awareness of the people, their technological choices are rational. For example, draught animals in many parts of the country are fed well only during the ploughing season because most of their traditional year-round functions–water-lifting, oil extraction, cane crushing, etc. – have been usurped by pumpsets, oil mills, cane crushers, etc. Another example is the fact that the load-bearing capacity of bullock carts is kept low because the average payload is only about 250 to 300 kg.

We must understand rural rationality if we want our technological suggestions and recommendations to be accepted. For example, if smoke from wood-stoves (*chulas*) is essential to check termite attack on thatched roofs, then it is unlikely that smokeless stoves will be accepted unless they are accompanied by a solution to the termite problem, for instance, a termite-proof roof.

LESSON 2: We must first be students if we want to be successful teachers.

Information must flow both ways: from the people to the rural technologists, and from the rural technologists to the people. There are several important steps in this information flow process.

Step 1: Scientific study of the lives of the people. This step is crucial because most rural technologists know more about, say, London or New York than about villages 20 km from their institutions. Hence, there is no option other than starting from zero.

Step 2: Identification of felt needs, rather than perceived needs. For instance, villagers are completely aware of the fact that thatched roofs (a) leak, (b) catch fire, (c) are attacked by termites, (d) harbour insects and rodents, and (e) need constant maintenance. If asked (for instance, through a questionnaire), they may express their perceived need for a tiled or reinforced-cement-concrete (RCC) roof because those are the only alternatives that they have seen and of which they are aware. But their *felt need* is really for an improved roof that does not have the defects of thatched roofs. An understanding of felt needs is essential for working out the design criteria for improved technologies.

Step 3: Presentation of options to the people. Before a major effort is launched to develop of new technologies, it is vital that the various technological options be presented to the people and their preferences elicited.

Step 4: Technology selection. If the ultimate intention is to spread the technology and to ensure that it does not remain a museum piece, it is imperative that the final decision on the selection of the technology be made by the people and not by the technologists. Technology choice is too important to be left to technologists and other "experts". "Experts" have made monumental errors even in the industrialised countries (as in the case of the Concorde supersonic aircraft, or the US breeder reactor). Our countryside is littered with blunders in the choice of technology. Rural technologists, as all people whose careers, fortunes and fame are linked with technologies, often have vested interests in the technologies that they favour: they are not as unbiased or objective as they claim or as they are portrayed. These vested interests may diminish the extent to which they bring their technical skills to bear on the problems of poverty and thereby help the poor.

Step 5: Technology generation. The arduous task of R & D has to be taken up at this stage.

Step 6: Technology testing. This important step consists of testing out the technology in the field and getting the reactions of the prospective users.

Step 7: Technology finalisation. The feedback from the field is used to improve the product or process before the technology is finalised for diffusion.

Step 8: Technology dissemination. The process of disseminating the technology has to be a multi-institutional effort involving development agencies, technologists, financial institutions and rural users.

The steps involved in this two-way information flow are quite similar to those involved in satisfying the demands of urban middle and upper class consumers, but the terminology is usually different. In the case of the generation and dissemination of technologies for the middle and upper classes, the following steps are usually distinguished:

Market Survey ==> Consumer Preferences ("the customer is always right") ==> Identification of Market Demand ==> R &D ==> Test Marketing ==> "Productionising" ==> Manufacturing==> Marketing.

All this, which is considered so self-evident in the case of affluent customers, is completely ignored in the case of the poor. This bias is perhaps because the poor do not have enough purchasing power to articulate their demands through the market mechanism and be rated as "consumers". But, because people are poor, we must not ignore their likes, tastes, preferences and needs. For example, government-subsidised housing (Janata houses) for the poorest sections tend to ignore the way in which the spaces in traditional houses are used by villagers.

We must also curb our natural tendency to develop technologies in response to imaginary and imagined needs identified in remote and alien settings. For example, a number of "modern" designs of bullock-carts were developed with the capacity to carry 1000-2000 kg of load even though such high loads do not arise frequently in typical rural situations but only in exceptional ones, for instance, in the catchment area of a sugar factory.

The technologist must ensure that all the objectives in a rural user's list are included in his/her design criteria. If the technology designer can achieve the simultaneous inclusion of all the rural consumer's objectives in the technology, then it does not matter whether the consumer's ranking of the objectives is different from the designer's ranking. This is what seems to have happened in the case of the brand of improved woodstove known as the ASTRA OLE – whereas the designer's priorities seemed to have been (l) reduction of fuel consumption, (2) smokelessness and (3) cutting down cooking time, the rural user's priorities were very different: (l) smokelessness, (2) cutting down cooking time and (3) reduction of fuel consumption.

If the designer cannot meet all the user's objectives simultaneously but only in stages, then it is imperative that the designer's sequence must be in the same order of the user's priorities – otherwise, the implementation may run into problems. This is what happened to ASTRA's community biogas plant at Pura – the villagers wanted the biogas to lift and pipe drinking water, generate electricity for lighting homes and provide cooking fuel. But they did not stress that order of priorities, and the ASTRA workers did not pick up the signals – they sought to provide cooking fuel first. The villagers went along with this effort out of solidarity, but the dung availability could not provide biogas even for one complete meal (let alone two meals), and the biogas plant had to be stopped for some time. The plant was later restarted at the request of the villagers, but this time, drinking water was taken up as the first priority – as desired by the villagers – and the project has taken off again.

LESSON 3: Start with the people, and only with the people!

Unfortunately, it is possible for scientists and engineers to get so involved with Steps (5) and (7), i.e., technology generation and technology finalisation, that they forget all the other steps in which the rural people (who are the prospective users of the technology) have a crucial role to play. This process of by-passing the people is even easier when the technology dissemination consists of simply transporting a device or piece of equipment (for example, a photovoltaic module or a biomass-fuelled engine-cum-generator) and installing or erecting it in a village. What these blinkered scientists and engineers disseminate may be rural technology, but it will certainly not be technology for rural development. For development cannot take place without the involvement of people. It is wise therefore to keep on asking: "Where are the people?"

However idealistic and romantic it may sound, it must be stressed that technologists must approach rural work with empathy and affection for the people. With these feelings, they look forward to interaction with the people (even when they are in groups). Otherwise, they tend to be afraid of them, and hide behind the walls of their rural centres. Then, the poor conclude that their poverty is being used as a resource for professional gain. Even if the people do not benefit from the interaction, the feelings with which technologists make efforts are extremely important in their eyes. Given the right attitude, the people are far more understanding of technical failures (which are the usual precursors of success) than the educated urbanites who cheer when the satellite goes into orbit and jeer when it falls into the sea.

Science and technology too stand to gain from these feelings of empathy and affection. The forging of an emotional bond with the people may result in the catharsis, redemption and the resurrection of science and technology which have become so amoral, immoral and violent. At that stage, the poor shall inherit science and technology and therefore the earth.

LESSON 4: Never forget the women!

Women are often the best agents of disseminating technologies for rural development. Even in projects where technologists work with the people, the tendency is to restrict popular involvement to the men. This gender bias is often difficult to avoid because most scientists and engineers are men, their technologies are often male-oriented, there are social taboos discouraging direct interactions with women, rural women do not come forward to articulate their views in the presence of their men, etc. But with many technologies, once the women get involved, the dissemination takes off. For example, once the women began to have a vested interest in the delivery of dung to the Pura community biogas plant, the operation of dung collection and delivery began to run smoothly.

LESSON 5: There is a learning curve for technologies.

In the case of most rural technologies (stoves, windmills, biogas plants, wood gasifiers, etc.), there is a marked difference between the first generation of unsuccessful devices (which were often the result of the enthusiasm of unqualified amateurs) and the second generation of successful devices (which emerged from the creative efforts of qualified professionals).

Thus, the penetration of the countryside with rural technologies involves a learning curve. In the initial part of the curve, there is a very slow penetration of the potential "market", then a rapid climb, and finally a saturation. Unfortunately, the plans of most development agencies forget this learning curve and prescribe linearly increasing targets.

During the initial part of the learning curve, there has to be intense back-and-forth interaction between the laboratory and the field. The feedback from users in the field must lead to modifications and improvements of the product or process, and the improved product or process needs further "test marketing" in the field. As a result of this interplay between technology generation and dissemination, and between technologists and potential consumers of the technology, the penetration of the "market" is necessarily very slow during this phase.

All these points are generally ignored when technology dissemination is planned and implemented. In fact, there is a general tendency for technology generation and technology dissemination to be thought of as two distinct non-overlapping sequential stages with the generation ending when the dissemination begins, and the generators "washing their hands off" the technology dissemination process.

LESSON 6: From the standpoint of current expectations, resource availability, materials and circumstances, most traditional technologies are inadequate and most modern technologies are inaccessible.

Traditional technologies have evolved through a long process of natural selection of innovations and therefore, must have been optimal solutions for the challenges of the past. For example, computer analysis has shown that the geometry of traditional bullock carts represents anoptimum solution to the problem of stability. Hence, traditional technologies must not be ignored as sources of innovation.

Although traditional technologies may have been optimal solutions in the past, almost all of them are sub-optimal and inadequate today because of changed expectations, resource availability, materials and circumstances. For instance, in the past when the country was heavily forested, teakwood may have been an optimum material for constructing the highly stressed wheels of bullock-carts, but today teak has become such a scarce material that it is a costly and therefore sub-optimal solution. On the other hand, the so-called "modern" technologies, which are often nothing more than bad xerox copies of western technologies, are invariably inaccessible to the poor. For example, the poor cannot afford a modern roofing technology such as reinforced cement concrete (RCC).

It is therefore a Hobson's choice for the poor – on the one hand, traditional technologies are inadequate, and on the other hand modern technologies are inaccessible.

LESSON 7: The role of rural technologists is to generate new technological options, each more effective than the traditional and more accessible than the modern.

These options must enable the poor to escape from the dilemma described above. Ideally, the options should constitute a hierarchy of technologies with upward compatibility. Then, with rising incomes, the poor can move from a cheaper less cost-effective option to a costlier more cost-effective option. Only in such a situation will the people have genuine choices. Thus the role of rural technologists is to be option-generators and choice-wideners. For example, in the matter of cooking fuels and stoves, rural technologists can widen the options of villagers so that they can also choose improved (smokeless and fuel-efficient) woodstoves or biogas cooking.

LESSON 8: There are three main approaches for generating technological options: (1) cheapen western technology, (2) develop ab initio **an alternative technology and (3) transform traditional technology.**

For example, in the case of low-cost building technologies, the approach of cheapening western technologies may consist of developing fibre-reinforced materials, that of developing *ab initio* alternative technologies, geodesic domes, and that of transforming traditional technologies, compacted unfired mud blocks.

Even though it is a hitherto untapped source, the transformation of traditional technologies is a rich source of, and promising route for, technologies appropriate for rural development. The transformation of traditional technologies involves an understanding of their scientific basis, followed by qualitative changes brought about by marginal improvements.

LESSON 9: As a consequence of the whole process that has been outlined above, the technologies that are developed are likely to be region-specific, location-specific and culture-specific.

The local culture may have many surprises. This is probably why Gandhi is reported to have advised one of the most creative architects in modern India, Laurie Baker, "When you design for the poor, restrict yourself to materials that are available within a radius of 10 miles!"

LESSON 10: Any fool can make a thing complicated, it takes a genius to make it simple.

The end-product may have to be, or may turn out to be, simple, but the thinking that goes into its development can be quite sophisticated. In fact, there is a desperate need for wise ideas and ingenious solutions. Rural technologies are neither trivial nor second-class, because they invariably pose the extremely tough challenge of having to be "zero cost".

LESSON 11: There are four main approaches to the dissemination of rural technologies: (l) the market, (2) the top-down approach, (3) the bottom-up approach, and (4) the franchising approach, and it is very important that the appropriate mechanism be chosen.

Each of the four approaches mentioned has its advantages and disadvantages. The market is an excellent allocator of resources, but it ignores three extremely important aspects: equity, the environment and the long-term. In particular, the rural poor are by and large outside the market because they do not have the requisite purchasing power to articulate their demands via the market.

The top-down approach – so favoured by bureaucracies – seems the obvious route when there is clarity at the top, but underrates the central role of popular participation in technology selection and finalisation and of the strengthening of self-reliance.

The bottom-up approach starts with popular participation, but may suffer from the people's lack of technical expertise.

The franchising approach in which a centralised technology-generating-cum-development agency franchises local groups or entrepreneurs, may be able to combine the advantages of the large and the small, public and private initiatives and technologists and grass-roots workers.

LESSON 12: Of various technologies contending for dissemination, those technologies succeed in spreading (i.e., penetrating the "market") that solve several problems simultaneously.

Charles Berg, who first enunciated this "theorem", illustrated it by stressing that energy-efficiency improvements were introduced into the US steel industry during a period of declining energy prices because those improvements were accompanied by other useful characteristics such as greater capital productivity. The Berg "theorem" is very relevant to rural technologies too. Thus, of the various designs that have been tried for improved woodstoves, the ones that have been successful (for example, the ASTRA OLE) have been those that simultaneously eliminated smoke, cut down cooking time and reduced fuel consumption.

LESSON 13: Rural technology has both power and limits: it is an essential requisite for development, but it cannot be a substitute for economic, social and political change.

Notwithstanding any successes with the generation and dissemination of rural technologies, technology alone cannot remove poverty, redress injustices, prove a panacea and solve development problems. Technology is only a sub-system of society, and the development of society hinges, not only on technology, but also on the other crucial sub-systems. Technology is only an instrument for the development of society. Like all instruments, it must be specifically chosen and/or designed to fulfil its intended function. But the will to use the instrument, and the skill to wield it effectively, do not depend so much on the instrument as on those who use it. Thus, improved technologies are a necessary condition for rural development, but not a sufficient condition. It is also essential that the political structure and the socio-economic framework are both committed to development goals. Rural technological missions will succeed only when they are part of successful societal missions.

LESSON 14: The perspective guiding rural technology is also vital.

Rural technology is not merely a matter of expediency, a transitory measure and a tactical device to cope with the current predicament of the poor in the countryside. Rural technology is a path to a new society. It is an instrument for development. And development must be seen as a socio-economic process directed primarily towards the satisfaction of basic human needs starting from the needs of the neediest particularly in the locations of development projects. In addition, development must involve the strengthening of endogenous self-reliance, based on social participation and control. Finally, if this development is to be sustainable over the long term, it must be in harmony with the environment.

18

POSTSCRIPT: Highlights from the Discussions

The quality, analytical depth and wide-ranging nature of many of the papers included in this book naturally created expectations that the discussions during the seminar would be equally interesting and stimulating, and this was indeed the case. No attempt will be made here, however, to reproduce the discussions. Instead of that, some of the points made in the course of the seminar will be used to throw light on two main questions: (i) what, if anything, *have* we learnt from the experience with IRDP over the recent past? and (ii) what new orientations, organisational innovations and lines of research seem to offer most promise, for the next decade or so? We shall limit ourselves to points that seem to us not to have been sufficiently emphasised in the papers or in the introductions to the two parts.

Not surprisingly, one of the points that generated a great deal of discussion was the strategy of "delinking the poor". The discussion quickly moved to the fundamental question of the objective of fighting poverty and of how seriously it should be taken, in the IRD context. If IRD is seen merely as a convenient way to keep the poor quiet at minimum cost, a strategy based on assistance will be sufficient. If, however, the objective is taken at face value, and if it is recognised that rural poverty does not result purely from a general lack of resources, then it will almost inevitably lead to attempts to change socio-economic structures and even to reform the State. Otherwise, even if resources *are* made available, the socio-economic processes at work will funnel those resources back to the rural rich. In such a situation, some form of delinking, in the sense of decreasing the dependence of the poor on the rich and the exploitation that usually goes with such dependence, becomes imperative. In this respect, the importance of the organisation of the rural poor was frequently stressed.

One lesson from experience that seems to have been drawn by most of the participants as well as by a good number of the projects reviewed in the seminar concerns the importance of *flexibility* as a characteristic of project design and organisation. During the discussions, participants often stressed the inadequacy of schemes based on blueprint approaches and the need to reinforce the pilot nature of IRD projects, not in the sense of restricting them to small areas, but in that of emphasising the need for continuous learning – by the planners, by the implementing institutions and by the beneficiaries themselves – and for the inclusion of the lessons learnt in constantly revised project designs. This continuous learning process will naturally concern different facets of the situation for each of the groups or institutions involved; its most important aspect, however, is that, if taken seriously, it will ultimately turn IRD into what can only be described as an open-ended process, the very targets of which undergo a continuous process of revision and readjustment.

One crucial implication of this change in perspective concerns the *time scale* of IRD projects. While the close scheduling of targets is possible in the case of blueprint-type projects, it makes very little sense to do it for open-ended projects, in which both the situation and the targets change more or less continuously. This brings to the fore the vital question of sustainability. If it is not possible to set specific targets with well defined time-horizons, it becomes essential to adopt project formats that can be sustained for long enough to have a significant impact. One consequence of this change in perspective is that institutional development acquires an even greater priority than it has hitherto been assigned.

In this connection, it is difficult to exaggerate the importance of the *mobilisation of the poor*. Although 'standard' uses of beneficiaries' organisations – such as the identification of needs and priorities, on the one hand, and of the needy themselves, on the other – remain important, the mobilisation process should have the more general aim of helping the poor understand and change their own environment. Ultimately, a successful mobilisation of the poor can, and probably will, lead to their much closer involvement in political activities, particularly those connected with the defence of their rights and legitimate interests.

Another aspect of institutional development that this change in perspective entails is the *reinforcement of the capacity of local government* to participate in, and ultimately to manage, IRD projects.

Again this seems to be a clear trend in more recent formulations of IRD projects in several Asian countries. The greater the technical and managerial capacity of local government, at a variety of levels, the smaller will be the need for the special project mode of project management and the higher the likelihood that the projects will continue to operate beyond the period during which they are set up. This is likely to prove especially true if that increased capacity is clearly acknowledged by the direct and close involvement of local government in the running of the projects, even prior to the transfer of responsibilities.

The renewed importance of flexibility and long-term sustainability and of a change in the time scale of IRD projects also raises questions concerning the role of *donor-support*. It may be possible to persuade certain donors to support projects

with an element of open-endedness and longer temporal horizons - and some of the cases mentioned in the seminar seem to indicate that, to a certain extent, that is already happening. On the other hand, the need to retain an element of accountability and to monitor progress creates an interesting organisational challenge as well as a problem for research, since the need to evaluate the progress of the IRD projects will remain, even if they are accepted by the funding organisations as open-ended projects

In addition to being flexible, it is important that the strategies adopted in the context of IRD be also *robust*. The concept of robustness has to do with the possibility for a strategy to retain its validity – or its usefulness – in the face of considerable uncertainty about the future. In this way, for instance, a strategy which ties the welfare the rural poor in a particular area to the continuing presence of an organisation or project that provides them with inputs and markets their output is less robust than one which assures them of access to inputs and helps them set up their own marketing systems. Given a change of circumstances that may cause the organisation to leave the area or the project to be terminated, the first strategy will collapse, leaving very little behind, while the second may continue to give fruit for a long time. The robustness of different strategies may be assessed with the help of a range of scenarios of the most likely evolution of conditions (e.g. macro-economic variables, government policies, donor attitudes, etc.).

Although mobilisation of the poor is extremely important, it needs to be complemented by a range of other measures destined to create the possibility for them to engage into productive work.

In this connection the case of Kerala, where an effective organisation of urban and rural workers resulted in an exodus of small and medium-sized industrial entreprises and even in changes in cropping patterns in order to reduce labour inputs, holds important lessons. *Rural industrialisation* seems to hold considerable promise in this respect. It must, however, be noted that such rural industrialisation can only be successful if the owners of capital in the rural areas – i.e. the rural rich – become involved in it. This goes beyond the scope of IRD; in fact, as the participants in the seminar stressed, IRD is only one of many possible forms of intervention in rural areas, for the purpose of stimulating rural development. What may be stressed, though, is that rural industrialisation can only be properly considered from a regional perspective. This point has been made elsewhere and will not be elaborated any further here.

An important aspect of the discussions in the seminar concerned the *differences between the approaches* to IRD in India and in the other countries covered by country papers. After an initial orientation towards area development and block planning, IRD in India became almost exclusively oriented towards the identification of target groups and the provision of employment or productive resources to them, in order to stabilise the wage level and to achieve a partial redistribution of productive assets. By contrast, the other countries retain an areal planning orientation, which finds its strongest manifestation in the Philippines. Participants in the seminar expressed the idea that it would be desirable to combine the best aspects of each of these two orientations. In that respect, the seminar – and this book – may be seen as a first step in the direction of greater mutual awareness by practitioners of the two approaches. Certainly the comparative material provided may go a long way towards stimulating research into ways of combining the respective strengths of the two approaches while avoiding their weaker points.

Finally, a very important observation, with considerable implications for research and policy-making, concerns the fact, recognised by all the participants, that although there are very *different types of poverty situations*, most projects and organisations adopt a single – although not the same in all cases – approach to all such situations. This often results in failures, as for instance when a project focuses its activities on providing resources to a target group which is poor because of mechanisms of exploitation. The participants recognised that there is a strong need to establish closer links between the strategies most likely to succeed in dealing with poverty and the different types of poverty situations.

INDEX